Contemporary Wales
Volume 16

CONTEMPORARY WALES

An annual review of economic,
political and social research

Volume 16

Editor

Richard Wyn Jones

*Published on behalf of the Board of Celtic Studies
of the University of Wales*

**Cardiff
University of Wales Press
2003**

www.wales.ac.uk/press

Published January 2004

British Library Cataloguing in Publication Data
A catalogue record for this book is available from the British Library.

ISBN 0-7083-1918-1

ISSN 0951-4937

Cover design and photograph by Marian Delyth
Typeset by Bryan Turnbull
Printed in Wales by Dinefwr Press, Llandybïe

CONTENTS

CONTRIBUTORS

David Adamson holds the Chair in Community and Social Policy at the University of Glamorgan and is Director of the Programme for Community Regeneration. He has acted as an Adviser to the Welsh Assembly Goverent on issues of community regeneration and is currently enaged in a number of research projects in community regeneration and the social economy in Wales.

David Brooksbank is Professor of Enterprise and Small Business Economics at the University of Glamorgan Business School and Director of the Welsh Enterprise Institute. He has published widely on enterprise and entrepreneurship, economic regeneration, unemployment policies and trends in the Welsh economy.

Andrew Davies is a Research Fellow at the University of Wales Centre for Advanced Welsh and Celtic Studies. Previously, he has worked as a researcher for the University of Wales Board of Celtic Studies, at Opinion Research Services, and at the National Assembly for Wales.

Jonathan Evans is a lecturer in the Cardiff University School of Social Sciences. He teaches on the postgraduate Social Work course and his main research interests lie in the field of juvenile justice.

Sally Holland is a lecturer in the School of Social Sciences at Cardiff University. Her research interests are primarily in the field of social work and social policies for children and families, and she is currently researching the use of family group conferences, with a particular focus on the conferences' effectiveness in empowering children and young people.

Simon Jenkins writes a twice-weekly column for *The Times* and a weekly column for the *London Evening Standard*. He has edited both the

London Evening Standard and *The Times* and written books on politics and on the history and architecture of London. His latest book, *England's Thousand Best Houses*, was published by Penguin in October 2003.

Melanie Jones is a Senior Research Officer for the Welsh Economy Labour Market Evaluation and Research Centre (WELMERC) at the University of Wales Swansea. Her research interests include local labour markets, unemployment and inactivity.

Richard Jones is a Senior Research Officer for the Welsh Economy Labour Market Evaluation and Research Centre (WELMERC) at the University of Wales Swansea. His research interests are regional labour markets, unemployment and low pay.

Stuart Jones is a Research Fellow based with the Programme for Community Regeneration at the University of Glamorgan. He has researched and published in the fields of youth homelessness and youth social exclusion and is currently engaged in projects on community regeneration and youth substance misuse.

Martin Laffin is Professor of Public Policy and Management, Durham Business School, University of Durham and was previously Professor of Public Policy and Management, University of Glamorgan. He is currently leading a project on 'the role of the parties in inter-governmental relations after devolution' as part of the Economic and Social Research Council Devolution and Constitutional Change Programme.

Ted Rowlands was the Labour Member of Parliament for Merthyr Tydfil from 1972 until his retirement in 2001, during this period being a Welsh Office Minister and Minister at the Foreign Office. He is a member of the Richard Commission established by the Welsh Assembly Government to examine the powers and electoral arrangements of the National Assembly, and has written a number of articles for academic journals.

Elin Royles is a Welsh-medium tutor at the Institute of Welsh Politics, University of Wales, Aberystwyth. The topic of her research is the development of civil society in post-devolution Wales.

Jonathan Scourfield is a lecturer in the School of Social Sciences at Cardiff

University. His current research interests include gender in social work, men and social policy, and children's identities. He is a member of the editorial collective of *Critical Social Policy* and, from 2004, joint editor of *Contemporary Wales.*

Roger Scully is a lecturer in the Department of International Politics at the University of Wales, Aberystwyth, and Director of the Jean Monnet Centre for European Studies. His research examines political representation and legislative behaviour, and he is the author of *Becoming Europeans?* (Palgrave, forthcoming).

Peter Sloane is a Professor of Economics at the University of Wales Swansea and is the director of the Welsh Economy Labour Market Evaluation and Research Centre (WELMERC). He is a Research Fellow at the Institute for Labor Studies, IZA, and a Member of the European Low Wage Employment Network (LOWER). He is also Vice President of the International Association of Sports Economists. He has published widely in the area of labour economics and the economics of sport.

Angharad Closs Stephens is studying for her Ph.D. in international politics under the guidance of Professor R. B. J. Walker at the University of Keele. The topic of her research is 'Political community, postcolonialism and the construction of Welsh political identity'.

Gerald Taylor is a Research Fellow at the University of Glamorgan. He is currently working on a research project on 'The role of political parties in intergovernmental relations' led by Professor Martin Laffin, and has previously published on the Labour Party, including a monograph called *Labour's Renewal? The Policy Review and Beyond*, for Macmillan.

Alys Thomas was until recently Senior Lecturer in Politics at the University of Glamorgan. She has published widely on Welsh and comparative politics and was part of a Glamorgan-based research team working on intergovernmental relations and devolution. She has worked in the Office of the Presiding Officer in the National Assembly for Wales since July 2003.

Fiona Wood is a researcher currently working within the Cardiff School of Social Sciences, Cardiff University. Her research interests lie primarily within the sociology of health and illness, most notably relating to cancer, mental illness and risk. Since July 2003 she has been working with the Department of General Practice, University of Wales College of Medicine.

EDITOR'S NOTE

To act as editor of *Contemporary Wales* is to be afforded an almost unique insight into the state of Wales-focused social science. Given the nature of the structures that govern academic life in Wales, no one else has either the reason or opportunity to develop the same synoptic overview of the state of play across the whole range of social science disciplines. As this issue marks my fifth and final volume as editor, it seems an appropriate point to provide some broad-brush impressions.

There can be no doubt that, generally speaking, Wales-focused social science is in a healthier state now than it was five years ago. There are more active researchers producing more work, and more properly funded research projects being undertaken. Particularly noteworthy is the fact that the basic social science infrastructure in Wales is much better developed now than it was even as recently as 1997. The establishment of the *Welsh Household Panel Survey* and the funding of successive election surveys have provided a wealth of high-quality quantitative data which is greatly enriching our understanding of contemporary Welsh society. Of course, quantitative work is only one dimension of social science research. Nevertheless, the fact that the ESRC – to its great credit – is willing to invest the substantial sums necessary to facilitate these headline projects demonstrates that one of the most powerful players on the UK social science scene has started to take its responsibility to support Wales-focused research seriously. This can only be good news for all those active in the field, whether they adopt quantitative research methods or not. Compared with the dark days of the late 1980s and early 1990s, in particular, when the then-editors of *Contemporary Wales* had to struggle to continue publication in an atmosphere in which the social sciences in general were under attack, and in which, in several social science disciplines, to adopt a Welsh focus was regarded as eccentric-bordering-on-deranged, we have come a long way.

There can be no doubt that it is devolution that has acted as the catalyst for this transformation. The establishment of the National Assembly for

Wales and the Welsh Assembly Government has helped legitimate Wales-focused research, provided a new public policy context and, if only gradually, generated demand for reliable data and analysis as a basis for policy-making. There is every reason to believe that this influence will continue to resonate in coming years and, to that extent, the prospects for Wales-focused social science are good.

That said, it is important not to overstate the extent of the change that has occurred in recent years. While in relative terms, Wales-focused social science research is much stronger than it was, this is in large measure simply a reflection of its past weakness. To survey Wales-focused research in discipline after discipline is to reveal a situation in which such work as does exist is still largely the preserve of a few isolated individuals. There are very few cases in which anything resembling a 'critical mass' of researchers exists. The debate between Lovering, Morgan, Cooke and others that has done so much to illuminate the state of the Welsh economy remains very much the exception – and all of those seeking to understand the contours of contemporary Wales are impoverished by the absence of such informed debates about the particularities, peculiarities and pathologies of the Welsh condition.

Graphic evidence of the continued marginal status of Wales-focused social science is provided by the submissions to the most recent Research Assessment Exercise (RAE). The number of Wales-focused pieces of research submitted by Welsh universities for consideration by the various subject panels was tiny. It will come as no surprise to learn that the amount of Wales-focused work submitted by institutions outside of Wales was almost negligible. RAE submissions are, of course, an imperfect measure of research activity. Nevertheless, the paucity of Wales-related work submitted should give even the most complacent pause for thought. Even more concerning are the persistent indications that several subject panels simply refuse to take Wales-focused work seriously. While this is never made explicit in the lawyer-proof feedback provided to departments and institutions by the panels, a number of panel members have confirmed that, for many of their colleagues, Wales-focused work is deemed to be incapable, by definition as it were, of deserving 'international' status. Given the importance accorded to the RAE within our higher-education institutions, even the perception that this may be the case is deeply damaging.

Of course, this is not solely a Welsh phenomenon or problem. Scottish readers will readily confirm that the impact of the RAE on Scotland-focused research has been the subject of considerable discussion and debate, including in the Scottish Parliament. Nevertheless, it is plausible to argue that the negative effects of the RAE are even more serious in the Welsh context than they are in Scotland or, indeed, Northern Ireland. The Welsh higher-education system is much more closely tied to that of England than is the case in the other parts of the Celtic periphery. Moreover, the tradition of Wales-focused research across a broad range of disciplines is much weaker in Wales than is the comparable case in either of the other countries. If the incentive structure within which higher-education institutions operate does not value Wales-focused research, and, indeed, is regarded as positively discouraging such work in some cases, few institutions are likely to have the vision or the resources to chart a different path.

The Welsh Assembly Government has trumpeted its commitment to evidence-based policy-making. If, however, we are to take this commitment seriously, then the continuing marginal status of Wales-focused social science research is an issue that must be addressed. At present the Higher Education Funding Council for Wales (HEFCW) spends well over £60 million a year on supporting academic research in Welsh higher education institutions. In terms of encouraging social research that can underpin the development of public policy in the devolved Wales, this very substantial sum is hardly generating value for money.

Thus far, neither the Welsh Assembly Government, nor, indeed, the National Assembly more generally, have covered themselves with glory in the field of higher education. Their main focus has been on the perceived need to consolidate various institutions: a policy with large associated costs and very few apparent benefits. That the new government in Cardiff seems bent on persisting with this course of action despite what one might think is the obvious lesson of the disastrous ELWa experience – namely, that policy-makers should be extremely wary of forcing very different institutions together in 'shotgun weddings' without very good reason – hardly inspires confidence for the future.

As for its policy on research, it appears that the Assembly Government has yet to proceed much beyond the usual populist platitudes about a 'world-class Wales' and a few high-profile initiatives which, however welcome in themselves, do not address the basic structural imperatives of the system as provided by the RAE, policy on postgraduate training, and so forth. In the absence of coherent policy for Wales, developments in the English system, such as the recent recommendations from the Roberts Commission on the future of research assessment, will inevitably fill the vacuum. And it hardly needs to be added that the need to encourage high-quality research on life in contemporary Wales is hardly at the top of the agenda set for such bodies! Does the Assembly Government have the will and vision to construct a higher education policy that both provides proper encouragement for Wales-focused research and preserves the traditional strengths of our higher education institutions? Readers of *Contemporary Wales* will be better placed than most to find out.

*   *   *

The new editorial team for *Contemporary Wales* will comprise Paul Chaney (*ChaneyP@cardiff.ac.uk*) and Jonathan Scourfield (*Scourfield@cardiff.ac.uk*), both of the University of Cardiff, and Andrew Thompson (*athompso@glam.ac.uk*) of the University of Glamorgan. Anyone wishing to contact the editors is invited to do so via any one of these e-mail addresses.

Finally I would like to thank all those who have contributed to the success of *Contemporary Wales* over the past five years, in particular those who have undertaken the unheralded work of refereeing contributions. But most of all, I would like to avail myself of the opportunity to thank Professor John Black and Gwenan Creunant. Without their cheerful efficiency and support, this editor would have found his task a great deal more arduous and much less enjoyable than it has been. *Diolch o galon.*

Richard Wyn Jones
Editor

1. CONTINUITY AND CHANGE IN THE VALLEYS: RESIDENTS' PERCEPTIONS IN 1995 AND 2001

David Adamson and Stuart Jones

INTRODUCTION

The Valleys of south Wales occupy a pivotal place in both historical and contemporary images of Wales. As the crucible of Welsh socialism they are celebrated for their critical contribution to the Labour movement and the development of modern politics in Britain. This history is associated with stereotypical images of the choral tradition, team sports and tight-knit communities. More recently, these have been replaced by new stereotypes as the economic decline of the region has created high unemployment, youth disaffection and rising crime. The region is now more associated with the images of lone parenthood, drug addiction and marginalized local authority estates. However, stereotypes and reality rarely match well and life in the Valleys has always been a varied experience, rather than the homogeneous pattern which both historical and contemporary stereotypes portray.

The Valleys are not abstract geographical or socio political spaces but are made up of communities and populations with varied social characteristics and cultural experiences, albeit with some clearly identifiable common elements. The population of the region has lived through significant social, economic and cultural change in the post-war period, yet little attempt has been made to understand how that change has been experienced and perceived by the residents of the region. In the popular stereotypes and in more sophisticated social policy versions, the Valleys communities are seen as passive and increasingly identified as hapless victims of economic decline and associated social problems.

This article presents some evidence to demonstrate that this is not the case, and maps residents' perceptions of social and economic change in the Rhondda Cynon Taff area of the Valleys. Derived from two surveys, the first in 1995 and the second in 2001; the 1995 survey was conducted by the University of Glamorgan Regional Research Programme and the second by its successor, the University of Glamorgan Programme for Community Regeneration. The 2001 survey was commissioned by the Rhondda Cynon Taff Youth Offending Team from funding secured from the Youth Justice Board. Both surveys employed house calls and street-based questionnaire delivery. Sampling was constructed to provide representative populations in terms of gender, age and location.

The 1995 survey was conducted against a backdrop of a wider project of census analysis which had identified a complex pattern of inequality that had emerged in the wake of economic restructuring, recession and the accompanying wide-ranging welfare reforms of the Conservative admin-istrations. In common with other parts of Britain (Gaffikin and Morrisey, 1992) increased differentiation between the economic fortunes of those in employment and those experiencing the consequences of recession and unemployment was drawing new social boundaries and creating a significant proportion of the population experiencing poverty and deprivation. Increas-ingly characterized as social exclusion, this 'new poverty' was multi-dimensional in character and displayed compound effects of low income, poor housing, low health and poor educational achievement. There was a clear spatial dimension to the pattern of poverty and considerable dis-cussion of the north/south divide which identified a prosperous south-east of England in stark contrast to the growing poverty of the north of England and key areas of the 'Celtic fringe' (Philo, 1995). At the same time there was a major change in social policy which 'demonized' welfare recipients and made key cuts to benefit entitlement including for those aged 16 to 18 years.

In Wales there was considerable divergence between the economic fortunes of the Valleys and the neighbouring southern coastal plain, with significantly higher levels of unemployment in Valley districts (Morris and Wilkinson, 1996) and lower average incomes (Mid Glamorgan Update: Summer 1994). Morris and Wilkinson identified an increasing polarization between local authority areas, with significant income disparities between Valleys communities and the more affluent areas of Wales. Such divisions were later to become the basis for identifying the Objective 1 region of Wales but at that time were only emerging from the census data for the first time. This polarization was particularly evident within the Valleys themselves, where, following national trends (Barclay and Hills, 1995), increases in poverty and social exclusion were predominantly concentrated in increas-ingly marginalized local-authority estates (Adamson, 1998; Jones, 1995).

Thus the polarizing trends which were emerging at county level were actually based in significant disparities at the local level within Valleys communities. Key local-authority estates were the source of depressingly high levels of economic inactivity and associated patterns of change in family structure, community life and social integration.

However, at the opposite end of the local socio-economic spectrum there was evidence of increasing affluence in the newly built private housing estates, often marketed as 'executive' housing, which were springing up on the Valleys' sides. This evidence of increased social and economic polarization both confirmed and built upon the work of one of the present authors, who argued that previous patterns of social and cultural homogeneity in the Welsh Valleys were being displaced by more fragmented forms of social class relations (Adamson, 1988, 1991).

Arguably, since the 1995 survey, further important changes have occurred in the Valleys and the wider context of Wales and the United Kingdom. At the UK level these have included major changes to the political climate, in the form of a Labour Party general election victory in 1997 followed by a second term of office. When the original survey was completed, the then Conservative government refused to accept the existence of poverty in the UK, and social policy reflected such beliefs. Explanations of poverty were framed in the judgemental and stigmatizing language of the 'underclass' debate (Murray *et al.*, 1996) and the problems affecting poor communities were deemed to be the consequence of a moral decline which included the growth of lone-parent families and absent fathers (Dennis and Urdos, 1992). Social policy reflected the domination of government by such an ideology and key welfare reforms, such as the loss of benefits to 16 to 18-year-olds, had major impact in poor communities on further reducing income and increasing poverty.

Since 1997 the language of poverty, disadvantage and social exclusion has dominated government policy, and there is a commitment to the eradication of child poverty in twenty years. There is clearly room for discussion about the extent to which this has been prioritized and targeted within the overall policy structure and whether 'New Labour' has significantly departed from the 'underclass' discourse of the Conservative era. A 'welfare to work' component can be readily identified in the full range of Labour social inclusion policies and entry to the labour market is the key policy approach to social inclusion (Levitas, 1996). However, key policy changes have occurred, and the eradication of poverty is a stated core objective of government. This intention has manifested itself in a wide range of policies, including the

Minimum Wage, Family Tax Credit, New Deal, Surestart and, more lately, the Strategy for Neighbourhood Renewal.

In addition to this major change in the social policy environment, the devolution process has created the Welsh Assembly Government, which has also brought poverty reduction to the fore of its Better Wales strategy. The result is a wide-ranging policy platform aimed at reducing unemployment, combating social exclusion and removing social disadvantage. As well as UK-wide programmes such as New Deal and Surestart, 'made in Wales' solutions have emerged in initiatives such as Sustainable Communities, People in Communities and more recently, Communities First. Seeking to capitalize on the demonstrated advantages of a wide range of community regeneration projects arising from community-based actions, the renewed interest in community-development has grown to occupy a core place in the policy tool-kit in Wales, as elsewhere in the UK.

Building on this 'bottom-up' experience and the early policy explorations of area-regeneration techniques, the Welsh Assembly Government has developed a far-reaching programme to combat social exclusion. The Communities First policy is targeting the hundred most disadvantaged communities in Wales, determined by the Index of Multiple Deprivation. In addition, thirty-two sub-ward pockets of poverty have been identified and a further ten communities as of interest. The programme will deliver long-term support and funding to community-based regeneration partnerships throughout Wales and engage community members and their local organizations actively in the regeneration process. In the geographical area covered by this article, seventeen Communities First localities have been identified and the local authority, voluntary sector and community agencies are collectively developing a response to the opportunities offered by the policy. Additionally, the Welsh Assembly Government's commitment to combating poverty has been reinforced in its second term by the creation of a specific ministerial office for Social Justice.

In addition to changes in the political and policy context there have also been significant economic changes. Arguably the most notable of these changes has been the considerable and sustained reduction in unemployment which occurred between 1995 and 2001.

In industrial south Wales employment growth has been concentrated along the so-called 'M4 corridor' where substantial flows of inward investment have produced a developing economy. Similar development has been elusive in the Valleys and unemployment has remained higher than the all-Wales figure throughout the period since the survey in 1995. However, the results from the 2001 survey, supported by secondary data from other sources, do provide evidence of reductions in unemployment in Valleys districts and a convergence with the wider pattern of unemployment in Wales. In 1996, shortly after the first study was published, the male unemployment rate in the area surveyed was 15.4 per cent compared with the Welsh rate of 11.6 per cent (Drinkwater, 1997). Figures for 2001, the year of the second survey, show not only a reduction to 7.30 per cent for the RCT area but a much closer fit to the all-Wales rate of 6.6 per cent (Brooksbank, 2001).

Consequently, the social, economic and political context of the 2001 survey is considerably different from that of the 1995 survey and represents a more optimistic social policy environment for tackling some of the issues identified in 1995. However, in many respects the theme of 'continuity and change' identified in 1995 remains constant. The underlying structural underpinnings of poverty and social exclusion remain intact. Whilst employment levels appear improved, there remain clear blackspots throughout the region, at county level in Blaenau Gwent and Merthyr Tydfil and within the workforce in the 18–24 age range (Brooksbank, 2001). Additionally, analysis of the 1991 census revealed major disparities at the local Enumeration District level, with key local-authority estates demonstrating very low levels of economic activity. Recent community audits conducted by the Regional Research Programme suggest that this local effect has prevailed, and the Small Area Statistics from the 2001 census are likely to verify this pattern on their release later this year.

Whilst the April 2001 survey has taken place in a social, cultural and political environment which is in many respects substantially different to that of the 1995 survey, and the concerns expressed by respondents have accordingly differed there remain many parallels. The social experience of life in the Valleys of south-east Wales has not been hugely changed by the intervening years.

THE SURVEY SAMPLE

In a time-comparative study such as this the major focus of analysis will inevitably be upon change over time. The validity of such analysis is obviously dependent upon the two samples of population being demonstrably similar in terms of their broad socio-economic and demographic characteristics. The sampling frame for the surveys ensured this, but it is important to emphasize that these are two different samples of population and that an element of caution needs to be exercised in drawing conclusions from comparisons of the two data-sets. Comparisons have been avoided where different sample characteristics exist. For example, one of the key differences in the 2001 sample has been the inclusion of respondents aged under 16 years. Their presence will obviously exert a direct effect upon some key results from the 2001 survey, and consequently this group has been excluded from certain areas of the analysis.

The main difference between the two samples of population relates to their size, with 572 responses being obtained in 1995 compared with 820 in 2001. Equally, whilst there appears to be a slight gender imbalance in the 2001 sample with 60 per cent of respondents being female and 40 per cent male, imbalance was also evident in the 1995 sample where 56 per cent of respondents were female and 44 per cent male. Although in the 2001 survey responses were elicited from those aged under 16 years, in overall terms the age distribution of the two samples is more or less identical, with the only major difference occurring in the proportion of the sample aged 51 and over.

TABLE **1.1**
Age distribution of the 1995 sample and the 2001 sample

Age Category	1995 (%)	2001 (%)
Under 16	n/a	8
16–20	10	10
21–30	17	17
31–40	16	16
41–50	14	13
51 & over	43	36

Where differences between the two samples are apparent they correspond with what might be expected from known trends occurring within Rhondda Cynon Taff and society generally. Thus, whilst in many respects the two samples of population are very similar in terms of marital status, almost twice as many respondents in the 2001 survey described themselves as co-habiting (see Table 1.2). This corresponds with a well-established trend of increasing diversity in household and family structures. Similarly, although owner-occupancy rates remain constant at around two-thirds of the population, the dimensions of the rental sector appear to have changed. Whilst overall numbers remain small, the 2001 survey recorded twice the proportion of tenants in Housing Association accommodation than was the case in 1995, and a greater number of tenants in private rented accommodation (11 per cent in 2001, compared with 9 per cent in 1995, see Table 1.3). Such statistics appear to confirm the continuation of a long-established decline in Local Authority accommodation as the principal form of social housing (Malpass, 1992; Taylor, 1996; WAG, 2001).

Finally, the 1995 survey was conducted in the immediate aftermath of a programme of pit closures which effectively marked the final demise of the deep-mining coal industry in south Wales, and in the context of successive recessions which produced persistently high levels of structural unemployment throughout the 1980s and 1990s. The 2001 survey was conducted against a markedly different economic background, in which there had been a period of sustained economic growth and declining rates of official unemployment. It is hardly surprising therefore that almost twice as many respondents (41 per cent) in the 2001 survey were in employment as was the case in the 1995 survey, where only 23 per cent of respondents were in employment.

TABLE 1.2
Marital status (excluding under 16-year-olds)

Marital status	1995 (%)	2001 (%)
Single	23	23
Married	51	49
Divorced	9	7
Separated	1	3
Cohabiting	5	9
Widow/er	11	9

TABLE 1.3
Housing tenure of sample

Housing tenure	1995 (%)	2001 (%)
Owner occupier	67	66
Council house	20	17
Housing association	2	4
Private rented	9	11
Other	2	2

ECONOMY, ECONOMIC ACTIVITY AND VALUES

In recent decades the economy of industrial south Wales has changed so radically that many commentators would now describe it as post-industrial. In common with other 'old' industrial areas of the UK and, indeed, across the western world, the traditional economic base of heavy manufacturing and coal extraction has followed a continuing trajectory of steep and unremitting decline. This demise has occurred alongside considerable growth in the service sector and light manufacturing, an expansion which has been greatly aided by new flows of inward investment. Indeed, in recent times Wales has succeeded in attracting a larger proportion of inward investment than any region in England or Scotland and, in contrast with the wider UK economy, the share of manufacturing output in the Welsh economy actually increased during the 1980s (Morgan and Price, 1992; Fevre, 1999). However, these expansions were from a low base and the proportion of GDP derived from manufacturing remains lower than the UK level.

Regrettably, these areas of new employment growth have done little to rectify the problems that have been generated by the decline of the traditional economic base in the south Wales valleys. Unlike the old industrial base, which was inextricably linked to the regional economy, inwardly investing firms tend to have a low positive economic multiplier effect (Turok, 1993; Roberts, 1994), whilst wage levels are typically around half that of a coal-miner or steel-worker (Drinkwater, 1997). Wales has persistently remained a low-wage region (Brooksbank *et al.*, 1997). Moreover inward investment has largely occurred around a relatively narrow 'M4 corridor' on the southern coastal plain, rather than in the valley districts to the north where new employment is most needed, following the demise of the coal industry (Blackaby *et al,* 1993). In the survey localities, inward investment is more evident in the Cynon valley. This in part reflects the natural geomorphology of the Rhondda valleys, which is noticeably narrower and steeper sided than the Cynon valley, creating a shortage of suitable land for developments such as business parks or road-widening schemes.

Recent changes to the south Wales economy have been underpinned by a process of unprecedented globalization which has also brought about wide-ranging changes to employment conditions and practices throughout the European Union. Labour markets have undergone a process of deregulation and increased flexibility, manifested in increases in part-time working, self employment, temporary employment contracts and in more general terms, by greater levels of job insecurity for employees in employment (Gaffikin and Morrisey, 1992). The notion of a 'job for life' is now widely assumed to be a thing of the past. However, the results from the 2001 survey show little evidence of increased flexibility and its expected effects in terms of respondents' reported labour-market behaviour and their perceptions of the labour market.

Critically, there is no evidence of widespread temporary employment or associated feelings of job insecurity. Fewer than one in ten respondents (7 per cent) reported being in temporary employment (exactly the same figure as in 1995), whilst perceptions of job insecurity were considerably lower amongst the 2001 sample. In 1995 almost one-third of respondents reported feeling insecure in their employment, compared with only 12 per cent of respondents in the 2001 survey. This is a clear reflection of the apparent improvement in local labour-market conditions discussed earlier. Moreover, as can be seen from Table 1.4, respondents in the 2001 survey were likely to have been in their current employment for a longer period of time than were respondents in the 1995 survey. For example, 35 per cent of respondents in the 2001 survey reported that they been in their current employment for over eleven years, compared with 26 per cent in 1995.

TABLE 1.4
Length of time in employment in current job

Length of time (years)	1995 (%)	2001 (%)
0–5	51	47
6–10	23	17
11–15	10	15
16–20	7	5
Over 20	9	15

However, in at least one key respect, the 2001 survey data demonstrate a close fit with the expected outcomes of economic restructuring and labour-market flexibilization; that is the wage-depressing effect which these processes are claimed to have exerted upon the incomes of broad swathes of the working population (Byrne, 1997). There is certainly much evidence of this in the Welsh economy, where the economic transformation described above has been paralleled by sustained decline in average incomes relative to other parts of the UK, most particularly in relation to the south-east of England (Brooksbank *et al.*, 1997). If anything the findings from the 2001 survey paint an even bleaker picture of wage levels in Rhondda Cynon Taff. Whereas official statistics reported that in 1997 only 12 per cent of full-time employees had earnings of less than £200 per week (Brooksbank *et al.*, 1997), nearly two-thirds (59 per cent) of respondents in the second survey in full-time employment reported earning less than £200 per week, whilst a small but nonetheless significant 5 per cent reported earning a weekly wage of less than £100 per week. Given these reported wage levels it is little wonder that the condition of the local labour market was identified by 40 per cent of respondents as one of the biggest problems facing the Valleys. Whilst a similar theme was powerfully evident in the 1995 survey, there was a qualitative shift in responses to the 2001 survey, where greater emphasis was placed upon the quality of employment, with much new employment being perceived as low paid and low quality.

As is briefly noted in the introduction, the proportion of the 2001 sample in either full- or part-time employment is almost double that of the 1995 sample (41 per cent compared to 23 per cent). However, even here the survey results are far from straightforward, as can be seen from Table 1.5. Whereas it might be expected that increased employment levels are reflected in corresponding reductions in registered unemployment, the principal reductions in the survey sample appear to have occurred amongst certain categories of economic inactivity rather than among the registered unemployed. Whilst there is a difference of four percentage points in the proportion of the sample describing themselves as unemployed, the proportion of the 2001 sample describing themselves as permanently sick/disabled or as a house-worker is approximately half that of the 1995 sample. This apparently considerable decrease in economic inactivity may well be the result of more buoyant economic conditions, encouraging the labour market return or entry of individuals who were previously numbered amongst the unofficial or hidden unemployed.

Beatty and Fothergill (1998) argue that a significant number of those who lost employment as a result of the demise of the mining industry moved on to sickness rather than unemployment benefits. This, they argue, occurred with the tacit support of government which was keen to lower official unemployment, and as a result of the relatively generous rates of allowance and eligibility conditions of these benefits. Their relative attractiveness was increased by the sustained programme of cuts to unemployment benefits (Pierson, 1994) and the introduction of increasingly stringent and coercive eligibility conditions (Wikeley, 1989).

The apparent reduction in the number of house-workers probably also reflects increased economic opportunities for these individuals and their consequent labour market entry/return. It is equally likely that this group is principally comprises individuals with partners who are already in employment and who therefore face fewer economic barriers to entering into employment. There is certainly strong evidence of polarization between 'work rich' and 'work poor' households in the 2001 sample. In nearly three-quarters (72 per cent) of cases where the respondent was in employment and had a partner, their partner was also employed. This compares with only one-third (33 per cent) of those respondents who described themselves as unemployed and one-fifth (21 per cent) of those who described themselves as permanently sick or disabled.

TABLE 1.5
Economic status

Economic status	1995 (%)	2001 (%)
Working	23	41
Unemployed	18	14
Retired	27	22
Permanently sick/disabled	12	6
House worker	10	4
Student	6	11
Government training	1	–
Other	3	–

Consequently, the 2001 survey data suggest that there is a stability in patterns of fragmentation, polarization and exclusion that were evident during the 1990s. Continuing local high levels of unemployment and polarization between 'work rich' and 'work poor' households may well be indicative of the continuing exclusion of a Marginalized Working Class identified in the 1995 survey. Equally, there is strong evidence of the continuation of these patterns of exclusion from the data relating to the family relationships of under 16-year-olds. For example over a quarter (27 per cent) of the under 16-year-olds interviewed during the 2001 survey lived in lone-parent families, and 40 per cent lived in households where there was no adult in employment.

Finally, it is worth briefly commenting upon the limited evidence about the causation of labour-market exclusion and its associated poverty which is available from the 2001 survey data. The 1995 survey was conducted at a time when stigmatizing, behaviourally-based explanations of poverty such as Murray *et al.*'s (1990, 1996) underclass thesis enjoyed considerable currency in public debate and in the development of social policy. These explanations essentially contended that much contemporary poverty was caused by the labour-market behaviour of the poor themselves, who, it was argued, lacked a work ethic. Then, as now, the survey results showed no evidence to support these claims. In responses to a series of questions which addressed this issue, the 1995 survey demonstrated a deep-rooted commitment to working for a living amongst respondents, despite the severe contraction of the labour market. If anything, this commitment appears to have strengthened amongst the 2001 sample. Respondents demonstrate a willingness to take actions to improve employability in both surveys. These findings are in line with other research conducted locally which explores this issue in considerably more depth (Jones, 1999).

TABLE **1.6**

Proportion of respondents answering 'Yes' to questions on improving their employment prospects

	1995 (%)	2001 (%)
Willing to move from area	57	60
Willing to retrain	73	74
Willing to start business	41	43

COMMUNITY, CULTURE AND SOCIETY

Although an ostensibly straightforward term, community represents a complex and contested amalgamation of ideas and notions which defy simple definition and frequently produce contradictory and paradoxical outcomes (Hoggett (ed.), 1997). However, whilst recognizing the contradictions and complexities which are inherent within concepts of community, the approach adopted within this analysis has been to adhere to the commonsensical usage and understanding of this term employed by respondents. Although inevitably tied in with processes of nostalgia, romanticization and sanitation, this notion of community is something which possesses enormous resonance for Valleys residents. Despite fundamental changes to the Valleys' economic base, respondents in the 1995 survey reported high levels of community association, both in terms of their perceptions and in reported behaviour. This has continued to be the case in results from the 2001 survey, which found that 85 per cent of respondents claimed that the level of community in their area was either 'excellent', 'good', or 'acceptable' (compared to 84 per cent of respondents to the 1995 survey). Equally, 32 per cent included 'community' when asked what three things they liked best about the area in which they lived, and 59 per cent expressed the view that it was the sense of community which made the Valleys different from other parts of Wales.

Additionally, respondents clearly placed great faith in their immediate social networks as a source of support during times of adversity. Whilst the greatest reliance was placed upon family networks, with 81 per cent of respondents claiming they would receive help from this source, more than half also expected to receive support from neighbours (58 per cent) and/or friends (55 per cent). This deep-rooted reliance upon close-knit social networks of kinship and friendship has also been demonstrated in other studies conducted locally, particularly in those which examine various aspects of young peoples' social exclusion (Jones, 2001; Hutson and Jones, 1997, 1999). Thus community continues to be firmly embedded in respondents' perceptions as a defining characteristic of Valleys life, whilst local social networks retain their importance as a source of support, particularly during times of adversity.

However, paradoxically, the 2001 survey results also appear to indicate greater privatization of Valleys social life in respondents' perceptions and in their reported behaviour. One-fifth (20 per cent) of respondents felt that a decline in traditional community structures, practices and values was one of the biggest changes occurring in Valleys life. Such views were typically expressed through comments such as 'people are more private' or 'are too busy for one another', but were also closely linked to perceptions of rising crime and drug abuse (19 per cent) and changes to the local labour market (27 per cent). Evidence of a more privatized social life in the Valleys can also be found in reported behaviour. Thus, whilst respondents in the 2001 survey reported similar levels of contact with near relatives as did respondents in the 1995 survey, the frequency of contact with neighbours was significantly lower, with 10 per cent of respondents claiming that contact with their neighbours occurred on a 'monthly or less' basis compared to 3 per cent in 1995 (see Table 1.7). Similarly, whereas almost a third (31 per cent) of respondents in the 1995 survey claimed membership of a local community group or association, less than a quarter (23 per cent) of respondents in the 2001 survey made this claim.

However, these overall trends in Valleys community life are often contradicted at the local level, particularly in those localities which have been the settings for recent community-based regeneration programmes. The findings from the 2001 survey provide some indication that these programmes can have a substantial effect upon levels of community association and levels of perceived community. Thus in Blaenllechau, which is home to the 'Bell Centre', an active community-regeneration facility, nearly three-quarters (74 per cent) of respondents claimed to be members of a local community group or organization, and 97 per cent reported that the sense of community in their area was 'excellent', 'good' or 'acceptable'. Equally, the 1995 survey found that over a third (39 per cent) of respondents from deprived local authority estates viewed the sense of community in their area as 'poor' or 'very poor', compared with only 16 per cent of the overall sample. The results from the 2001 survey indicate a clear reversal of this trend in certain localities with, for example, only 6 per cent of respondents from the Penrhys estate reporting that the sense of community in their area was 'poor' or 'very poor' (compared with 15 per cent of the overall sample).

TABLE 1.7
Levels of reported social contact with near relatives and neighbours

	Near-relatives (%)		Neighbours (%)	
	1995	2001	1995	2001
At least once per week	84	84	62	54
At least once per fortnight	6	5	5	9
Monthly or less	11	9	3	10

Possibly reflecting greater dynamism in the labour market, the 2001 survey data also show a less settled pattern of residence than was apparent amongst respondents to the 1995 survey. Although when looking at the overall sample this might be explained by the inclusion of under 16-year-olds in the 2001 survey, this trend remains intact when this group is removed from the analysis. As can be seen from Table 1.8, whereas 57 per cent of respondents in the 1995 survey had lived in their area for over 21 years, this was the case for less than half (45 per cent) of respondents to the 2001 survey. Moreover, evidence of greater turnover of population within Valleys communities is also apparent in respondents' perceptions of the changes occurring around them, with respondents citing either in-migration (5 per cent) or out-migration (5 per cent) as one of the biggest changes to Valleys life.

TABLE 1.8
Length of residence (excluding under 16-year-olds)

Length of residence (years)	1995 (%)	2001 (%)
0–5	16	19
6–10	9	12
11–15	8	8
16–20	10	9
Over 20	57	45

It is likely that a further key factor in respondents' perceptions of declining community life can be found in the acutely perceived lack of services and local amenities. The issue of local amenities illustrates how in many ways Valleys residents can be seen as being doubly disadvantaged, in the sense that their disadvantage includes components of both rural and urban disadvantage (Bennett, Beynon and Hudson, 2000). Socially, economically and culturally, Valleys society is rooted in urban industrial structures, and has experienced problems which would be familiar to inner-city areas across the western world. However, the geography of the Valleys, and the corresponding elongated ribbon-like development of housing, creates problems for the provision of services and amenities which would be more familiar to rural areas. Particularly, in the more isolated and inaccessible areas there is a lack of even the most basic public or private sector amenities, such as schools, medical centres, dentists, shops, post offices or public houses. The sense of physical isolation and social exclusion which this can create amongst residents in these localities is further exacerbated by an inadequate or declining public-transport infrastructure.

Respondents frequently cited the lack or absence of local services and amenities as a contributory factor in the emergence of social problems in their area. Thus, 20 per cent of respondents expressed the view that a lack of recreational facilities and boredom amongst younger generations was a major cause of crime in their area. Less dramatically, but arguably of greater severity, a lack of amenities can be directly implicated in young people's ostensibly harmless behaviour becoming viewed by other residents as problematic or even delinquent. Through lack of alternative venues, young people frequently congregate in and socialize in prominent public spaces where their presence, and often essentially innocuous behaviour, can be a source of disturbance and even fear for other residents.

However, responses relating to local amenity and service provision are both complex and contradictory. Thus whilst 26 per cent of respondents cited the absence or poor quality of local services and amenities as one of the three things they liked least about their area another 33 per cent cited proximity to local services and amenities as one of the things they liked best about their area. Clearly, these responses are in large part conditioned by locality and proximity to town centres. Thus as can be seen in Table 1.9, residents of the small and isolated communities of Blaenllechau and Stanleytown were twice as likely to cite lack of services and amenities as one of three things they liked least about their area as were residents of the valley towns of Pontypridd, Porth and Aberdare. However, this does underline the post-code lottery of service provision and the strong sense of physical isolation in the upper reaches of the Rhondda Valley especially, where medical services are particularly difficult to access.

TABLE 1.9
Perceived lack of amenities in different localities

	% of responses
Porth	23
Pontypridd	20
Aberdare	22
Stanley Town	42
Blaenllechau	40
Blaen-cwm	50
Entire sample	26

CRIME AND SOCIAL PROBLEMS

In the 1995 survey, perceptions of rising crime proved to be one of the key issues emerging from the data, and, alongside perceptions of rising unemployment and drug use, were entwined with perceptions of community change and decline. This has also proved to be the case with the results from the 2001 survey. Crime and drug abuse comprised nearly one-fifth (18 per cent) of responses to the question which asked respondents to list the three things they liked least about their area, whilst a further third (30 per cent) cited minor crimes such as littering, dog fouling, vandalism and graffiti. Similarly, crime and drug abuse ranked second in respondents' perceptions of the most serious problems facing the Valleys, with 36 per cent of respondents expressing this view. However, the 2001 survey data does indicate a trend towards some reduction in the fear of crime.

TABLE 1.10
Respondents' perception of the level of crime in their area

Perceived level of crime	1995 (%)	2001 (%)
Very high	21	13
High	38	29
Average	31	35
Low	8	15
Very low	2	6

Nearly twice as many respondents believed crime in their area to be 'low' or 'very low', whilst the number of respondents who believed that crime in their area was either 'high' or 'very high' was a third lower than in 1995. That said, it remained the case that a greater proportion of the sample believed that crime in their area was either 'high' or 'very high' (42 per cent) than 'low' or 'very low' (21 per cent).

There is further evidence of reduced fear of crime in the responses to a series of questions which asked respondents about their perceptions of safety within their local area. In 2001 only 22 per cent of respondents claimed to have altered routines because of crime in their area compared to 46 per cent in 1995. Moreover, the fear of crime is generally low amongst respondents in the 2001 survey, with only 3 per cent of respondents claiming to feel unsafe in their neighbourhood during daylight hours and 2 per cent of respondents feeling unsafe in their homes during daytime. Unsurprisingly, the proportion of the sample who feel unsafe rises at night, with 11 per cent claiming to feel unsafe in their homes and 35 per cent reporting that they felt unsafe in their neighbourhood. These fears are greatest amongst women and older sections of the population with only 53 per cent of women and 54 per cent of respondents aged forty-one and over reporting that they felt safe in their neighbourhood after dark.

Although there is overall evidence of reduced fear of crime amongst respondents to the 2001 survey, this pattern obscures considerable local variations. Indeed, these local differences constitute a key issue which has emerged from the crime data in the 2001 survey. In certain localities, within the Cynon Valley in particular, many respondents complained of an escalating problem of heroin abuse and associated problems of criminality (often coupled by a perception that these problems had been imported into these communities through the council-housing policy or through private-sector absentee landlords).

TABLE **1.11**
Localities where there are perceived high crime levels

	% of respondents viewing crime as high or very high
Fernhill	84
Hirwaun	72
Penrhiwceiber	76
Pen-y-waun	67
Overall sample	42

In the 1995 survey respondents cited the state of the local labour market as the dominant explanation of crime in their area. In the 2001 survey this position was occupied by drug abuse. In four localities in the Cynon Valley the proportion of respondents expressing the view that crime in their area was either 'high' or 'very high' was almost double that of the overall sample. Equally, respondents in these localities focused almost exclusively upon crime and drug abuse when asked to list the three things they liked least about their area. Thus in an area of high rise-flats in Hirwaun the issue of drugs and crime accounted for 68 per cent of responses to this question, and in Pen-y-waun it accounted for 34 per cent compared with 18 per cent for the entire sample. During the course of a single morning in one locality one of the authors of this report interviewed three different individuals who had had direct and recent experience of these types of difficulties. One woman claimed that within a single year a peer had died of a drug overdose, her child had found a discarded 'dirty needle' and that a heroin user had collapsed in the street outside her house. Whether apocryphal or not, the references to such social experiences are sufficient to demonstrate major anxiety at a community level over issues of drug abuse and associated criminality in these specific communities.

Pessimistically, the survey points very clearly to areas of Rhondda Cynon Taff where fear of crime is significantly higher than should reasonably be expected. Additionally, assessments of crime levels remain high for a majority of the respondents. More optimistically, the 2001 survey also points generally to a much lower fear of crime for the survey population as a whole and a corresponding lower impact on feelings of community and personal safety. In 2001 significantly more people feel safe in their community and home, at both day- and night-times, and fewer respondents have altered their activities in relation to perceptions of crime. Explanation of these partial improvements is difficult to provide from the survey data, and it is likely that a combination of improved economy, higher employment levels, local community safety initiatives, community-regeneration activities and youth-crime initiatives have all had a role in reducing fear of crime levels in the majority of areas covered by the survey.

CONCLUSIONS

The results of the 2001 survey clearly indicate that the central analytical themes of continuity and change, that were identified in results from the 1995 survey, are of continuing relevance to Valleys society. In comparative terms, a healthier labour market has raised feelings of job security and the wider UK economic upturn since 1995 has impacted on the pattern of unemployment and economic inactivity in the south Wales Valleys. Improvements in these areas demonstrated by the comparison between 1995 responses and those given in 2001 are to be welcomed for their general impact on social exclusion and disadvantage in south Wales. However, the findings reported in this article demonstrate the persistence of key social problems affecting the quality of life in the region and the existence of significant continuities in the pattern of social, cultural and economic life of residents of Rhondda Cynon Taff. In particular, the structural patterns of poverty and social exclusion identified by the Regional Research Project in the mid-1990s appear to have remained intact, as does the polarized spatial form that these phenomena have taken.

That said, in certain key respects, the dimensions of these social problems appear to have undergone significant change during the last six years. During the mid-1990s, these problems were largely defined by the poverty and social exclusion associated with high levels of unemployment and economic inactivity amongst those of working age. The 2001 survey shows that, whilst these problems of unemployment and economic inactivity persist, there appears to have been considerable growth in the number of individuals in employment during the course of the last six years, as might be expected from national economic trends. Yet this growth appears to have occurred in employment which offers low levels of remuneration, despite the relatively recent introduction of a statutory minimum wage. It is therefore unsurprising that the condition of the local labour market is still regarded by many residents as one of the 'biggest problems' facing the Valleys.

As in 1995, some contradiction exists between reported high levels of social interaction and community relations and expressed feelings of a decline in community. The level of contacts between relatives and neigh-bours, although lower in the 2001 than in 1995, continues to demonstrate close social relationships and strong social networks. High appraisal of the quality of community stands in contrast to responses to other questions which cite declining community as being evident. Whilst in part this points to the difficulty of operationalizing a concept like 'community' in survey work, it also points to the ways in which different components of social life make up a sense of community. In their close everyday relations, contacts with friends and neighbours reinforce a sense of community, despite issues such as fear of crime, unemployment and drug abuse creating a sense that community is being undermined by negative changes. Moreover, perceived acute lack of services and amenities is something that many respondents regard as a key factor in problems as diverse as youth crime and drug abuse and the social isolation of the elderly. More generally, it would seem highly probable that declining levels of community association, whether evidenced by respondents' perception or reported behaviour, are powerfully influenced by a lack of such provision. If nothing else, these services and amenities can provide the physical venues in which the routine and mundane forms of social interaction which underpin community life take place. Declining services inevitably impact on the levels of community association.

Counteracting this trend is the growth of community-centred initiatives which are providing local services in a variety of innovative and different ways. The highest density of community regeneration programmes in Wales can be found in the area covered by this survey (*www.glam.ac.uk/ regeneration*). Major projects such as those found in such communities as Penrhys, Pen-y-waun, Blaenllechau, Ferndale and many other locations are providing essential services to the community as well as building a renewed sense of community in all age groups. The results from the 2001 survey provide clear evidence of the positive effects which these programmes have had in communities such as Penrhys. Not only did the survey record a greater sense of community amongst respondents in Penrhys than was apparent amongst the overall sample, but it also provided evidence that the sense of community had increased since the 1995 survey – a trend which stands in contrast to the prevailing trend of community decline which is evident amongst the wider sample.

Finally, one of the key symbolic indicators in perceptions of declining community spirit recorded in responses to the 1995 survey was constituted by perceptions of rising crime levels. The problem here was not simply the direct effects of actual crimes but the wider-ranging effects it had upon community relationships, most especially in the loss of trust in others that these perceptions brought about. This was perhaps best illustrated by the number of respondents who claimed that they now felt the need to lock their front door, in contrast to a past perception of immunity from local crime. Pessimistically, the survey points very clearly to areas of Rhondda Cynon Taff where fear of crime is significantly higher than should reasonably be expected. Additionally, assessments of crime levels remain high for a majority of the respondents. More optimistically, the 2001 survey also points generally to a much lower fear of crime for the survey population as a whole, and a corresponding lower impact on feelings of community and personal safety. In 2001 significantly more people feel safe in their community and home, at both day- and night-times, and less respondents have altered their activities in relation to perceptions of crime. In the aspects of social, economic and community life investigated by the two surveys, the data present a complex view of life in the south Wales Valleys. Variations in perception and experience belie the myth of a unified Valleys lifestyle, which currently preoccupies media coverage of the region and finds its way into social policy. Policies such as Communities First, which allow a role for local experience and embed change in community processes, are likely to be more successful than past policies driven by centralism and top-down economic measures. In conducting this and other surveys in the region no fieldworker can remain unimpressed with the optimism and commitment of residents of those communities, even in the least desirable locations. Here we record our gratitude for the assistance and support given to this research by local residents and hope that we have added to the information and understanding needed to drive a full regeneration of the communities we visited.

REFERENCES

Adamson, D. (1988). 'The new working class in welsh politics', *Contemporary Wales*, 2, 7–28.
Adamson, D. (1991). 'Lived experience, social consumption and political change in Wales', in Day, G. and Rees, G. (eds), *Nations and European Integration: Remaking the Celtic Periphery*, Cardiff: University of Wales Press.
Adamson, D. (1998). 'The spatial organisation of difference and exclusion in a working class community', in *Full Employment: A European Appeal. The Spokesman*, 64, 141–52, Nottingham: Bertrand Russell Peace Foundation.
Barclay, P, and Hills, J. (1995). *Inquiry into Income and Wealth*, York: Joseph Rowntree Foundation.
Beatty, C, and Fothergill, S. (1998). 'Registered and hidden unemployment in the UK coalfields', in Lawless, P., Martin, R, and Hardy, S. (ed.), *Unemployment and Social Exclusion: Landscapes of Labour Inequality*, London: Jessica Kingsley.
Bennett, K., Beynon, H. and Hudson, R. (2000). *Coalfields Regeneration: Dealing with the Consequences of Industrial Decline*, Bristol: The Policy Press in association with the Joseph Rowntree Foundation.
Blackaby, D., Murphy, P. and Thomas, D. (1993). 'Wales: an economic survey', in *Contemporary Wales*, 8, 213–304.
Brooksbank, D., Pickernell, D. and Morse, L. (1997). 'Low pay and inward investment: lessons for Wales', Paper 2, *Occasional Papers in the Regional Research Programme*, Pontypridd: University of Glamorgan.
Brooksbank, D. (2001). 'The Welsh economy: a statistical profile', in *Contemporary Wales*, 14, 164–92.
Byrne, D. (1997). 'Social exclusion and capitalism: the reserve army across time and space', in *Critical Social Policy*, 59, 17, 27–51.

Dennis, N. and Urdos, G. (1992). *Families Without Fatherhood,* Choice in Welfare Series, No. 12, London: IEA Health and Welfare Unit.

Drinkwater, S. (1997). 'The Welsh economy: a statistical profile', in *Contemporary Wales,* 9: 171–90, Cardiff: University of Wales Press.

Fevre, R.(1999). 'The Welsh economy', in Dunkerley, D. and Thompson, A. (eds), *Wales Today.*

Gaffikin, F. and Morrisey, M. (1992), *The New Unemployed: Joblessness and Poverty in the Market Economy,* London and New Jersey: Zed Books.

Hoggett, P. (ed.) (1997). *Contested Communities: Experiences, Struggle, Policies,* Bristol: The Policy Press.

Hutson, S., and Jones, S. (1999). *Building a Better Future? The Evaluation of the Taff Ely Self Build Scheme,* Ilford: Barnardo's.

Hutson, S., and Jones, S. (1997). *Rough Sleeping and Homelessness in Rhondda Cynon Taff,* Pontypridd: University of Glamorgan.

Jones, R. (1999). 'Breakdown of the work ethic? An analysis of labour force attachment in a marginalised community', unpublished M. Phil thesis, School of Humanities and Social Sciences, University of Glamorgan, Pontypridd.

Jones, S. (2001). 'Young men, community and social exclusion', conference paper presented to the Anthropology Wales Conference, Rhondda Heritage Park, Trehafod.

Jones, S. (1995). 'Social polarisation in Mid Glamorgan', paper presented to the *Ideas of Community Conference,* University of West of England, 11–13 September 1995.

Levitas, R. (1996). 'The concept of social exclusion and the new Durkheimian hegemony', *Critical Social Policy,* 16, 5–20.

Malpass, P. (1992). 'Housing policy and the disabling of local authorities', in Birchall, J. (ed.), *Housing Policy in the 1990s,* London: Routledge.

Mid Glamorgan Update (Summer 1994). 'Incomes in Mid Glamorgan: the north south divide', No. 19, Policy, Research and European Affairs Unit.

Morgan, K., and Price, A. (1992). *Re-building Our Communities: A New Agenda for the Valleys,* Cardiff: Institute of Welsh Affairs.

Morris, J., and Wilkinson, B. (1996). 'Poverty and prosperity in Wales: polarization and Los Angelesization', *Contemporary Wales,* 8, 29–45.

Murray, C. *et al.* (1990). *The Emerging British Underclass,* London: Institute of Economic Affairs.

Murray, C. *et al.* (1996). *Charles Murray and the Underclass: The Developing Debate,* The Institute of Economic Affairs (IEA) Health and Welfare Unit in association with *The Sunday Times Magazine,* Choice in Welfare No. 33, London.

Philo, C. (1995). *Off the Map: The Social Geography of Poverty in the UK,* London: Child Poverty Action Group.

Pierson, P. (1994). *Dismantling the Welfare State? Reagan, Thatcher and the Politics of Retrenchment,* Cambridge: Cambridge University Press.

Roberts, A. (1994). 'The causes and consequences of inward investment: the Welsh experience', in *Contemporary Wales,* 6, 73–86.

Taylor, M. (1996). 'Combating the social exclusion of housing estates', paper presented to Housing and Social Exclusion Housing Studies Association, 1996 Autumn Conference.

Turok, I. (1993). 'Contrasts in ownership and development: local versus global in "Silicon Glen" ', *Urban Studies*, 30, 2, 365–86.

Welsh Assembly Government (WAG) (2001). *The Tenants' Views of Social Rented Housing*, Housing Research Report No: HRR 2/01-May 2001, Cardiff: WAG.

Wikeley, N. (1989). 'Unemployment benefit, the state and the labour market', *Journal of Law and Society*, 16, 3, 291–309.

2. ELY: A 'DANGEROUS PLACE' REVISITED

Jonathan Evans and Fiona Wood

Cardiff's Ely estate, the largest local-authority housing development in Wales with more than 30,000 residents, has been reported upon on a number of occasions in academic literature (see, for example, Smith, 1983; Williamson and Weatherspoon, 1985; Drakeford, 1993). It emerges as an area in which a range of social difficulties have coalesced progressively during the last quarter of the twentieth century. A combination of regular stigmatization in the local media and a paradoxical pride by local residents in their Ely identity still produces a sense of the area being a 'township' beyond the main city walls.

Although Ely's public image has often been very negative, the area was never particularly associated with the problem of racism until the so-called 'riots' in August 1991. The proportion of the local population drawn from minority ethnic populations is below both the UK and Cardiff averages, although such percentages still represent some 1,000 people from visible minorities living in the area. In the aftermath of what were seen as racially motivated disturbances, many local white people adopted an under-standably defensive posture in response to the negative portrayal of their community. This was particularly evident, however, when the 'race' dimension to the riots was broached. On one level, of course, the riot took the form of young white men in blue jeans squaring up to young white men in blue uniforms. Unlike Brixton in 1981, though, Ely's was a 'white riot' (Sturges, 1995). Nevertheless, there can now be very little doubt that the incendiary events that detonated the riots were explicitly racist in motivation. When a Pakistani grocer was drawn into a trading dispute with a white newsagent, certain sections of the white community aligned themselves with the newsagent. One of the central organizing principles of this mobilization was undoubtedly racism. Indeed, scenes involving white people chanting 'Pakis out' can be explained in no other terms.

These scenes were, in fact, the culmination of a pattern of racially motivated incidents. The Pakistani grocer concerned had already been subjected to at least eleven racially motivated offences between 1987 and January 1991 (Campbell, 1993: 27). This repeated harassment also took place against a growing trend of racially motivated offences in the area. Although the sharp rise in these figures can be partly explained by improvements in the police's recording practices, the wider social context of racist activity seems evident.

Despite the evidence of racism in Ely, the police, local media and white community leaders were all complicit in downplaying the significance of racism as an issue. Williams and Short (Williams, 1995; Williams and Short, 1997) have written about the wide currency of certain Welsh myths in contemporary popular culture. One such myth is the belief that Wales is a tolerant society; a place that accepts and welcomes difference. Such popularly held beliefs are often in vivid contrast to the daily reality of many people's lives. Evans (1985) has also argued that white Cardiff is very reluctant to confront its racist past. This same process of collective denial – a communal defence mechanism, perhaps – seemed to operate in Ely in the months that followed the riots. For example, the Reverend Bob Morgan, a popular local councillor, declared in the *South Wales Echo* in September 1991: 'The public reads "race riot", which couldn't be further from the truth. Ely people, regardless of colour, inter-marry and live harmoniously together' (Campbell, 1993: 125); indeed, it was declared that: 'Only ignorant outsiders see race as a community issue in Ely' (Campbell, 1993: 159).

It is likely that Revd Morgan was anxious to defend his embattled and stigmatized community against the charge of 'white trash' racism. There was, no doubt, a very real danger that some sections of the media would seek to pathologize Ely and diagnose it as a 'sick community'. It was, perhaps, in this context that Revd Morgan also referred to the chair of the Race Equality Council, Dr Rita Austin, a black woman, as an 'ill-informed outsider' (Campbell, 1993: 159). Ideas about 'insiders' and 'outsiders' appear to be very important in places like Ely, and Dr Rita Austin probably *was* perceived by many local white people as an agent of unwelcome outside interference.

The depth of the white community's continuing denial is evident in the report of a 'One Day Residents' Conference' (1992) held some seven months after the riots. The document is an excellent record of a community confronting *most* of its social problems in a candid and creative way. The document is equally notable for its silences: the absence of a distinctive black or minority perspective is certainly its most profound weakness. Insofar as the experience of minority ethnic residents is addressed at all, it is dealt with in a somewhat dismissive fashion:

> the media coverage of the disturbances in Ely caused tension by inferring that racism was at the root of the trouble. Those in the group felt strongly that this had not been the case, and that Ely suffered very little from racist issues.

> where there were any incidents of racist behaviour, these were isolated incidents and were due to a lack of education on the part of the aggressor.

> That there was a danger of misinterpreting remarks and actions as being of a racist nature when they may well have not been intended as such.
> (Ely Community Development Forum, 1992: 35).

In the report's recommendations, it is stated that: 'every opportunity should be taken to integrate members of ethnic minorities further into the community, and [they should be] encouraged to join local activities and community groups' (Ely Community Development Forum, 1992: 37). The concept of integration within the document is not defined. Furthermore, the possibility that ethnic minorities may desire separate provision of services in some areas of social life is not mentioned. Members of ethnic minorities are, instead, to be 'encouraged to join local activities and community groups'. Without in any way wishing to denigrate the altruistic sentiments that probably lay behind these words, it is nevertheless important to question the model of 'integration' white people in Ely had in mind. Asad (1990) has commented that modern nation states appear to offer minorities a stark choice: 'complete assimilation' or 'despised difference and exclusion'. As Solomos puts it: 'While this argument may seem somewhat overstated it is also reflective of an ongoing struggle in contemporary societies, including Britain, over the definition of who belongs and who does not' (Solomos, 1993: 218). One might add that it also raises the supplementary practical question of *how* minorities might belong to communities like Ely.

It is clear from a review of the literature that discussions about Ely have taken the form of an exclusively white discourse. The experiences of minority ethnic people have been pushed to the margins of 'authorized' community texts. The research reported here represents a modest attempt to bear witness to those experiences of marginalization.

THE RESEARCH

The research was commissioned by the voluntary sector children's charity, Barnardo's. The initial impetus for this research came from an Ely-based Barnardo's project, the Community Shop. The staff at the Community Shop identified three main reasons for the research. Firstly, the community project was failing to engage meaningfully with minority ethnic residents in Ely. Consequently, it was not known whether their needs were actually being met. Secondly, some racially motivated incidents had taken place in the locality. This raised wider questions concerning the nature of relations between the different communities in Ely. Was Ely a community at ease with itself? Thirdly, Barnardo's is an organization committed to developing best practice in anti-racist work. It was hoped that the lessons learned from Ely could be applied to other neighbourhoods.

It was against this background that we, as white researchers from Cardiff University, embarked upon a series of exploratory meetings with the agency in order to develop a research strategy. Those involved in this process included representatives from Barnardo's, Ely police officers, the South Wales Police Minorities and Racial Incidents Unit, the Director of Cardiff and the Vale Race Equality Council (subsequently renamed Race Equality First), the manager of the Cardiff-based Combating Racial Harassment Project and a local councillor. On the basis of extensive consultation the research aims were negotiated and formalized. The research would be conducted with visible minority ethnic residents in Ely on four broad themes: the experience of living in Ely; the experience of service delivery; the experience of racial discrimination and harassment; and individual profiling around such issues as income, household structure, language and religion. It was also agreed that data collection would be conducted by interviewers drawn from minority ethnic communities (using section 52D of the Race Relations Act 1976). The principle of 'ethnic matching' – in terms of linking the profiles of interviewers and research participants – was seen as an important ideal to which to aspire. It was the collective view that such interviewers were best placed to access the more sensitive 'lived experiences' of minority residents in the neighbourhood. This perspective is broadly consistent with the position taken by Russell (1992), Bhopal (2001) and Phillips and Bowling (2003). The decision did, however, raise the possibility of a problematic division of intellectual labour along racial lines. The prospect of 'white experts' analysing the data generated by 'minority data collectors' was a scenario fraught with tensions and pitfalls. In the interests of developing an inclusive research practice it was therefore seen as essential to form a 'reference group' that included minority ethnic community residents from Ely as well as the interviewers and representative professionals. The 'reference group', which gave itself the name of EMBRACE (Ethnic Minority and Black Reference Action Coalition in Ely), came to play a crucially influential role in the five key stages of the research: designing the interview schedule; interpreting the collated data (including field notes); determining the format, structure and content of the final report; framing a set of key recommendations for further action; and disseminating the Report's findings to the wider community (public meetings, media coverage, and so on.). The presence of a 'reference group' as an active agent in the research process was an acknowledgement that the production of knowledge is a socially and culturally contested activity. Our meetings with EMBRACE provided important fora within which to negotiate the possible 'meanings' of the data produced.

The form of research conducted in Ely was both quantitative and qualitative, combining the techniques of questionnaires and semi-structured interviews. Potential research participants were approached through a process of 'snowball sampling'. This approach eventually produced a total of thirty-nine face-to-face interviews with black and minority ethnic residents. A summary of the major results follows.

Demography
The thirty-nine respondents were from a wide age range (19 to 68 years), although the majority were aged between 30 and 49 years. A wide range of ethnic groups were represented in the sample and the one person who identified herself as white had children of mixed race. Fifty-six per cent of participants were female. Questions relating to household composition revealed that 64 per cent of participants had children living with them and nearly half (49 per cent) were the only adults in the household. Nearly half (46 per cent) described themselves as Christian, and 28 per cent described themselves as having no religion. Participants were also asked about their approximate annual household income. Annual household income is, of course, only a proxy indicator of social and economic deprivation. The measure is problematic in that there is little indication of how many people in the household are supported by the income. Nevertheless it was considered important that some attempt be made at calculating the income of the respondents. Thirty-six per cent of respondents were living on an estimated total annual household income of less than £5,000 and a further

26 per cent were living on an estimated household income of between £5,000 and £10,000. Household income was found to be associated with age (the younger the respondent the less the household income tended to be). Furthermore, single adults, lone parents, those living with relatives, and pensioners tended to be living on a lower household income than couples. The majority (90 per cent) of the respondents spoke English at home and a third of the sample spoke languages other than English. It could be surmised that many people from ethnic minority groups in Ely are bilingual and attention could be given to viewing bilingual communities as an economic resource rather than being an educational challenge (Casson *et al.*, 1994). Whereas the positive benefits of Welsh/English bilingualism are rightly highlighted in the Welsh context, a deficit model tends to be applied to those languages that do not enjoy the same claim to territoriality. Whereas a 'deficit analysis' focuses attention on the disadvantages associated with use of a minority community language (creating a 'language barrier' or 'cultural obstacle' to the achievement of 'social inclusion'), 'resource' or 'opportunity' analyses can reframe exactly the same situation in a positive light (recognising bilingualism/multilingualism as an additional qualification or value-added skill).

Living in Ely
About half (49 per cent) of the participants were living in council-owned accommodation. A further 10 per cent lived in housing association properties and 41 per cent were owner-occupiers. Data produced by Cardiff County Council (1996) states that 51 per cent of tenure in Ely is local authority, 3 per cent Housing Association and 43 per cent owner occupied. For Caerau the figures are 32 per cent, 9 per cent and 54 per cent respectively. Therefore, the participants reflect a representative sample of housing tenure. The majority of the sample had lived in Ely for over thirty-five years; eleven people (26 per cent) had lived in Ely all of their lives; and a further thirteen (33 per cent) had lived in Ely for more than half of their lives. The majority (64 per cent) of respondents stated that they were satisfied with their accommodation. However residents of council-owned houses were less likely to be satisfied with their accommodation than were residents of privately-owned houses. Where there was dissatisfaction with council houses this was usually because of delays in repair works or the property being too small and cramped.

Participants were asked what they liked best and what they disliked the most about Ely. The most common response was that they most liked the sense of belonging to Ely and having friends and family nearby. Respondents were most likely to express a dislike of the troublesome children on the streets, abuse from other local residents and the poor public image of Ely.

Ely is all I've known. Yes I do like it but I don't know anything else.

I know everyone and all my family live here.

I don't like the trouble that we have experienced with a family living in Ely who harassed me and my family and my personal belongings. Gangs of kids have been causing trouble recently.

In order to ascertain a measure of social support, participants were asked to agree or disagree with statements about the level of contact and support with friends and family. Only 18 per cent agreed that most of their friends were drawn from their own race/ethnic group. This clearly implies that the majority of respondents had friends from other ethnic groups. The majority also agreed that they received a lot of support from their family and that they had a good relationship with their neighbours. However, 13 per cent stated that they did not have a good relationship with their neighbours. Furthermore, 26 per cent stated that they did not have friends or family in Ely.

Experience of service provision
Generally speaking, respondents had a good knowledge of services that were available to them in Ely. Services that were least well known, or perhaps least well used, were Social Services, youth services, adult education, community centres and financial services. In the case of youth services, however, it should be noted that all respondents were adults. It is, therefore, unsurprising their knowledge of the service was limited. In terms of service use, the most frequently used services were transport, shops and schools. The least used services were the Barnardo's community centre/shop and Social Services Department. Participants were also asked whether they had experienced any difficulties, of any sort, in using services in Ely. The services that respondents found the most difficult to use were schools (six respondents) and the police (five respondents). Reasons given for the difficulties ranged from limited disabled access to concerns about racial harassment.

I find the service [police] patronizing and don't really want to go back.

Racist bullying goes on in school. It wasn't so bad when the children were younger, but it's becoming worse.

Teachers don't understand my son's needs, nor are they willing to understand.

There is no literature on black or ethnic minority history [libraries].

There's a lack of sensitivity towards racial harassment complaints [housing].

There's not enough variety unless you have a car to travel further [shops].

Overall, nineteen people (50 per cent of the sample) thought that services could be improved in some way. Suggestions offered ranged from practical suggestions of improving access to some services to retraining staff to be aware of race issues.

The police should be more open and helpful to ethnic minority problems.

Adult education should have its own building so that classes could be during daytime instead of using schools and attending classes in the evening.

Training [school teachers] on racial issues might help.

Well over half the respondents considered that the shops in Ely were inadequate for their needs in terms of choice and price. Consequently, they preferred to shop elsewhere. Over half of the respondents stated that they banked outside Ely. The most frequently mentioned suggestions for other services were youth activities. Some respondents were concerned about the lack of structured or supervised activities for children and young people. There was also support for more leisure and entertainment for the community as a whole, perhaps in the form of social clubs, gyms or a cinema. Only one person mentioned that they required more specialist food shops. Thirty-nine per cent of the sample felt that they had been discriminated against at some time. The police service was the most common source of discrimination, although some participants also felt that they were discriminated against in shops and whilst using public transport. Discrimination from the police was usually related to the police failing to take a complaint seriously. People were reluctant to report crime and harassment because they felt that the police were unwilling to act on the complaint. Fourteen of the thirty-nine respondents (36 per cent) discussed this problem. In a couple of instances, not only was the complaint not acted upon, but the victim was blamed for the crime or accused of harassment.

> The bus driver didn't stop at the bus-stop that I wanted. He said that he hadn't heard me when I asked him to stop. He shouted at me 'This is the problem with YOU people'.

> Yes in the shops, it's the way that some cashiers look at you and treat you.

> The police didn't support me when I lodged a complaint. Instead I was blamed for the problem. They criticized me and didn't give me any advice.

> Sometimes I think that some [police] officers don't want to get involved or don't care.

Experiences of racial harassment
Over half of the sample had experienced racial harassment in Ely. For many, this seemed to be a feature of everyday life. This experience of almost routine racial harassment, particularly racial abuse, echoes the findings of another survey (Chahal and Julienne, 1999). Harassment was experienced from neighbours, local children or youths, customers of shops, the police, and participants at sports events. Much of this was in the form of verbal abuse or mockery from local people and bullying at school. In some cases this appeared to be an occasional event, but in others the abuse was more repeated. For example, one participant reported gangs chanting racist abuse outside her home and writing racist graffiti on the house. In some other cases harassment was of a more physical nature. It ranged from being spat at and having dogs set on individuals, to more extreme forms of physical abuse such as violent attacks. Of the twenty participants who had reported harassment, none of them stated that there had been a positive outcome or that the situation had been resolved satisfactorily. There was a consistent acceptance that verbal abuse was something that happens regularly and that one learns to live with it.

> It doesn't bother me enough as there are so many other problems I have. To survive in this area you need to rise above such comments.

> I don't believe in reporting these issues.

In the past I reported verbal abuse from my neighbours. I don't report it now, no point really as I felt that nothing would be done and it's your word against theirs.

Some participants commented that reporting racial harassment could make the situation worse for them.

I've not reported it. Nothing ever gets done, instead it makes things worse.

No I don't believe anything worthwhile could be achieved and did not want to provide them with the satisfaction of knowing they bothered me.

The few incidents that were reported included school bullying (reported to teachers, but no action), youths giving verbal abuse (reported to police, no action), and violent attack (reported to police). Two participants stated that the harassment had come from the police. In both cases, the people involved were repeatedly being stopped and questioned by the police.

I was stopped by the police on numerous occasions for a long period of time. The police were very patronizing, mocking and laughing and asking ridiculous questions such as 'Do you love your girlfriend?'. It was a waste of my time, their time. I didn't report it as I didn't believe anything could be achieved and I didn't want to give them the satisfaction of knowing they bothered me.

Fewer people had definitely experienced racial harassment outside Ely, although a sizeable number were not sure whether to classify the incident as racial harassment or not. The form of harassment experienced outside of Ely tended to be more verbal in nature. In particular there were many accounts of the participants being the recipients of verbal abuse by strangers on the street, in parks, pubs, clubs and sports fields/venues. A few participants stated that they had experienced racial harassment by people they knew, such as neighbours or colleagues. Incidents, though, were reported only where physical contact had been made (assaults, stone throwing, and so on.).

Fifteen per cent of participants stated that they did not feel safe in their own homes during the day and the same percentage stated that they did not feel safe on the streets of Ely in the day. Twenty per cent did not feel safe in their own homes at night; while 49 per cent did not feel safe on the streets at night (this includes those participants who didn't know whether they would feel safe on the streets at night because they seldom ventured out at this time). People were asked whether there were places in Ely and outside Ely where they felt particularly vulnerable. Fourteen people stated that there were such places in Ely and ten stated that there were such places outside Ely.

Evidence from the British Crime Survey (Fitzgerald and Hale, 1996) suggests that variables such as age and gender affect a person's perception of security. Women and older people generally feel more vulnerable to most forms of crime. Furthermore, the length of time that a person has been living in an area may well affect their integration into a community and, as a consequence, the perception of personal security. It may also influence the experience of harassment, discrimination and the corresponding capacity to cope. However, it is important to emphasize the point that a survey of this size cannot provide definitive explanations of these complex social processes. It is with this 'health warning' in mind that we found there were no significant differences between men and women in terms of their perceptions of racial harassment and personal safety. Whilst men generally felt safer on the streets at night, there were no statistically significant differences between men and women and their statements on safety.

CONCLUSION

There are many important and interesting themes that emerge from the data. Of particular interest are issues of learning to live with harassment and discrimination; poor service provision (especially in relation to shops and banks); a sense of 'belonging'; the existence of territorial boundaries; the poor public image of Ely; and a belief in the 'problem' of troublesome children. Some of these issues would not be experiences that are exclusive to black and minority ethnic populations. Indeed, it would be instructive to explore these themes with local white residents. Nevertheless, it is vitally important to recognize the validity of those experiences that are particular to minority ethnic residents: *racial discrimination* and *racial harassment*. Against that background, the following represent our main conclusions:

- One of the positive messages from the research is that respondents appear to be reasonably well supported by family and/or social networks. Relations with white people in the neighbourhood are also generally good. It is important, therefore, not to stigmatize Ely as a 'hotbed of racism'.
- Although respondents probably suffer from many of the same problems as

their white neighbours, there is a discrete strand of experience that is unique to minority ethnic communities: the experience of racial discrimination and harassment.

- Positive recognition should be given to those members of the community who speak languages other than English. The ability to speak more than one language is an educational, economic and community resource (Casson *et al.*, 1994).

- A key strength of the research is that it has focused on those communities in Ely who have been previously dis-voiced. That said, the results of the research raise many questions about the white majority in the area. The issue of racism, for example, needs to be understood from the perspective of the white community. There would be considerable value in mapping the *routes of racism* (Hewitt, 1996) within the local white community.

- The research *and* the wider literature would suggest that there is probably a need for a variety of creative interventions with children and young people. It is particularly important to challenge the culture of racism that can emerge amongst young people. The literature contains some advice and guidance about how this can be best achieved (detached youth work, for example). This need not necessarily involve launching new, high-profile initiatives. It may, though, have training implications for those who work with young people: teachers, community workers and youth workers. Awareness also needs to be raised about young victims of racial harassment.

- The MacPherson Report (1999) has succeeded in raising public awareness around institutionalized forms of racism. The time may be opportune to press for a Cardiff-wide policy audit of all the major public services: education, housing, personal social services and health. Given the complete absence of minority community representation in the National Assembly, it seems perfectly reasonable to widen the audit to the whole of Wales. Whilst important work on this front has already been undertaken by the Assembly (Chaney, 2002; Chaney and Fevre, 2002), such an audit needs to reach deep down into all local authorities, non-governmental organizations and professions. It should engage the different communities in an inspection and reappraisal of the procedures, practices and occupational cultures of all major service-providers. Searching and uncomfortable questions need to be asked of them. Racism is not just a problem for the police and those they patrol on social housing estates. The more discreet, 'genteel racism' of liberal professions, like social work, teaching and academic research, should also be scrutinized. Questions should be asked, too, about the way in which audits are conducted. What, for example, is the purpose of ethnic monitoring? What conclusions can we draw from the information available to us? How is the information used by organizations? Has monitoring become a meaningless bureaucratic exercise, or does it genuinely inform policy and service delivery outcomes? Only a few years ago, a Welsh-wide debate on such issues would have seemed ambitious and idealistic. In the present climate, however, such ideas are likely to receive a more positive reception. Indeed, the National Assembly is well placed to confront the sentimental myths of the 'Welsh radical tradition' and promote, in place, an inclusive form of citizenship.

- Despite the differing experiences of minority ethnic and white communities in Ely, there are many common concerns and shared interests to unite them. Low income, poor services and inadequate amenities are just three possible areas around which local people are capable of forming meaningful alliances. It is, of course, entirely possible for diversity and unity to occupy the same space. The fact that there exists a community of interest between white and minority ethnic people suggests that there is a sound base on which to construct anti-racist strategies. As Sibbitt puts it:

> barriers can begin to come down where there is a non-racial focal point, where people can come together actively, to address issues of mutual concern. These issues may consist of leisure activities, the local quality of life or local problems. People's *active* participation in – and ownership of – local projects is likely to be a significant factor in the success of any project. . . . active involvement in multi-racial community development work can itself benefit race relations. (Sibbitt, 1997: 109–110)

Given the strong community traditions of Ely, the ground for such initiatives may well be quite fertile. It is therefore the responsibility of the wider community to ensure that Ely, and places like it, are given the resources and equipment to do the job.

REFERENCES

Asad, T. (1990). 'Ethnography, literature and politics: some readings and uses of Salman Rushdie's *The Satanic Verses*', *Cultural Anthropology*, 5, 3, 239–69.
Bhopal, K., (2001). 'Researching South Asian women: issues of sameness and difference in the research process', *Journal of Gender Studies*, 10/3, 279–86.
Campbell, B. (1993). *Goliath: Britain's Dangerous Places*, London: Methuen.

Cardiff Research Centre (1996). *Key Statistics, Cardiff*, Cardiff County Council.
Casson, M., Cooke, P., Jones, M,. and Williams, C. (1994). *Quiet Revolution? Language, Culture and Economy in the Nineties*, Aberystwyth: Menter a Busnes.
Chahal, K. and Julienne, L. (1999). *'We Can't All Be White': Racist Victimisation in the UK*, London: JRF/YPS.
Chaney, P., (2002). 'An absolute duty – the Assembly's statutory equality of opportunity imperative,' in Osmond, J. and Jones, J. B. (eds), *Building a Civic Culture – Institutional Change, Policy Development and Political Dynamics in the National Assembly for Wales*, Cardiff: Institute of Welsh Affairs, pp. 225–44.
Chaney, P. and Fevre, R. (2002). *An Absolute Duty: Equal Opportunities and the National Assembly*, Cardiff: Institute of Welsh Affairs.
Drakeford, M. (1993). 'Poverty and local authority action: the example of Ely in Cardiff', *Contemporary Wales*, 7, 29–46.
Ely Community Development Forum (1992). *One Day Residents' Conference*, Cardiff: E.C.D.F.
Evans, N. (1985). 'Regulating the reserve army: Arabs, blacks and the local state in Cardiff, 1919–45', in Lunn, K. (ed.), *Race and Labour in Twentieth Century Britain*, London: Routledge.
Fitzgerald, M. and Hale, C. (1996). *Ethnic Minorities: Victimisation and Racial Harassment: Findings from the 1988 and 1992 British Crime Surveys – Home Office Research Study 154*, London: Home Office.
Hewitt, R. (1996). *Routes of Racism: The Social Basis of Racist Action*, Stoke-on-Trent: Trentham.
MacPherson, W., Cook, T., Sentamu, J. and Stone, R. (1999). *The Stephen Lawrence Inquiry – Presented to Parliament by the Secretary of State for the Home Department (Report)*, London: The Stationery Office.
Phillips, C. and Bowling, B. (2003). 'Racism, ethnicity and criminology: developing minority perspectives', *British Journal of Criminology*, 43, 2, Spring.
Russell, K., (1992). 'Development of a black criminology and the role of the black criminologist', *Justice Quarterly*, 9/4, 667–83.
Sibbitt, R. (1997). *The Perpetrators of Racial Harassment and Racial Violence – Home Office Research Study 176*, London: Home Office.
Smith, S. M. (1983). 'The level of deprivation existing in the council estates of Cardiff: incorporating a case study of North Ely', diploma dissertation, UWIST/Cardiff University.
Solomos, J. (1993). *Race and Racism in Britain*, London: Macmillan.
Sturges, G. (1995). 'Civil disorder in the 1980s and 1990s: a comparison of the Brixton experience with local events in Ely, Cardiff', diploma dissertation, Cardiff University.
Williams, C. (1995). '"Race" and racism: some reflections on the Welsh context', *Contemporary Wales*, 8, 113–31.
Williams, C. and Short, C. (1997). *Working with Difference: A Resource for People Working to Promote Anti-Racism in Social Work and Social Care in Wales*, Cardiff: CCETSW Cymru.

Williamson, H. and Weatherspoon, K. (1985). *Strategies for Intervention: An Approach to Youth and Community Work in an Area of Social Deprivation*, Cardiff: Social Research Unit, University College, Cardiff.

3. WHITEHALL'S LAST STAND: THE ESTABLISHMENT OF THE WELSH OFFICE, 1964

Ted Rowlands

The generally accepted account of the establishment of the Welsh Office centres upon the role of Jim Griffiths, Charter Secretary of State for Wales, whose refusal (to the point of resignation) to accept an office without executive powers overcame Whitehall's grim determination to prevent this decisive act of devolution (Jones, 1989). The papers now available at the Public Record Office covering the deliberations of the committee on the machinery of government in 1964 certainly verify this account (see Treasury Records, T330). Indeed, they show to what lengths the most senior Whitehall mandarins went to prevent an executive Welsh Office. In one sense this was Whitehall's last stand against Welsh devolution. However, the papers also intimate that this was not the whole story. Whitehall opposition fed off a significant political ambivalence to devolution which ran through the Labour party, and the Labour government.

The Labour party, in opposition, had been slow to adopt the agenda of a Welsh Office and a Secretary of State. The strong centralist tendencies within the party, from Herbert Morrison to Aneurin Bevan, resented and resisted the 'home rule' tendencies. However, in September 1959, the party policy document, 'Forward with Labour', committed a future Labour government to appointing a Secretary of State with cabinet responsibility for health, housing and local government. A similar commitment was confirmed after the 1959 election by Hugh Gaitskell, made easier by Bevan's reluctant neutrality on the issue. A pre-election party document, 'Signpost for the Sixties', reaffirmed the party's position. The conversion, however, was less than full-hearted. A significant group within the Welsh Parliamentary Labour Party, led by Ness Edwards (Caerphilly) and Iorwerth Thomas (Rhondda West) remained unconvinced; and, within the highest echelons of the United Kingdom party, a derisive scepticism prevailed. Dick Crossman confided to his diary after the 1964 election victory that the appointment was 'an idiotic creation . . . a completely artificial new office . . . all the results of a silly election pledge' (Crossman, 1975: 117).

Nevertheless, in the spring and early summer of 1964, Whitehall had to assume that the commitment to a Welsh Office and Secretary of State of cabinet rank was for real, albeit a small part of a much greater shake-up of the machinery of government. The Labour party had also committed itself to major new ministries of technology, land and natural resources and a Department for Economic Affairs (see Clifford, 1997).

As convention dictated, senior Whitehall officials had began an evaluation of the Labour party programme in 1963, and, following Prime Minister Harold Macmillan's assent, Sir Lawrence Helsby, head of the Home Civil Service, set up a machinery-of-government steering group to consider the potentially volcanic reorganization of Whitehall promised (or threatened) by the Labour party. The much greater challenges to chisel out a Department of Economic Affairs (DEA) and the Ministries for Technology and Land inevitably dominated the steering committee's deliberations. Consideration of a putative Welsh Office did not begin until May 1964, little more than six months before the latest possible date for a general election. The tardiness in addressing the issue of a Welsh Office reflected a barely concealed irritation within Whitehall that this matter should be reopened; reopened because, as far as senior Whitehall officials were concerned, the question of a Welsh Office on the Scottish model had been definitively rejected in 1957, when Harold Macmillan had formally replied negatively to the Council for Wales and Monmouthshire recommendations. Macmillan's letter to the Council's chairman, Huw T. Edwards, was, as far as Whitehall was concerned, the last word on the matter. During the course of their deliberations in the summer of 1964, the 1957 letter assumed the proportions of a biblical text.

Whitehall's consideration of the Labour party's pledge began in earnest with an internal letter to the leading permanent secretaries from Sir Philip Allen, drawing attention to the possible commitment by the Labour party, 'though we are not aware that the Labour party has worked out in any details what the function of a Secretary of State might be'. Allen's letter reminded the recipients of the powerful arguments against having a Secretary of State which had been canvassed on a number of occasions, notably in Harold Macmillan's letter to the chairman of the Council for Wales. Notwithstanding, Allen felt it 'sensible' that his Whitehall colleagues should consider what the plan should be, if a Secretary of State were appointed. They should work upon two possible assumptions, the first of which was a Welsh Office on the pattern of the Scottish Office which would include the Ministry of Agriculture, Fisheries and Food, the Department of Education and Science, Ministry of Health and the Home Office functions relating to the police, probation, child care, fire service, civil defence, remand houses and approved schools.

Officials, however, had 'heard rumours' that the Labour party's plan 'may be less ambitious', confining the takeover to the four departments already part of the decentralized administration: Agriculture, Education, Health and Housing, and Local Government. Sir Philip Allen sought his colleagues' observations, as well as raising one additional point for consideration: whether such changes would require legislation or just a transfer-of-function order (letter to department heads, 8 May 1964).

During the following six weeks, the knighted mandarins of the four departments submitted their observations. Without exception their responses were negative – a chorus of disapproval describing varying adverse consequences upon the administration of Welsh affairs. Sir Thomas Padmore (Ministry of Transport) feared the disruption of road planning between the two countries.

> Apart from the important consideration that our attempts to plan a national transport system would become more complicated and difficult, an argument based on the analogy of Scotland had little real force. The Welsh border is much larger than the Scottish. It is crossed by many more roads and road communications are much more dependent on, and interlinked with those in England. Traffic in the North flows to and from Merseyside and in the South the main links are with the Midlands and London. The most heavily trafficked route is between North and South Wales through Herefordshire and Shrewsbury in England.
>
> (letter from Padmore to Allen, 23 June 1964).

For these reasons Sir Thomas felt that a separate Welsh Office would make road planning 'time consuming' and administratively 'wasteful'. He hoped that, if a Welsh Office were established, transport would be excluded.

Sir Herbert Andrew (Ministry of Education) had very different concerns. He felt that the separation of England and Wales would throw up a severe practical problem 'over the supply of teachers'. Wales provided many more teachers than Welsh local authorities were allowed by the quota system and therefore 'exported many to England'. A separate Welsh administration would certainly lift the quota and thus enable the Welsh schools to absorb the great bulk of the future of Welsh supply of trained teachers, and probably draw upon a good many Welsh teachers now serving in England . . . Worse, Wales might develop a different pay structure which might well be manipulated to reinforce the process. Theoretically it would be possible to impose financial controls to discourage such movements, though 'politically that would be impossible as the government would be accused of starving Wales of money to force young Welsh people to immigrate to England' (letter from Andrew, 20 May 1964).

Sir John Winnifrith (Ministry of Agriculture) feared other dire consequences. A Welsh agriculture department on the Scottish model would require five or six assistant secretaries with divisions running their own subsidy schemes and land policy. 'They would be virtually a net addition to our Welsh Office at present run by an Under Secretary and SEO.' Sir John feared worse. 'It was not easy and seldom quick for policy decisions to be reached between three agricultural departments (and three farmers' unions). To add a fourth animal to the troika would inevitably add to the potential difficulties and delays.' For good measure Sir John warned that any attempt to create a specific Welsh national agricultural advisory service might lead to 'a very inbred unit losing some of the benefits of the cross-fertilisation which takes place under the present system' (letter from Winnifrith, 14 May 1964).

Two other departments presented contrasting problems for a devolved Welsh executive. None of the Home Office functions were delivered within Wales; the analogy with the Scottish Office was, therefore, inapplicable. There were grounds for resisting a similar pattern for Wales in that Wales had the same systems for law and courts as England, whereas Scotland had a separate system.

> Transfer of the Lord Chancellor's functions should certainly be resisted such as tending towards separate laws and a separate judiciary in Wales ought to be avoided at all costs. If the Home Secretary's and other responsibilities were not transferred it would be sensible to retain the status quo with regard to his other function . . . (9)

The Ministry of Health and its permanent secretary (Bruce Fraser) could not make such a case. 'The Ministry of Health already exercised most of the functions in Wales through a Welsh Board of Health under a chairman paid at an under-secretary rate and two others' . . . 'Devolution has, in fact, gone about as far as it can . . .'. Further forms of devolution raised complicated issues relating to the administration of the NHS superannuation scheme, general policy on the Whitley Council for Health Service remuneration and the Service's central purchasing arrangements.

Sir Bruce Fraser drew attention to three other difficulties. An inordinate amount of subordinate legislation would be duplicated. Duplicating many bodies (both executive and advisory) would present major staffing issues, such as the medical practices committee. Even if these were joint creations of the Minister of Health and Welsh Secretary of State, 'they would in future all have to include Welsh men which by no means all of them do at present'.

> It is worth noting that where medical expertise is called for Wales, with half Scotland's population, is less than half as well able to look after itself because of Scotland's strong medical traditions and disproportionately large share, qualitatively and quantitatively, of the UK's Medical Schools.
>
> (letter from Fraser, 1 June 1964).

Even the obvious decentralized department Ministry of Housing and Local Government found substantial objections to the Labour party's proposal. Its formidable permanent secretary, Dame Evelyn Sharpe, admitted that virtually all the work of the department had already been delegated to the Cardiff Office. The real snag, however, 'would be the cutting-off of this relatively small staff, with its relatively narrow range of experience from the staff at Whitehall'. In theory, of course, they would have access to Whitehall for advice or information they wanted, but in practice, they would go 'much more of their own way'. 'Already inbreeding is a real problem in the Cardiff Office and exchanges are extremely difficult to arrange. There is consistency between the staffs of Whitehall and Cardiff. This would inevitably diminish.' However, Dame Evelyn was equally dismissive of the suggestion of her colleague, Sir John Winnifrith (Ministry of Agriculture), of a Secretary of State for Wales without executive responsibilities. In light of the fact that this became Whitehall's preferred option it is worth quoting in full. Drawing upon her experience of the existing arrangement of a minister within her department responsible for Welsh Affairs she concluded:

> I am unable to envisage, as Sir John Winnifrith suggests, a Secretary of State for Wales who would have no policy or executive responsibilities. This would be simply our Minister of State (who finds life frustrating enough) with

high-flown name – a kind of common Parliamentary Secretary to four ministers, with a title superior to theirs and a seat in the Cabinet! Much though I would like to avoid the duplication and inefficiency certainly entailed in a separate department, I cannot imagine that this is a possible device.

If we get a Secretary of State I think there is nothing for it but to create a separate department as in Scotland, though limiting it, if possible, to the work of the HLG, Education, Health and Transport (letter from Sharpe, 3 June 1964).

It was, therefore, an extremely sceptical gathering of permanent secretaries which met in Sir Philip Allen's room on Tuesday, 7 July, to review the departmental responses. They were greeted with more gloomy news. Only a fortnight earlier (25 June) Jim Griffiths had reaffirmed the Labour party's commitment to a Secretary of State 'with executive authority over a number of departments and overall responsibility for government activity, policies and plans in Wales' (note of meeting held in Allen's room at the Treasury, 7 July 1964). This unequivocal reaffirmation overrode advice received from one of the most senior and experienced civil servants in Wales, the secretary at the Welsh Office, Ministry of Housing and Local Government, J. W. M. Siberry. He had minuted Dame Evelyn Sharpe that, having just read the Labour party's 'Signpost to the New Wales', he thought: 'One cannot, of course, read any certainty into such vague generality but I still think we cannot rule out the possibility that a Labour government would not want to go far except in name' (minute, 23 June 1964).

Therefore, while wearyingly rehearsing the arguments against any such office, the group grudgingly felt compelled to turn its attention to the structure and organization of an executive Welsh Office. It was hoped that it could be confined to three departments: a development department, incorporating housing and local government, plus certain transport functions: an agricultural department and one other, combining health and education. They envisaged a deputy secretary to act as a chief adviser to the Secretary of State, though he might also act as head of the departments.

Philip Allen minuted the conclusion of the group to the Machinery of Government Steering Group on 15 July. It emphasized the collective hostility of all departmental heads to the whole idea, and reiterated that the case made by Harold Macmillan as far back as December 1957 remained 'as valid as ever'. It would mean having small pockets of staff with limited opportunities for experience cut off from the main stream and with all its consequences in inbreeding . . . Wales, unlike Scotland, had the same system of law, local government and land tenure so there was no need for a division on the

Scottish pattern. The Welsh population was only just over two and a half million (half that of Scotland). Wales did not have 'the special problems' of the Highlands and Islands. It did not require 'separate policies'. An appointment of a Secretary of State 'would do nothing to strengthen Wales' voice in matters of economic development', which is what the Welsh are 'really interested in'. At ministerial level it would require three ministers having to act together whenever policies or legislation affecting matters were dealt with by the Welsh Secretary of State. Nevertheless, faced with the commitment made by the Labour party, Philip Allen felt it necessary to advise the steering group that the minimum which it could be expected for a Secretary of State to take over were the four decentralized departments – housing and local government, agriculture, education and health as well as responsibility for the road programme ('Secretary of State for Wales', note from Allen, 15 July 1964).

The steering group, comprising the five most senior mandarins in Whitehall (Sir Lawrence Helsby, Sir Philip Allen, Sir William Armstrong (all Treasury officials), Dame Evelyn Sharpe and Sir Richard Powell (Board of Trade), met to consider Allen's note on 22 July. The bare minutes of the meeting record Sir Philip Allen's introductory remarks as wholly negative, underlining three particular disadvantages of creating a post of the kind envisaged by the Labour party: once created it would be very difficult to do away with; secondly, seeking the authority of three ministers would add to the complication of legislation; thirdly, 'a Secretary of State would have to justify his appointment by producing positive benefits although Wales was being well enough looked after already, and there were, in fact, no complaints on this score . . .'. Allen, however, admitted that, if the Labour party remained committed to a Secretary of State with executive powers, then the four-department solution would be 'the minimum required'.

The senior steering group gave short shrift to any such minimum solution. Discussion, immediately, turned to alternatives, 'the most promising line' being a Secretary of State supported by an office rather than a department and with coordinating rather than executive responsibilities. Instead of a Minister of State in the Ministry of Housing, there would be an independent Secretary of State who could give expression in the Cabinet to the 'voice of Wales'. 'If he sat in the House of Lords he could also be responsible for the business of some or all of the departments with functions in Wales. This would be preferable to the creation of a Welsh department' (Machinery of Government Steering Group, 22 July 1964).

Matters were taken no further within Whitehall before the October election. Following the Labour party's narrow victory, Harold Wilson promptly appointed Jim Griffiths as the first Secretary of State for Wales, but without stating the extent of his powers or responsibilities. There proceeded, over the following month, hectic and, at times, fractious exchanges to resolve the nature of the new Office.

While Wilson had promptly fulfilled one part of the election pledge with the appointment of Jim Griffiths, it quickly transpired that he did not feel obliged to create a Welsh Office on the Scottish Office model. A note from the Prime Minister's private secretary to Sir Lawrence Helsby (22 October) drew attention to the Prime Minister's two thoughts that 'the Welsh themselves did not want to go as far as the Scottish pattern of devolution', and that officials 'ought to consult the Chancellor of the Exchequer both qua Chancellor and also because of his interest in Welsh affairs'. Wilson referred officials back to the Council for Wales memorandum (minute from J. Anson, Prime Minister's private office, 22 October 1964).

When, some days later, senior officials under Helsby's chairmanship met to consider the position, Sir Lawrence reported that the Prime Minister did not consider the organization proposed by the Council for Wales and Monmouthshire 'sensible', and he had not felt 'committed to adopt that organization by appointing Mr Jim Griffiths as Secretary of State for Wales'. The group, therefore, decided to explore

the possibility of establishing arrangements under which the relationship between the Secretary of State for Wales and the department's operations in Wales would be similar to that envisaged for the relationship between the Minister for Economic Affairs and other departments in the organization to be established for regional planning and development throughout the country . . .

Officials remained adamant that the transfer of any executive powers would 'weaken' the administration in Wales. For instance, the Department of Education and Science had delegated functions extensively to their Cardiff office a year ago. The 'opinion of the officer in charge of the Cardiff Office after his experience of working his arrangement was that it was bad for Welsh education because it had taken Wales out of the mainstream of educational development'. The same was likely to arise for agriculture and health.

It would be important that the new Welsh Office should be wholly disassociated from any of the departments operating in Wales, including the Ministry of Housing and Local Government.'The absurdity of establishing a separate department for Wales would be clearly revealed by the large number of separate and small votes that would be required.'

Whitehall collectively clung to the hope that oversight powers for the new Secretary of State would suffice. Summing up the discussion, Sir Lawrence Helsby admitted that 'the main problem' would be to persuade the Secretary of State that the oversight arrangements would be sufficient 'to release him from the commitment which some would find in the words he had used in Parliament last June'. A prime ministerial statement supporting such an arrangement, which the Secretary of State could quote authoritatively, could be sufficient for the purpose (minutes of meeting held in Helsby's room, Treasury, 26 October 1964).

Helsby duly submitted the unanimous Whitehall opinion to the Prime Minister, though not before pursuing Wilson's other earlier recommendation to consult Jim Callaghan as a Welsh member. Sir Lawrence's minute to the Prime Minister attached a record of the conversation with the Chancellor and deserves quoting *in extenso*.

The Chancellor feels that it would be wrong to under-rate the weight of opinion in Wales which supports the setting-up of separate Departments of State. He agrees that this opinion may not be altogether representative, but it is the vocal opinion that is what a Welsh Member is bound to be conscious of. He agrees in logic a strong case can be made out against fragmentation of the work of the government departments which at present cover both England and Wales; but he was inclined at first to suggest that it might not be impracticable to arrange for separate Votes for some part of the work that is done in Wales. He mentioned that he has himself taken a personal interest in the road programme, and asked whether there could not be a separate allocation of funds for roads in Wales, with a separate Vote, as is done in Scotland. To this I replied that under the Scottish system there are 26 separate Scottish Votes, and any provision of separate Votes for Wales would probably lead us fairly quickly into the creation of at least 15, and perhaps more, new substantive Votes. The Chancellor agreed that this would create some awkward problems and said that he would not wish to press this line of thought.

The Chancellor's conclusion was that he would support the line taken in my separate minute, but he warned me that I ought not to regard him as a wholly reliable ally on this, for the conclusion which I had reached was not one for which he would want to fight in the very last ditch.

(minute from Helsby to Prime Minister, 27 October 1964)

The most senior Whitehall officials had, however, misunderstood and misread the politics of the issue. Their stiff-necked resistance even to a minimal transfer of executive power to the new Secretary of State had placed one of the most senior and respected politicians in the Labour party in an impossible position. For Jim Griffiths the commitment to a Welsh Office with executive powers was not just a party manifesto pledge, but essentially a personal political lifelong ambition. It was not, as officials had cynically observed, a question of finding a way 'to release the Secretary of State' from his 'commitment'. Jim Griffiths had no wish to be released. The 'commitment' was personal, and failure to deliver a minimal part of it would be both a personal and a political humiliation.

When the steering group met on 9 November to take stock, Helsby had to report that the Secretary of State had pressed for separate Welsh departments of housing, education, agriculture and health on the lines of the Council for Wales memorandum. Put under such pressure the group reluctantly conceded the transfer of housing and local government functions linked to a commitment to consider subsequent transfers 'in due course' (minutes of the Machinery of Government Steering Group, 9 November1964). Three days later, on 12 November, a crestfallen Sir Lawrence reported that 'a further talk' between the PM and the Secretary of State had led to a renewed request that the new office assume 'operational control within Wales for the implementation of national policy in the fields of health, education, housing, planning and agriculture'.

Jim Griffiths's persistence prompted another round of administrative soul-searching. The notion of a Secretary of State assuming 'operational control' of national policy would lead to all sorts of administrative headaches. Agricultural subsidies, for example, could only, in practice, be operated on a national England and Wales basis. 'Consistency in the application of policy could only be achieved if the casework were handled by a single department'. Such a division of education responsibilities would 'tear a ragged line down the middle of the Education acts'.

Whitehall's final compromise package consisted of a Welsh development department incorporating virtually all the housing and local government functions, some additional environmental responsibilities and, possibly, local health and welfare services. Transferring roads was to be resisted 'in view of the long land border' while national parks had already been assigned to the new ministry of land and natural resources. The Secretary of State's 'oversight' responsibility was to be dressed up with fortnightly meetings with heads of Whitehall departments in Wales, and in taking the lead in formulating and implementing the regional plan. He could answer general parliamentary questions 'of the kind which asks why a particular service falls short in Wales of the standard in England and Scotland' (note of meeting in Helsby's room, Treasury, 12 November 1964).

Matters, however, were hastily taken out of official hands. Clearly fearing that the delay and dithering might lead to growing parliamentary impatience, the Prime Minister and Jim Griffiths settled bilaterally the new department's functions. Seizing the opportunity of a tabled written parliamentary question by Roderick Bowen, Wilson answered it orally on 19 November (to some embarrassment to Mr Bowen, who was not present). The statement, interestingly, dropped any reference to a 'development department', simply referring to the takeover of 'virtually all the executive responsibilities of the Ministry of Housing and Local Government's housing and new towns, town and country planning and the organization of local government'. More significantly, the Prime Minister also included the responsibility for the planning of roads, including trunk roads, something the official steering group had been resisting to the last. The statement spelled out the Secretary of State's oversight role and concluded with the claim that the changes would 'achieve the object of giving Wales a strong voice in Government counsels and a strong hand in her own administration'.

Defensive briefing accompanying the draft parliamentary statement anticipated pressure to explain the exclusion of health, agriculture and education: 'This may well be searching in regard to the Welsh Board of Health created as a separate Welsh department by an act in 1919.' The Prime Minister was advised simply to respond that he would be 'giving further consideration to this matter'. Pressed upon education and, particularly, the bilingual character of Welsh education, he was advised to suggest that 'operational control over departments in Wales' would 'enable effective supervision of educational policies'.

The brief parliamentary exchanges arising from the statement were scarcely searching. They drew lukewarm endorsement from Ness Edwards and Iorwerth Thomas, an enthusiastic welcome in Welsh from Tom Jones (Merioneth) and congratulations from Lady Megan Lloyd George 'on being the *second* Prime Minister to recognize the nationhood of Wales', though also asking whether the Secretary of State will assume responsibility for the Departments of Education, Agriculture and Health. These issues had already been pursued more forcefully by Sir Keith Joseph, the former minister responsible for Welsh affairs, who alleged that, with the exception of roads, executive responsibility for agriculture, health and education, transport and labour remained the same as under the previous administration, and contrasted strikingly with the pledges made in the Labour party's 'Signpost to the New Wales'.

Joseph's intervention drew from the Prime Minister a lengthier response, explaining that 'a great deal of time had been spent' to get 'the right degree of devolution in Wales without breaking up existing Departments where that would have been inimical to the interests of Wales'. Wilson, however, accepted that the government would be prepared to change 'in any direction if they found that such changes were needed'. He dismissed Joseph's allegation that little had effectively changed. In the past Welsh affairs had been 'tacked on' to other ministerial duties (for papers relating to the parliamentary questions see Cab 21/5608, HC Debates, 19 December 1964, cols 623–30).

The Conservative opposition continued to chide the government for the gulf between its pre-election commitment to establish a Welsh Office with wider executive responsibility and the proposed modest transfer of functions. At a Welsh Grand Committee on 16 December, Sir Keith Joseph and others pressed the Secretary of State to explain his responsibility for water and the promises for a Welsh Water Resources Board. Joseph had created, prior to the election, a survey and redevelopment section to carry out, in conjunction with the Secretary of State for Trade and Industry and the Regions, a plan for Wales. He also reminded Jim Griffiths of a commitment to carry through local government reorganization, before concluding that Wales had 'a widely respected minister' with 'a sonorous title' but with reduced powers.

Jim Griffiths had little difficulty in rebutting the general political charge. 'Simply whatever the arrangements were before, and however good or bad they might have been, they did not fulfil the deeply felt desire to have Wales recognized . . .'. However, he was in no position to respond to the detailed probing on his powers in respect of water, forestry and national parks, which, since the Prime Minister's statement had become the subject of a tug of war with the new Ministry of Land and Natural Resources (Welsh Grand Committee, 16 December 1964).

At least, in this Whitehall battle, the nascent Welsh Office had its champions at Court, a new Minister of State and a Whitehall-wise under-secretary, Goronwy Daniel, transferred from the Ministry of Power. Whereas the Ministry of Land, understandably, sought to guard its new central policy role for land and natural resources, it was eventually forced to concede that the Secretary of State would be responsible in Wales for the implementation of policy and legislation. Welsh representation would be assured on appropriate agencies and commissions. The Secretary of State would become the third forestry minister (alongside his Scottish counterpart). After much detailed haggling at both official and ministerial level all were incorporated into the draft transfer of functions order laid before Parliament in March 1965 (papers related to the Transfer of Functions, December 1964 to March 1965).

For nearly a year, Whitehall at the most senior levels had fought a protracted and determined battle to prevent the establishment of a Welsh Office with executive responsibilities. In the light of subsequent experience, many of the fears would appear grossly exaggerated if not absurd. However, reading the internal papers and minutes one cannot doubt that the Whitehall mandarins clearly considered a principle of considerable importance to be at stake. Whitehall viewed the creation of a Welsh Office as a significant challenge to the integrity and cohesion of a centrally administered state.

The Sir Lawrence Helsbys and Dame Evelyn Sharpes of their day were heirs to a Whitehall machine which had first been forged and unified during the period following the First World War, the development of a Home Civil Service with a common entrance qualification, training, remuneration and philosophy. It embodied an ethos and a culture which had grown as a result of wartime experiences, and, although after the Second World War it had witnessed an expansion of regional offices, they had remained essentially outposts of the central administrative Whitehall empire. Regional officials' own careers, prospects and cultures were inextricably bound to Whitehall. In a letter circulated to all departments, spelling out the manner and arrangements by which the Secretary of State for Wales would exercise his 'oversight' and executive role, Sir Lawrence Helsby took great paternalistic pains to ensure that standards of the service to and in Wales would not fall as a result of the changes.

The Welsh Office is bound to be a relatively small department; and it is essential therefore that there should be an interchange of staff, particularly administrative staff, between the Welsh Office and Whitehall in order to make sure that the Cardiff staff do not suffer by comparison with their English departments in breadth of experience. The Treasury will use its good offices in securing interchange of staff on an adequate scale.

(letter from Helsby to departmental heads, 3 December 1964)

But Whitehall resistance was not just a question of practicalities. It was an issue of administrative and executive principle. While, as a result of their long rearguard resistance, officials had whittled down the original political demands, conceding any executive function was considered a defeat. As Sir Philip Allen had observed during the early stages, there would be no going back. The demand for further transfers would be inevitable; the challenge to the integrity of a central unified administration would continue.

In 1964/5 officials benefited from a deep-seated political ambivalence to the whole project within the leadership of the Labour government. That ambivalence remained throughout the two Labour administrations, from 1964 to 1970. When renewed pressure for the transfer of health, education and agriculture arose in 1966/7 it was not only defiant Whitehall mandarins but also Cabinet ministers who resisted.[1] However, Whitehall had also learnt in 1964 that politicians could not be relied upon to hold fast. In Jim Callaghan's words to Sir Lawrence Helsby it was 'a conclusion' for which one 'would not want to fight in the very last ditch'. The time and manipulative skills devoted by the most senior Whitehall officials to resisting an executive Welsh Office indicate that they saw it very much as a last ditch stand against devolution.

NOTES

1. There will be a sequel to this account covering 1966–1970.

REFERENCES

Clifford, C. (1997). 'The rise and fall of the Department of Economic Affairs 1964–1970: British government and indicative planning', *Contemporary British History*, 11 (2), 94–116.

Crossman, R. H. S. (1975). *The Diaries of a Cabinet Minister*, London: Hamilton Cape.

Jones, J. G. (1989). 'Socialism, devolution and the Secretary of State for Wales, 1940–64', *Transactions of the Honourable Society of Cymmrodorion*, London, 135–59.

4. DEVOLUTION AND PARTY ORGANIZATION: THE CASE OF THE WALES LABOUR PARTY

Martin Laffin, Gerald Taylor and Alys Thomas

Devolution raises new issues of how public policy can be controlled and coordinated across the four 'countries' of the UK. The devolution settlements for Wales, and for Scotland, created new elected bodies which enjoy considerable autonomy from central government. Before devolution, Welsh policy was closely aligned with central policy as collective responsibility in the Westminster Cabinet bound the Welsh Secretary to centrally-determined policies. Now the Welsh Assembly Government can pursue its own policies within the broad framework of Westminster primary legislation and its block spending allocation. The unspoken assumption behind the settlement was that Labour party discipline and solidarity would remain the mechanism of control and coordination between the centre and Wales and Scotland (Laffin and Thomas, 2000). This article reports on one part of a larger investigation into how the Labour party is acting as such a mechanism and on the implications for the party, both at the British level and in Scotland and Wales, of the new challenges involved in holding on to power at the centre and governing the devolved territories. Accordingly, it addresses the post-devolution questions of how the Welsh Labour party itself is changing and how its relationship with the Labour party nationally is changing.

More specifically, regionalization and devolution might be expected to change significantly the Welsh devolved-level party system. How has the Welsh party system changed and what are the implications for the Labour party in Wales? And are those changes the result of devolution itself or of other factors, such as the different electoral arrangements of the National Assembly for Wales and the modernization project of the British Labour party?

Furthermore, the corollary of McKenzie's (1955) supposition that a centralized party structure arises from, and then reinforces, governmental centralism by subordinating the politics of regional or territorial interests to national party interests, is that devolved or regionalized government will give new life to territorial politics. Indeed, building on Eldersveld's concept of 'stratarchy' (1964: 4–5), it can be hypothesized that British parties centrally are facing pressures to devolve significant responsibility downwards to their Welsh and Scottish branches rather than incur the risk of over-centralization. As a matter of survival, 'the party develops its own hierarchical pattern of stratified devolution of responsibility for the settlement of conflicts, rather than jeopardize the viability of the total organization by carrying such conflicts to the top command levels of the party' (Eldersveld quoted in Gyford and James, 1983: 4). In other words, the problem with an over-centralized, 'control-freak' approach to the new, post-devolution challenges of party and political coordination is that it overloads the centre, particularly at a time when devolution has diffused power in a variety of new structures. To what extent is devolution unleashing new political forces militating towards a devolved party structure? How are those within the Welsh Labour party dealing with the centre, and how is Labour centrally responding to the new challenges posed by devolution?

Y DDRAIG GOCH A'R FANER GOCH – THE RED DRAGON AND THE RED FLAG: THE POLITICAL CULTURE OF THE WELSH LABOUR PARTY

From its beginnings, the Welsh Labour Party has been divided between focusing on the politics of the state and the politics of the locality, with state power tending to dominate, subordinating issues of territory and identity to those of class. Aneurin Bevan expressed this dominant view in his claim 'that the prime issue was the unity of the working class and that questions of territorial management merely served to undermine this aim' (McAllister, 1981: 84). Welsh issues were less central to the party's electoral fortunes in Wales than issues such as unemployment, health and education (Morgan, 1994: 117). Support for the creation of a Welsh Secretary of State and Office in 1964 reflected a claim for parity with the Scots (McAllister, 1981: 84–5) and was seen to provide 'privileged channels of access to the centre' (Jones and Keating, 1985) rather than an expression of territorial identity. This dominant strand was reflected in the opposition of many major Welsh Labour figures to, and lukewarm, at best, grassroots support for devolution in the 1979 referendum campaign (Balsom, 1983: 203–4, Table 10.4).

The division between pro-devolutionists and those who saw devolution as an irrelevant distraction, or, even worse, as undermining the advantages of integration into the British state, have overshadowed any left–right or activist–leadership divisions in Wales. This point was well illustrated at the time of the 1979 devolution referendum when Neil Kinnock, prominent in the 'No' campaign, was attacked for disloyalty to the party both by established Welsh trade-union 'barons' and by established political rebels such as Michael Foot (Jones and Wilford, 1983: 131–2). Of course, subsequently Welsh Labour party opinion swung much more towards devolution, fostered by the experience of Conservative government (Jones, 2000: 1–2), and bolstered by a feeling that the Conservatives lacked the legitimacy to impose their policies on Wales (Davies, 1999: 5).

The Wales Labour party has also traditionally been characterized by weak party organization; paradoxically, its very electoral dominance has tended to discourage active involvement within the party (McAllister, 1981: 79–81). Consequently small numbers of activists have dominated the grassroots level. A strong trade union membership might have ameliorated this dominance, but social and economic factors since the 1960s have meant trade unionism has declined as a countervailing power centre within the Welsh Labour movement (McAllister, 1981: 82). Consequently, the Welsh party has developed many of the features associated with one-party rule – such as a tendency towards paternalism and nepotism, reflected in the frequent resort to 'favoured son' successors in the party organization. Only recently have professional values and 'modernization', driven by New Labour from the centre, begun to overturn this cosy localism and community-based paternalism (Taylor, 2003b).

THE NEW WELSH PARTY POLITICAL SYSTEM: THE DECLINE OF LABOUR AND RISE OF PLAID CYMRU

Since the 1970s, Labour's organizational weakness and perceptions of poor performance by Labour-led local authorities in the south Wales valleys have enabled Plaid to gain an electoral foothold in this Labour heartland. Plaid's steadily improving electoral performance appeared to be levelling out in general elections after the 1970s (McAllister, 2001: 113), but Plaid's electoral breakthrough in the 1999 National Assembly elections marked a watershed in Welsh politics. Plaid's vote share trebled and both Labour and Conservative shares of the vote declined from the 1997 general election, in Labour's case by 17.1 per cent, as turnout fell to below 50 per cent, with nearly half of Labour's voters in 1997 failing to vote and a further 10 per cent defecting to Plaid (Johnston *et al.*, 2000: Tables 9.1 and 9.2). At the same time, local election victories saw Plaid take control of the Valleys' councils of Caerphilly and Rhondda Cynon Taff (Balsom (ed.), 2000).

Labour's failure, in 1999, to win the widely anticipated outright majority in the Assembly was an enormous culture shock for the party. Many in the Welsh party conveniently blamed the British party's imposition of Alun Michael as the new leader of the Welsh Labour party shortly before the election (Taylor, 2003a: 168), and overlooked problems within the party itself. Tellingly Plaid made significant inroads in the south Wales valleys, winning Assembly seats in areas like the Rhondda, Llanelli and Islwyn. Post-devolution, then, Plaid is acquiring a new role as the opposition to Labour's dominance of Welsh politics, epitomized by Plaid's role as the official opposition in the National Assembly. The division between the pro-devolutionists and those still sceptical of devolution has now became a strategic choice in how to combat the nationalist, and socialist, threat of Plaid. One Welsh Labour official observed:

> It's always an internal debate in the party about whether Welsh Labour can ever win by being more Welsh or should they just try and be more Labour. There's one school of thought that says you can never out-nat the Nats, so the thing is to go on your Labour credentials.
>
> (interview, May 2002)

Whilst the 2001 general election saw a decline in turnout in Wales which was 'only' in line with the UK average, that is to say, down by 12 per cent, Labour's fall in its share of the vote in Wales was twice that in any other UK region, and its decline in industrial south Wales, at 7.3 per cent, was greater than in any other area of the UK (Butler and Kavanagh, 2002: Table A1.2, 262–3). In the 2003 Assembly elections Labour was able to regain the ground it had lost to Plaid, but as the result of a further decline in the turnout which this time affected Plaid more than Labour (*Western Mail*, 5 May, 2003). Labour had not regained its lost electoral support, but Plaid had lost its support. Labour still has real problems motivating its electorate in Wales; the implications of this when, and if, voters return to the polls remain uncertain (Taylor, 2003d).

THE NEW WELSH PARTY POLITICAL SYSTEM: THE POLITICS OF COALITION GOVERNMENT

The 1999 Assembly elections created a further new dimension in the Welsh party system. Labour was left a minority ruling party in the Assembly, thanks largely to the proportional representation system. Labour initially resisted coalition but succumbed to the necessity, given the increasing problems of getting Assembly business done. The coalition was duly consummated with the *Partnership Agreement* with the Liberal Democrats in October 2000. The creation of the coalition was by no means uncontroversial within the party. The Assembly Labour Group, despite rumblings from notable critics, acquiesced and approved the coalition proposals after the Cabinet had agreed them, with the endorsement of the Welsh Executive apparently received in advance (Osmond, 2000: 6). However, many local government leaders and MPs, who, in the main, were not consulted (with the exception of Paul Murphy, the then Welsh Secretary), were highly critical of the idea of entering a coalition. The *Partnership Agreement* provided for two Assembly Cabinet seats for the six-strong Liberal Democrat group, and endorsed a raft of policies for the Assembly Government (Thomas, 2003: 185). The Liberal Democrats claimed that their policies, enshrined in the *Partnership Agreement*, were those underpinning the Labour-led Assembly Government despite vehement denials by Labour and a pamphlet published by them tracing Assembly policies back to their election manifesto of 1999 (Labour Party, n.d.), a claim which became a major campaigning theme in the 2003 Assembly elections.

Welsh electoral politics can no longer be characterized as driven by the 'dynamics of one-partyism' (McAllister, 1981). Plaid has been able to consolidate a position as the official opposition and carve out a distinctive role for itself (McAllister, 2001: 221–2), which is likely to continue, despite its poor performance in May 2003. Even though Labour has reversed the defeats of 1999 in the 2003 Assembly elections, and won half of the seats in the Assembly, Labour will still have to take note of an opposition in which Plaid will continue to play a significant role. Moreover, future coalitions may well be necessary or even desirable for Labour, so the Liberal Democrats will continue to play a significant role in the Welsh political system.

THE CHANGING PARTY: NEW STRUCTURES AND RELATIONSHIPS IN WALES

Post-devolution the Welsh Labour party (WLP) contains a proliferation of real and potential power centres. In addition to the Welsh Parliamentary Labour party (WPLP) in Westminster, the Welsh Executive Committee (WEC), the Labour Group in the Welsh Local Government Association (WLGA) and the Welsh Labour party bureaucracy, the WLP now has new power centres in the Assembly Cabinet, the Assembly Labour Group, the Welsh Policy Forum (WPF), and particularly the WPF's Policy Commissions and Welsh Joint Policy Committee (WJPC). The WPF and Assembly have had to be fitted into the Welsh Labour party's existing structures. Indeed the WPF has acquired a new significance as a mechanism to develop manifesto policies for the Assembly. As one interviewee commented: 'I think people realised that it wasn't in the masterplan but it could actually fit reasonably well' (interview, May 2002). The forging of other new relationships have been more difficult, notably the relationship between Welsh MPs and Assembly Members (AMs).

The introduction of the policy forum in Wales arose from the implementation of the Labour party policy document *Partnership in Power* within the party nationally (Taylor, 1999: 14–20; Baston, 2001: 164–5), a development which occurred alongside the reform of the party's ideological basis in Clause 4 of its constitution (Taylor, 1997: 168–91), and reform of the party's National Executive Committee (NEC) (Baston, 2001: 163–4, Taylor, 1999: 18–19). Equally importantly, the party's membership lists and recruitment were centralized and constituency labour parties (CLPs) reformed (Taylor, 1997: 178; Baston, 2001: 164). In contrast to these centralizing processes, the new policy forum policy-making system promises potential decentralization, 'allowing a conspicuous measure of party democracy' (Kelly 2001: 334). How far these reforms really are a move towards greater decentralization and democracy remains a matter for debate. Kelly interprets Labour's system as representing the kind of 'hidden system' which he had earlier described in his work on the Conservative party (Kelly, 1989). The benefits of this development are in the recognition 'that unity can no longer be imposed from above, but can be achieved only by reflecting, and shaping, rank-and-file opinion':

> The trick, it seems, is to provide such democracy without sparking high-profile rows at the main party conference. The Tories, with their conference system, were the first to discover what the trick was. Labour, with its policy forums, found a better way of performing it.
>
> (Kelly, 2001: 334)

Notably, Kelly, as a conservative theorist, tends to favour conservative aspects of democracy, particularly the ability of leaders to lead, to 'shape' party views, and democratic systems which tend to operate through reform rather than through innovative proposals.

This pluralistic interpretation of these changes was reinforced by the adoption of 'one member, one vote' (OMOV) in internal party election and selection procedures. These reforms explicitly sought to include and engage a wider party membership than the constituency-based meetings which used to select and elect candidates, and the annual conferences that supposedly decided party policy. Even so, these reforms were driven at least as much by the same imperatives as those underpinning changes in candidate selection, namely the need to sideline supposedly unrepresentative and 'extreme' party activists (Scarrow *et al.*, 2000: 131). The centralizing of some functions, on the one hand, and appealing directly to members and supporters, on the other, effectively removes the power of party activists, and, as Kelly suggests, creates in the process at least the semblance of party unity.

Candidate selection
The creation of the devolved bodies gave the party the opportunity to create a new system of candidate selection. Labour's open 'B' list system for parliamentary candidates had included, as one Welsh Labour official commented, 'all sorts of people . . . that basically you didn't want on it in a month of Sundays' (interview, July 2002). The intent behind the new candidate-selection process was to exclude 'established notables', particularly in local government, whose 'longevity in office was not always matched by their talents'; improve the prospects of selection for women candidates; and raise candidate calibre (Shaw, 2001: 38). Some have argued that those who were less articulate or who did not fit 'the New Labour mould' were excluded (Edwards and Chapman, 2000: 370).

Even more controversial was the imposition of 'twinning', an attempt to ensure equal selection of women and men candidates in constituency seats by pairing CLPs together and requiring that members of both CLPs should select one man and one woman. Many long-serving constituency activists considered this a major challenge to 'constituency sovereignty' and many of the women selected experienced resentment from these activists (Edwards and Chapman, 2000). In 2002, the party faced the prospect of another controversial round of selections for the 2003 Assembly elections, and the possibility that those who had opposed twinning might challenge women AMs in some constituencies. To prevent this, the party adopted the 'affirmative nomination' procedure, first used in the 2001 general election as a means to reduce the number of seats likely to be contested (Butler and Kavanagh, 2002: 187).

'Affirmative nomination' required sitting AMs to receive the approval of at least 50 per cent of their CLP or face a reselection contest. Not one existing Labour AM was forced into a contested reselection, although John Marek opted for reselection rather than face a disciplinary hearing for bringing the party into disrepute which would have effectively excluded him from a reselection contest if he had lost (Taylor, 2002: 57). The Party then had sixteen vacancies, three resulting from the retirement of incumbents, and thirteen which Labour had failed to win in 1999. Of these, it was calculated that six constituencies needed to 'volunteer' for all-women shortlists to maintain Labour women AM numbers. The consequent procedures were easily agreed, despite some residual acrimony over 'constituency sovereignty', notably from Valleys constituencies like Islwyn and Blaenau Gwent, at the April 2002 Wales Labour party conference. Labour officials divided the vacant constituencies into the eight most winnable and the eight least winnable seats. Then three constituencies in each were asked to agree to all-women shortlists. Despite concerns about constituencies equivocating over an all-women shortlist, the six constituencies came forward with little acrimony. As a result, Labour now has an Assembly Group dominated by women, a fact which has contributed to women gaining exactly half of the Assembly seats in 2003.

Notably this time, unlike the first candidate-selection process, the candidate panel process has permitted constituencies to consider alternative nominees not on the panel list. However, the party stressed the relative ease of getting, and benefits of being on the panel, such as guaranteed endorsement by the Welsh Executive Committee (WEC) and the regular information provided to those on the panel database. For the 1999 Assembly elections application forms and criteria were used to assess those to be invited by the panel for interview; for the 2003 election, applicants who clearly met the criteria in their application forms could be placed on the list without having a panel interview.

The Welsh Policy Forum
The creation of the WPF had already forced some adjustment in the structures of the Welsh Labour party. As with the National Policy Forum (NPF) at UK level, the WPF acquired most of the Welsh Executive Committee (WEC) policy-making functions. Inevitably, this change has detracted from the WEC's already limited status, as one former WEC member told us 'The WEC was not somewhere you went to enhance your career in the Labour party, unlike the Scottish Executive Committee for instance' (interview, March 2003). Many Welsh MPs were even more scathing about the WEC, most regarding it as a 'damp squib', or as 'useless and malign', with one

claiming that the WEC had 'a history of domination by strong personalities with tiny brains' (interviews, September 2000).

As one party official observed: 'The Welsh Policy Forum process reflected the National Policy Forum because this was the only policy process up and running' (speech at WPF meeting, November 2002). Like the NPF, it is a policy forum with wide party representation, driven by Policy Commissions and the Welsh Joint Policy Committee. The crucial differences are in the composition of these bodies rather than in their role. The WJPC, like the National JPC, includes representatives from government, the policy forum and executive bodies, but whereas the government representatives are outnumbered on the JPC, this is not the case for the WJPC. The Assembly Government provides five members – the First Minister, and four of the eight Labour Ministers and Junior Ministers in the Assembly – the remainder comprise the Welsh Secretary, three members of the WEC, two from the WPF, ostensibly a trade union and a CLP representative, and one elected member. The WPF Policy Commissions are smaller in number than the NPF Commissions – three as opposed to eight – and focused on Assembly policy priorities, and again government representation is stronger than on the NPF Commissions. Two of the WPF Commissions contain ten members, and one, the Communities, Environment and Health Commission, contains eleven. The First Minister and Secretary of State have seats on all the Commissions, and two more seats, three on the Communities Commission, are reserved for other Labour Assembly Ministers, each has two WPF members, one trade union and one CLP, three WEC members, one of whom is a NPF delegate, and one elected member.

Unlike the NPF, the WPF consists predominantly of CLP delegates, two from each CLP, alongside a number of delegates from affiliated organizations including the trade unions (interview, May 2002). The NPF contains a smaller proportion of CLP representatives but a wider range of other party interests (Labour Party, 2001: Appendix 1). After the 2003 Assembly election, this process may be reformed, possibly through new subcommittees of the WJPC replacing the Policy Commissions. Such a reform would strengthen the already dominant role of the WJPC. Indeed, the WJPC has become the effective policy-making body of the party, responsible for agreeing policy documents after consultation within the party outside the manifesto-writing policy cycle. As one party official noted: 'The WJPC has sole responsibility for policy-making now, and yes, of course there is going to be a tension. I think that Assembly Ministers are going to feel, quite rightly, that they want a very direct, key input into their section of the manifesto' (interview, May 2002).As members of the Policy Commissions and WJPC, Assembly Ministers have enjoyed just this kind of input and have thus been able to adopt WPF policies for immediate implementation. At the UK level, where the NPF has a more established and settled working process, ministers also play an important role (Kelly, 2001: 331) but, in addition, other participants in the NPF Policy Commissions have also made a significant contribution. As one commented: 'As a member of the Policy Commission I had a very, very substantial input, I effectively wrote quite a lot of the policies, I was very pleased about that' (interview, July 2002). Non-government participants in the WPF Commissions may, by comparison, be less directly involved. Nevertheless, the WJPC and the Commissions do decide on document content, on how WPF submissions are considered and the WPF agenda. Furthermore, even the Labour Assembly Group must make submissions to the WPF, which are treated in the same way as submissions from elsewhere in the party; although presumably the WJPC and Commission members may notice them more readily. Revealingly perhaps, even MPs saw the process as Assembly rather than activist-driven; the agenda 'is still under the control of the centre, just because they set it'. These views were most strongly articulated by those with the closest experience of the WJPC and Commissions.

These new bodies have not inherited the kind of powers once held by the NEC and Annual Conference, or at a Welsh level the WEC and Welsh Conference and, therefore, are less at risk of becoming a focus for the sort of internal tensions exhibited at that level in the 1970s and 1980s. This risk is reduced by the Welsh Labour party political culture, particularly the absence of left–right or leadership–activist divisions, and not least the 'hidden' nature of the new policy system (Kelly, 2001; Taylor, 1993). Indeed, this hidden nature has created problems for WPF advocates, especially as those making submissions have no idea of how their submission contributes to policy.

Interestingly, Labour's pitch for the 2003 Assembly elections was based on 'ten key pledges,' following recent Labour tradition both in Wales and in UK general elections, which were presented to the Welsh press over two days, with the announcement of a promised abolition of prescription charges and the introduction of free breakfasts for all primary-school children (*Western Mail*, 2 April 2003), followed the next day by an announcement of ten key pledges, of which these two were part (*Western Mail*, 3 April 2003). Yet not one of these ten key pledges was included in Labour's pre-manifesto draft discussed at a Cardiff meeting of the WPF in November 2002, and Rhodri

Morgan claimed that free school breakfasts was an idea that 'he hit upon' after visiting a school which had introduced the policy (*Western Mail*, 2 April 2003). These developments suggest that the manifesto may not be closely tied to WPF policy, especially given the vague nature of many of the policy forum documents and the very specific nature of electoral 'pledges', which do allow considerable leeway for the Welsh party elite to interpret WPF policy. In addition residual scepticism exists among party activists still suspicious of the way in which they engage with the WPF process and who still see Conference, Welsh and Annual, as their forum.

Labour party centres of power: the unions, local government and party activists
How have these changes affected the other key power centres in the party, notably the trade unions and local government in Wales? The role of the unions has declined much as it has elsewhere in the UK. As one Welsh party official reflected, whereas in the 1980s, the WEC 'was full of the big trade-union barons, all the big trade-union barons in Wales were on it', this has now declined, perhaps reflecting the increasing distance between the party and the trade unions (interview, July 2002). All the Welsh Commissions and the WJPC include one place for trade unions, but these do not seem to be regarded as particularly significant or high status. The Wales Labour party does hold regular meetings with the trade unions, but contributions to the WPF and connections with the Assembly appear inconsistent. In terms of WPF submissions, as one party official explained, some unions, like Unison, used delegate-based meetings to decide submissions to the WPF, but few organized membership meetings to provide submissions (interview, May 2002), which reflected the situation in respect of the NPF (Labour Party, 2001: Appendix 5). One Labour AM observed that few unions were well organized in terms of their contact with the Labour Group or lobbying of the Assembly (interview, March 2003). It is also worth noting that Welsh Labour MPs were hardly unanimous about the trade unions' relationship with the party, with one arguing that 'we've valued the trade union movement in a way that perhaps other people elsewhere don't' (interview, December 2002), and another claiming that 'I'm a kind of sworn enemy of special-interest groups and they include trade unions' (interview, November 2002), perhaps reflecting a contrast between established Welsh Labour views and more recent New Labour-influenced perspectives.

In Wales, as in England, Assembly–local government relations are couched in the concept of 'partnership', which in the Welsh case has statutory force. The Local Government Partnership Council is a key element in this relationship (Laffin, Taylor and Thomas, 2002: 26–7). For the Labour party, local government pressures have reinforced the emphasis on the public sector, driven by the citizen rather than consumer, perspectives outlined in Rhodri Morgan's Swansea speech (Taylor, 2003a: 173–5). These pressures have also reinforced policy preferences which have focused on local government delivery and autonomy in a way which has not been the case in England. Notably some Welsh MPs view the relationship with local government as problematic, cementing a 'producerist' interest in Welsh politics. As one said to us: 'I want to be an exception to those local government leaders . . . who fight fiercely to defend the position they are in because they are in it, rather than because it has any merit', and another commented on the nature and quality of AMs 'if they come from local government and are afraid to kick against local government then you've got problems, because they won't take them on' (interviews, October 2000 and November 2002).

There have also been tensions with local government, specifically with Cardiff's Leader and formerly Lord Mayor, Russell Goodway, over the site for the Assembly and over his personal remuneration as Council Leader and Lord Mayor, and more generally with local government over issues such as the extra work generated for local government over constituency issues by repeated approaches from constituency MPs, AMs and regional list AMs over the same issue (Laffin, Taylor and Thomas, 2002).

Relations between MPs and AMs

To establish a relationship between the Welsh PLP and the Assembly and WLGA Labour Groups, a protocol has been agreed among these three groups representing, as one party official told us, 'an attempt to get us to focus more on developing a better informal network then we've had up to now' (interview, July 2002). The protocol allows for regular meetings of officers and observers at each other's meetings (Wales Labour Party, 2002). Cardiff MP Jon Owen Jones, as Chair of the Welsh PLP, has frequently attended Assembly Labour Group meetings; Cllr Graham Court attends from the WLGA Labour Group, Lorraine Barrett AM attends WLGA Labour Group meetings; and Welsh Labour Party General Secretary, Jessica Morden, attends Assembly Labour Group meetings. Notably, although Jon Owen Jones has assiduously attended Assembly Group meetings, reciprocal attendance at Welsh PLP meetings from the Assembly Labour Group has been on an entirely different basis. One MP pointed out: 'We send Jon Owen Jones as the chair of the Labour Group down to represent us in the Labour group there, and they send up to us a whole series of people, mainly Ministers, to talk to us about emerging policy in the Welsh Assembly Government' (interview, December 2002).

Relationships between Welsh MPs and AMs exist then largely at an individual, constituency level. Many MPs interviewed referred to their personal relationships with their Labour constituency AM in the organization of local offices, constituency surgeries and dealing with constituency issues. The role of regional AMs did grate with some Labour MPs, with one suggesting that an 'excellent description' of them would be as political 'ambulance-chasers' (interview, November 2000). Otherwise, these relationships exist almost exclusively on a ministerial level between Welsh and Westminster Ministers, and not at backbench level. One Welsh backbench MP described relations between AMs and MPs as 'bloody awful', while an informed commentator on the Assembly Group and the Welsh PLP claimed 'the problem is a lack of knowledge of each other' (interview, September 2002). This may be true not only in terms of the working practices of the two different bodies but also in terms of the policy pressures upon them.

Many MPs regret and even resent how the Assembly has eclipsed Westminster in Welsh media coverage. MPs complained about not having 'the balance right', that 'MPs get rather fed up that Westminster doesn't get the coverage in the Welsh media now that it used to do', commented on 'a tremendous polarization of the media towards the Assembly', that 'the media coverage of the Assembly is enormous' and 'the media see it through the eyes of the Assembly, the investment they make in covering the Assembly, almost to the complete exclusion of covering Parliament in London' (interviews). Even so, it should be stressed that Assembly Ministers lack both the resources and the inclination to attempt media management on the scale practised in Westminster. Indicatively, the special advisers in Wales are now policy rather than media specialists.

Turning to the relationship between Welsh Labour MPs and the Welsh Labour party, in our interviews Welsh MPs showed no great awareness of or contact with the Welsh Labour party as an organization. Historically, many Welsh Labour MPs have focused on their constituency and Westminster, and have not engaged with the Welsh Labour party organization (McAllister, 1981: 83). This is true as much for pro-devolutionists as for those sceptical of devolution, and for recent as well as established MPs. One MP, asked whether the party should adopt a federal structure commented that: 'It will be de facto. It is going that way but there is no design behind it' (interview, October 2002). These party links may be weak, yet institutional links are developing through the necessity of dealing with Welsh primary legislation. The Wales Health Service Act 2002 may have created a precedent for a new process of pre-legislative scrutiny involving MPs on the Welsh Affairs Committee and AMs on the Health and Social Services Subject Committee. This issue of the scrutiny of Welsh primary legislation was a matter which did concern many Welsh MPs.

Nonetheless, MPs have taken some initiatives in developing links with AMs. Arguably, MPs face greater incentives to build these links than AMs given that the Assembly's functions (in education, health, transport, local government and so on) have a direct impact on constituency issues and on MPs' chances of re-election. MPs do seem to feel distanced from their constituencies following their loss of direct influence over such policy areas. One initiative to create a closer relationship is the Valleys Forward group which aims to bring south Wales valleys' MPs and AMs together in one campaigning organization; but to date far fewer AMs than MPs have shown a commitment to this group. Nonetheless, it has prompted the formation of a north Wales group, but purely of MPs, to campaign for their regional interests.

The Assembly Labour Group and its political dynamics
The Assembly was intended to embody a 'new' politics for Wales and to be filled with the 'best talent in Wales' (Laffin and Thomas, 2000), reflecting the move in the Labour party noted above, to improve the 'standard' of Labour candidates. The selection process set out to 'attract a wider pool of applicants to ensure the best possible candidates', and under the influence of 'those who sought a more open and participatory' party sought to encourage women candidates (Bradbury *et al.*, 2000: 161).

The Assembly itself has provided a new career path for aspiring politicians within Wales. Cabinet members such as Jane Davidson, Carwyn Jones and Edwina Hart have emerged as new figures on the Welsh political stage and as potential future First Ministers (Laffin and Thomas, 2001). The Assembly Labour Group is not divided into recognizable factions. It tends to avoid votes and to be characterized by considerable policy consensus, this despite the presence of a very few members who are widely regarded as 'mavericks'. According to one source:

> the dynamics of the numbers, the way in which [Labour AMs] relate to Ministers and the way in which the agenda in this place is set, which is not driven by the kind of legislative timetable [which exists in Westminster] makes it much more like a local government group.

> (interview, July 2002)

One party official added that the AMs' backgrounds were further, key factors:

actually we've got a wide range of backgrounds in the party, and that reflects, to some extent, the way the group approaches its work. It has not been all the time harking back to Westminster or harking back to local council practice; it's been finding its own way to do things.

(interview, June 2002)

In addition, Labour AMs, overwhelmingly constituency-based, tend to have a workload which prevents the Group from operating along the same lines as Plaid or other Assembly Groups, which have a far greater proportion of list members. Inevitably, too, the Assembly Labour Group operates in a very different way from the Westminster PLP, not least as there are only twenty-eight Labour AMs compared with 410 Labour MPs. The Labour Group meets with Ministers present, and AMs frequently meet Ministers inform-ally around the Assembly building. They are well aware of each others' views on particular issues, and any factions within the Group are much more likely to be visible at an earlier stage, and more difficult to organize than might be the case with the much larger PLP. The politics of the Assembly Labour Group are very personal. To quote one of Labour's backroom staff: 'because the Group is so much smaller, the way the Group interacts is extremely important to the way things get handled' (interview, June 2002). The consequent group-dynamics militate against serious factional infighting, although these dynamics did not prevent Alun Michael as First Minister from becoming isolated within the Labour Group and then effectively forced to resign. Indeed, it was the indication by the group that it would not renominate Michael following a successful vote of no confidence that was the decisive factor in his departure (Thomas and Laffin, 2001).

Central–Welsh relations within the Labour party

The early post-devolution period was associated with attempts by the centre to control the new territorial bodies which it had established. This was apparent in the imposition of Alun Michael as leader of the Wales Labour party, Frank Dobson as the Labour candidate for London Mayor in opposi-tion to Ken Livingstone, and attempts by Blair supporters to shape candi-date selection in Scotland (Shaw, 2001). One major factor underpinning the attempt to maintain central control was the desire to ensure that nothing impinged on the election of Blair for a historic second term, which was duly delivered in 2001 (interview, March 2000). The way in which the then party

General Secretary, Margaret McDonagh, chose to interpret her role may also have been a contributory factor (M. Taylor, 2003: 55). The relative importance of these factors will remain uncertain, especially given McDonagh's replacement immediately following the election by David Triesman. Since the achievement of the second term, however, there has been a noticeable sea-change in the relationship between the centre and Wales in particular. In fact, at the policy level, one former Minister suggested to us that the view that the centre were essentially 'control freaks' was misplaced:

> Unless there are actual disputes where the thing does surface into the policy domain, not just differences, but differences which are held up in the national media as being significant differences like university fees, like social care, then it doesn't really impact that much to be honest.
>
> (interview, July 2002)

The idea that London was in control of events at Cardiff Bay had also been bolstered by the exclusive leadership style of Alun Michael (Taylor, 2003a: 169). In contrast, Rhodri Morgan has sought to emphasize the policy distance between Wales and the centre, at least in the run-up to the 2003 election (Taylor, 2003a: 173–5). Meanwhile, Blair himself has accepted that devolution will mean policy differences (*Western Mail*, 28 September and 4 October 2002). Morgan has, of course, been careful to keep Blair and the centre on side, supporting Alun Michael when he was leader of the Wales Labour party and allowing Assembly Ministers to develop contacts with their Westminster counterparts, including Morgan's twice-weekly meetings with the Welsh Secretary. From a party perspective, the position is more complicated. To some extent the party is underpinned by deeper bonds, as party officials told us: 'It doesn't matter whether you are devolved or not, what binds the party together is a set of values and they are enshrined in our new Clause 4' (interview, June 2002). Nonetheless, there are also organizational issues, as our interviews with officials at Millbank Tower, now moved to Old Queen Street, observed: 'One of the things we are concerned about are parameters. We do not want a federal system within the party. One of the issues we are interested in is how to continue to ensure that' (interview, June 2002).

The increasing number and frequency of elections across the UK serve to shape the policy considerations within the party, and inevitably this shapes the management of the policy-forum system, both in the run-up to general elections and Assembly elections. As one party official noted:

the fact that a policy forum is focused on a future election circumscribes what they are able to look at. Natural constraints on what needs to be done and how it can be done are built into the process. With any policy forum at any level what we seek is that the participants recognize the constraints upon us and that is that we are a party seeking to remain in government.

(interview, June 2002)

Nonetheless, it would be misleading to assume that the party at the centre is simply driven by an imperative to seek common policy ground between the centre and the Welsh and Scottish parties. Differences are, as party officials recognize, dictated by circumstance as well as by belief:

A lot of issues are practical rather than political. If you take student fees as an example they have been decided differently in Scotland than in England because resources are different, and the party has made a judgement, rightly or wrongly, that the UK electorate won't buy it.

(interview, June 2002)

The focus on elections and the electoral focus on service delivery, now a key feature of British electoral politics, leads to potential tensions. Tensions between the Assembly and the Westminster Cabinets have eased. Yet, for Welsh Labour MPs, the Assembly's ability to perform in key areas of service delivery may have a telling impact on their ability to maintain their electoral place in their constituencies. For them, the perception is clear: what it comes down to is should there not be the same expectation of the right to care and other services, and should the same priorities not apply wherever you happen to be and whatever the administration? (interview, June 2002). The fact that Welsh Labour MPs' views may contrast starkly with those of the Prime Minister was well made by one MP, who stated:

I didn't like what the Prime Minister said after his speech [at the Annual Conference in Blackpool] when he held that kind of Prime Minister's press conference on the Thursday I think, when he was asked by, I believe, David Cornock, 'What if the reforms that you've said are absolutely vital for the English Health Service aren't carried through in Wales?', and he said 'Well that's up to the Welsh, they are responsible for running Health in Wales'. There were some of us old veterans who were worried about that.

(interview, November 2002)

A number of MPs mentioned Health and the Assembly's performance on Health as a particular worry; the 'producerist' relationship of the Assembly with local government and other public-sector 'vested interests' was also mentioned. In addition, the Assembly's limited use of Private Finance Initiative (PFI) schemes has been raised by Cardiff MP and Welsh PLP delegate to the Assembly Labour Group, Jon Owen Jones, in an article in the Institute of Welsh Affairs' publication *Agenda*, and subsequently in the *Western Mail* (Jones, 2002; Taylor, 2003c).

CONCLUSION

The Welsh Labour party is moving away from being a traditional, 'one-partyist' Labour party, that is, a party with one organizational hierarchy focused on a dominant 'centre', towards a 'modernized' party, with multiple centres of activity and a less hierarchical organization. Devolution has been a major factor. It has created the conditions for the emergence of a new generation of Welsh Labour politicians almost overnight, a generation which is a contrast with the older generation of Welsh Labour councillors in their background and abilities, their status and powers, and their gender. In addition, the 2001 general election has seen an intake of MPs who appear also to represent a generational change, perhaps indirectly as the result of the successes of Plaid Cymru in the 1999 Assembly election. Yet devolution is only one part of the explanation of this change. Devolution could simply have further embedded traditional Welsh Labour leaders. The two other crucial and necessary factors have been proportional representation and organizational change within the Labour party.

Firstly, proportional representation has reduced considerably the like-lihood of Labour becoming the perpetual government of Wales. The 1999 elections left Labour as a minority administration and then as the senior partner in a coalition government. In 2003, Labour gained ground and has been able to form a 'majority' government with its thirty AMs. The import-ant point is that Welsh Labour, both in the Assembly and now in many of its formerly unchallenged local-government strongholds, is now electorally vulnerable. 'One-partyism' is no longer an option.

Secondly, centrally-driven organizational change within the Labour party has been critical in two ways. The drive towards a 'new' politics and candidates with wider experience and talents has served to foster the genera-tional shift in Welsh politicians, engineering a gender-balanced Labour Group with younger candidates, less indebted to party patronage and more professional in their political outlook. Meanwhile, almost as important has been the Britain-wide centralization of power within the party away from constituency-level activists and towards central- and Welsh-level party officers, whose role also has shifted from being centred on internal party politics to external campaigning.

The new Welsh political party system is now distinctive from the British party system. At least partly as a result Welsh Labour is diverging from British Labour, although we should be careful not to confuse rhetoric with substantial difference. Welsh Labour does face electoral and, to some extent, public policy challenges distinct from those facing Labour nationally, and operates in a different political culture and set of policy networks. In the 2003 Assembly election campaign, the Welsh political leadership emphasized its policy divergence from the centre, even packaging up its achievements in government in faintly left-wing rhetoric, although it is worth noting that this occurred only after Blair's public acceptance of policy difference at Labour's Annual Conference in Blackpool in 2002. Until then, Welsh Labour ministers had trodden carefully and presented any policy divergences from central Labour government policy more in terms of Welsh exceptional conditions rather than as ideological differences.

Notably, Labour at the centre has now pulled back from the tight control it sought to exercise earlier in the devolution process. It has accepted some degree of informal regionalization and devolution within the party, although no formal steps have been taken in terms of internal devolution or a 'federal' party constitution. The early tight control over the leadership selection process is now generally seen as having been counter-productive and as having damaged Labour's electoral prospects in Wales. This change in approach appears to confirm Eldersveld's 'stratarchy' hypothesis that the problems of internal party conflict management do tend to create pressures to decentralize. However, to date, decentralization within the party has been driven particularly strongly by very pragmatic electoral rather than just organizational dynamics. Labour at the centre now recognizes that it makes sense to allow the Welsh party, if it is to respond to the political environment in Wales and mobilize Labour voters, room for strategic manoeuvre and, therefore, some policy discretion. How far that policy discretion extends, and how keen the Labour Assembly Government is to push the boundaries of that discretion, will become clearer during the Assembly's second term.

AUTHORS' ACKNOWLEDGEMENT

The research for this paper was supported by an ESRC grant under the ESRC's Devolution and Constitutional Change Programme: Grant No.

L219252116 (D279). This is a revised edition of a paper originally presented to the Annual Conference of the Political Studies Association, April 2003, University of Leicester.

REFERENCES

Balsom, Denis (1983). 'Public opinion and Welsh devolution', in Foulkes, D., Jones, J. B. and Wilford, R. A. (eds) (1983), *The Welsh Veto: The Wales Act 1978 and the Referendum*, Cardiff: University of Wales Press.

Balsom, Denis (ed.) (2000). *The Wales Yearbook 2001*, Cardiff: HTV.

Baston, Lewis (2001). 'The party system', in Anthony Seldon (ed.), *The Blair Effect: The Blair Government 1997–2001*, London: Little, Brown & Co.

Bradbury, J., Bennie, L., Denver, D. and Mitchell, J. (2000). 'Devolution, parties and new politics: candidate selection for the 1999 National Assembly elections', in *Contemporary Wales*, 13.

Butler, D., and Kavanagh, D. (2002). *The British General Election of 2002*, Basingstoke: Palgrave.

Davies, R. (1999). *Devolution: A Process Not an Event*, Cardiff: Institute of Welsh Affairs.

Edwards, J., and Chapman, C. (2000). 'Women's political representation in Wales: waving or drowning?', in *Contemporary Politics*, 6, 4.

Eldersveld, S. J. (1964). *Political Parties: A Behavioural Analysis*, Chicago: Rand McNally & Co.

Gyford, J., and James, M. (1983). *National Parties and Local Politics*, London: George Allen & Unwin.

Johnston, R., Trystan, D., Pattie, C. and Wyn Jones, R. (2000). 'From parliament to assembly: changing voting behaviour in Wales between the 1997 general election and the 1999 National Assembly election', in *Contemporary Wales*, 13.

Jones, J. B. (2000). 'Introduction', in Jones, J. B., and Balsom, D. (eds), *The Road to the National Assembly for Wales*, Cardiff: University of Wales Press.

Jones, J. B., and Keating, M. (1985). *Labour and the British State*, Oxford: Clarendon Press.

Jones, J. B., and Wilford, R. A. (1983). 'The referendum campaign: 8 February–1 March, 1979', in Foulkes, D., Jones, J. B. and Wilford, R. A. (eds), *The Welsh Veto: The Wales Act 1978 and the Referendum*, Cardiff: University of Wales Press.

Jones, J. O. (2002). 'The price of saying No', *Agenda*, Winter 2002/3, Cardiff: IWA.

Kelly, R. (1989). *Conservative Party Conferences: The Hidden System*, Manchester: Manchester University Press.

Kelly, R. (2001). 'Farewell conference, hello forum: the making of Labour and Tory policy', *Political Quarterly*, 72, 3, 329–34.

Labour Party (2001). *National Policy Forum: Reports to Conference 2001*, London: Labour Party.

Labour Party (n.d.). *The Partnership Agreement and the Labour Party Manifesto*, Cardiff: Wales Labour Party.

Laffin, M., Taylor, G., and Thomas, A. (2002). *A New Partnership? The National Assembly for Wales and Local Government*, York: Joseph Rowntree Foundation.

Laffin, M. and Thomas, A. (2000). 'Designing the National Assembly for Wales', *Parliamentary Affairs*, 53, 3 (July), 557–76.

Laffin, M., and Thomas A. (2001). 'Learning to work together: political–official relations in the Welsh Assembly', *Public Money and Management*, 20, 2 (April), 45–51.

McAllister, I. (1981). 'The Labour Party in Wales: the dynamics of one-partyism', *Llafur: The Journal of Welsh Labour History*, 3, 2, Spring.

McAllister, L. (2001). *Plaid Cymru: The Emergence of a Political Party*, Bridgend: Seren.

McKenzie, R. T. (1955). *British Political Parties: The Distribution of Power within the Conservative and Labour Parties*, London: Heinemann.

Morgan, K. O. (1994). 'Leaders and led in the Labour movement: the Welsh experience', *Llafur: The Journal of Welsh Labour History*, 6, 3.

Osmond, J. (2000). 'The coalition government', in Osmond, J. (ed.), *Coalition Politics Come to Wales: Monitoring the National Assembly September to December 2000*, Cardiff: IWA.

Scarrow, S., Webb, P. and Farrell, D. M. (2000). 'From social integration to electoral contestation: the changing distribution of power within political parties', in Dalton, R. J., and Wattenberg, M. P. (eds), *Parties Without Partisans: Political Change in Advanced Industrial Democracies*, Oxford: Oxford University Press.

Shaw, E. (2001). 'New Labour: new pathways to parliament', *Parliamentary Affairs*, 54, 1.

Taylor, G. (1993). 'Changing conference: embracing an illusion of democracy', *Renewal*, 1, 4.

Taylor, G. (1997). *Labour's Renewal? The Policy Review and Beyond*, Basingstoke: Macmillan.

Taylor, G. (1999). 'Introduction' and 'Power in the party', in Taylor, G. (ed.), *The Impact of New Labour*, Basingstoke: Macmillan.

Taylor, G. (2002). 'Political parties', in Osmond, J. (ed.), *Dragon Takes a Different Route: Monitoring the National Assembly for Wales September to December 2002*, Cardiff: IWA.

Taylor, G. (2003a). 'Labour', in Osmond, J. and Jones, J. B. (eds), *Birth of Welsh Democracy: The First Term of the National Assembly for Wales*, Cardiff: IWA/WGC.

Taylor, G. (2003b). 'Can New Labour save Wales from itself?', in *Planet*, 158, April/May.

Taylor, G. (2003c). 'Political parties', in Osmond, J. (ed.), *Dragon Debates its Future: Monitoring the National Assembly for Wales December 2002 to March 2003*, Cardiff: IWA.

Taylor, G. (2003d). 'Back to the future: business as usual in Welsh politics?', *Planet*, forthcoming.

Taylor, M. (2003). 'Saving the party: looking out not up', in *Renewal*, 11, 1.

Thomas, A. (2003). 'Liberal democrats', in Osmond, J., and Jones, J. B. (eds), *Birth of Welsh Democracy: The First Term of the National Assembly for Wales*, Cardiff: IWA/WGC.

Thomas, A., and Laffin, M. (2001). 'The first Welsh constitutional crisis: the Alun Michael resignation', *Public Policy and Administration*, 16, 1, Spring.

Wales Labour Party (2002). *Protocol Between Labour Representatives in Welsh Local Government, Members of the National Assembly for Wales Labour Party, and Members of the Welsh Parliamentary Labour Party*, Cardiff: Wales Labour Party.

5. BUSINESS AS USUAL?
COMPARING WESTMINSTER AND NATIONAL
ASSEMBLY ELECTIONS IN WALES[1]

Roger Scully

1 May 2003 will see the second elections to the devolved chambers in Scotland and Wales. At the time of writing, it is impossible to say for certain whether the second election to the National Assembly for Wales (NAW) will prove as dramatic as the first, which witnessed the now legendary 'quiet earthquake' as Plaid Cymru stormed some of the most totemic of Labour bastions in the south Wales valleys – winning the constituency seats of Llanelli, Islwyn and Rhondda. Without entering into the hazardous business of election prediction, however, it is now possible to begin understanding the relationship between the two most important electoral contests that now occur in Wales: general elections to Westminster, and elections to the National Assembly. That is what I attempt to do in this article. Specifically, I wish to:

- why the results of the 1999 National Assembly and 2001 Westminster elections in Wales were so different;
- evaluate some of the interpretations placed on the 2001 result (and its relationship with the 1999 election);
- and suggest some interesting possibilities (without making any predictions!) for future NAW and Westminster polls.[2]

THE CONTEMPORARY ELECTORAL POLITICS OF WALES

The electoral dominance of the Labour party in Wales is a long-established and widely-noted fact. Even in times when Labour has done poorly in the rest of the UK, and particularly England, Wales has generally remained a Labour bastion (Wyn Jones, 2002). Thus, in the context of a record-breaking victory across the UK, it was utterly unremarkable that the 1997

Westminster election should see the Labour party in Wales extend its dominance even further, with all other parties falling a long way behind (see Table 5.1).

TABLE **5.1**
The 1997 general election in Wales – seats and vote share

Party	Vote share %	Seats
Labour	54.8	34
Conservative	19.5	0
Lib-Dem.	12.3	2
Plaid Cymru	10.0	4

It was largely because of Labour's hegemonic position in Wales that the 1999 NAW election was, despite the semi-proportional voting system employed, and even in the face of negative publicity experienced by Labour in the wake of Ron Davies's resignation and the divisive leadership contest that followed, widely expected to produce at least a narrow majority in the Assembly for Labour.[3] And it was because of these expectations that the result of the 1999 NAW election was shocking, witnessing as it did a number of remarkable contrasts with the Westminster election held only two years previously (see Table 5.2):

- The Labour party saw a substantial fall in its electoral support. Having won almost 55 per cent of the Westminster vote in Wales in 1997, Labour's support dropped to 37.6 per cent on the first (constituency) vote and 35.4 per cent on the second (regional list) vote. Thus, Labour fell short of a majority of the sixty seats in the Assembly.
- Less widely noted was a significant fall in Conservative support from the already mediocre Tory performance of the 1997 election. The Welsh Conservatives were no longer even a distant second party, but a (poor) third.
- Most dramatic of all, however, was the substantial advance in support for Plaid Cymru – up from 10 per cent in 1997 to 28.4 per cent on the first vote and 30.5 per cent on the second vote.

This election result has thus often, and appropriately, been described by the phrase used at the time by Dafydd Wigley – a *daeargryn tawel* ('quiet earth-quake'). The result prompted understandable jubilation in Plaid Cymru;

TABLE 5.2
Vote shares by party, 1997 and 1999

Party	1997 %	1999 (first vote) %
Labour	54.8	37.6
Conservative	19.5	15.8
Lib-Dem	12.3	13.5
Plaid Cymru	10.0	28.4

bitter disappointment in the Labour party (as well as concern in the other major parties); and it has, of course, had very important consequences for how the NAW has functioned subsequently. The result also prompted an internal inquest in the Labour party, with a search for sources of blame.[4]

In the aftermath of 1999, and despite the replacement of Alun Michael with the more popular Rhodri Morgan as Leader in spring 2000, the Labour party in Wales approached the 2001 general election with a degree of trepidation – fearing at least some losses similar to 1999. Conversely, Plaid Cymru had some reason for optimism about making significant gains on its 1997 performance – in both seats and votes. In this climate of expectations, what was striking about 2001 was the absence of change from 1997, and the disparity with 1999. Seat totals for Westminster among the parties remained identical with the previous parliament (although two individual seats changed hands).[5] Labour, despite seeing its vote share fall further in Wales than elsewhere in the UK, remained the dominant party in all respects (see Table 5.3).

TABLE 5.3
Seats and vote share in Wales, 2001

Party	Seats %	Vote share (change from 1997)%
Labour	34	48.6 (–6.2)
Conservative	0	21.0 (+1.5)
Lib-Dem.	2	13.8 (+1.5)
Plaid Cymru	4	14.3 (+4.3)

Reactions to the 2001 election result have been, perhaps, predictable. Within Plaid Cymru, the result was greeted with some considerable disappointment; there was even criticism of the party's new Leader, Ieuan Wyn Jones, for failing to make a more substantial electoral impact. This criticism, and sense of disappointment, persisted despite the fact that 2001 was, in terms of vote share and even, despite the low turnout, actual votes cast, Plaid Cymru's best-ever Westminster election performance. Party morale for the 2003 NAW election was reported to have been damaged, amidst a perception that the party's 'forward march' had been halted almost before it started (Wyn Jones and Trystan, 2001). Conversely, the 2001 election result prompted considerable jubilation amongst the Labour party in Wales. Numerous claims were made that 'Wales has come home to Labour', and that politics in Wales had returned to 'business as usual'; among many Labour politicians and activists, the 2001 result was apparently seen as indicating that the 1999 NAW election had been an aberration – perhaps that it really was all the fault of Ron Davies or Alun Michael.

These respective interpretations of the 2001 general election result are based on something that is obviously true: Labour did do better in 2001 than 1999, Plaid Cymru did do worse. But the central argument I will develop here is that these interpretations of the 2001 election result, and its relationship with the 1999 election, depend upon some highly dubious assumptions. Principal among these is the apparent belief that Westminster and NAW elections are, in electoral terms, essentially similar contests. Thus, in some quarters, the 2001 Westminster election result was seen as an indicator of the likely outcome in 2003 for the NAW poll. There are few things we can be certain of in political science; but one of them is that these interpretations of the 1999 and 2001 elections results are, to a substantial degree, *wrong*. I will now discuss, with some illustrations, why.

COMPARING WESTMINSTER AND NATIONAL ASSEMBLY ELECTIONS

The electoral shock experienced by the Labour party in Wales in 1999 doubtless did have something to do with events like Ron Davies's resignation, the Michael–Morgan leadership contest, and perhaps also the campaign run by Labour (Mungham, 2001). Labour did not go out of its way to make itself conspicuously attractive to the voters in 1999, and the party clearly had lessons to learn from that. However, it is important to understand that even amidst these problems, 1999 did not see a general rejection of the Labour party, and an adoption of an alternative like Plaid Cymru, by large numbers of Labour supporters.

The figures in Table 5.4 illustrate the point clearly. Taken from the post-election survey conducted in 1999, they show that while large numbers of voters did desert the Labour party in the *specific* context of a NAW election, this did not mean that they had abandoned Labour generally. When they were asked how they would have behaved in a Westminster election held in May 1999, however, voters responded very differently. In the context of a UK election, the majority of the voters of Wales remained loyal to the Labour party: indeed, the survey data suggest that Labour's vote share in 1999 was barely dented from that recorded in 1997. Whatever mistakes Labour had made in the build-up to the 1999 NAW poll, these had not been enough to lose the support, for a Westminster election, of the majority of those who had supported it in previous such contests. These figures for a hypothetical 1999 Westminster election also show that while Plaid Cymru was doing better than it did in 1997, the gains for Plaid in a *Westminster* context were of a much smaller magnitude than those it received for the NAW election.

TABLE 5.4
NAW vote share and hypothetical 1999 Westminster vote share

Party	NAW vote (first vote) %	Hyp. West. vote %
Labour	37.5	53.3
Conservative	14.0	18.4
Lib-Dem.	12.4	11.6
Plaid Cymru	30.8	14.9
Weighted N	678	1004

Source: Welsh National Assembly Election Study.

Indeed, from the standpoint of how things actually turned out in the 2001 general election in Wales, what is notable is that, despite the change in party leadership and changes to campaigning methods instituted by Labour prior to 2001, the Labour party actually did a little *worse* in terms of Westminster vote-share in 2001 than one might have expected in 1999. The larger point, however, is simply this: many voters in Wales in 1999 made different electoral choices depending on whether they were voting for Westminster or Cardiff.

In further analysis of the 1999 NAW election, the research team at Aberystwyth has probed further into the reasons why many people voted differently for the National Assembly than they would have done for Westminster (Trystan *et al.*, 2003). To do this, we separated the majority of the electorate in Wales into three groups:

- those who did not vote Labour in May 1999 and would not have done so for a Westminster election;
- those who supported Labour for Westminster AND remained loyal to Labour for the NAW poll;
- and the *key group*, those who reported supporting Labour in a Westminster context but who switched to Plaid for the NAW election.

The findings of this study suggested that the latter group did not switch for more-or-less random reasons, or simply because they were disillusioned with Labour in 1999. (After all, the party that had come fourth in vote share in the 1997 Westminster election would not have been the most obvious repository for 'protest' votes.) Those switching to Plaid tended to place particular importance on Welsh issues, and to be most likely to see the NAW election as a very different contest from the Westminster one.

These findings about the 1999 election were, inevitably, limited in being based on data from only one election. However, similar information is now available from the survey administered after the 2001 general election. Using data from this survey, we can therefore compare how people actually voted in the Westminster election of that year and how they state they would have voted in a NAW election. This comparison gives us some further insight into whether the 1999 election really was an aberration (see Table 5 5).

TABLE **5.5**
Vote share, actual Westminster and hypothetical NAW election, 2001

Party	Westminster %	Hyp. NAW vote (first vote) %
Labour	51.9	49.4
Conservative	16.7	10.6
Lib-Dem.	15.6	11.9
Plaid Cymru	14.3	26.2
Weighted N	733	667

Source: Welsh Life and Times Study.

Looking at the figures in Table 5.5, two key points are apparent. The first is that, once again, we can see very considerable differences between behaviour across the two types of election. The second point is that, in the aggregate at least, the differences are very much in the same direction as before. That is, we see both the Labour party and the Conservatives doing better in Westminster elections (although the differential for Labour is smaller in

2001 than for 1999, perhaps suggesting that the party has become more effective at winning support for a specifically 'Welsh' electoral contest); Plaid Cymru gets many more votes for NAW polls.

It would be both naive and foolish to attempt to project or predict the result of the 2003 NAW election from the 2001 survey figures. At time of writing we can have no means of knowing what events may happen (or may have already happened) to change the levels of party support seen in the 2001 survey. However, it would seem clear that the prospects for the Labour party (and the Conservatives) for 2003 are somewhat worse than might seem apparent from an immediate examination of the 2001 general election results, while the prospects for Plaid Cymru are rather better. Whether the respective parties take *advantage* of those prospects is, of course, another matter.

CONCLUSIONS

Both immediate and longer-term conclusions can be drawn from this paper. The immediate conclusion is that the 2001 election in Wales was far less about voters 'coming home to Labour' and deserting Plaid Cymru; rather, the result is evidence of the continuation of a pattern of differential party support across different electoral contexts in Wales. The longer-term conclusions we can draw are three in number. First, that substantial number of voters in Wales see elections for Westminster and the National Assembly as being very different contests, and vote differently in response. Second, such voting patterns seem to reflect a public belief in Wales, as occurs in Scotland and elsewhere in Europe, that sub-state level regionalist/nationalist parties are more focused on the concerns of a particular region; and, conversely, that they have much less relevance to state-wide electoral contests. This suggests, finally, that Plaid Cymru is likely to do *systematically* better in NAW elections, and worse in Westminster elections, as long as such voter perceptions persist. For Labour (and also the Conservatives), the opposite is the case. These disparities between different types of elections may be what 'business as usual' comes to mean with regard to future electoral politics in Wales.

NOTES

1. An earlier version of this paper was presented to the conference on 'Business as usual? The 2001 general election in Wales', Aberystwyth, October 2002. The author would like to thank participants at the conference for their helpful comments.

2. In addition to the election results themselves, this paper draws on the findings of the 1999 Welsh National Assembly Election Study and the 2001 Welsh Life and Times Survey, the first major election surveys conducted in Wales since 1979. The surveys were funded by the Economic and Social Research Council of the United Kingdom (ESRC Grant Nos R000 23 8070 and L219252042). Fieldwork for the surveys was undertaken by the National Centre for Social Research, and both were co-directed by Richard Wyn Jones and Anthony Heath.

3. The final opinion poll of the Assembly election campaign, by NOP, was reported on 5 May 1999 to show Labour's support at 47 per cent (expected to secure thirty-four seats in the Assembly) compared with Plaid Cymru at 26 per cent (expected to garner thirteen NAW seats). On polling day, experienced pundit Peter Kellner opined that 'In Wales, Labour should win a clear overall majority' (*Evening Standard*, 6 May 1999, 16; see also the *Guardian*, 5 May 1999, 2, and *Daily Telegraph*, 5 May 1999, 15 for similar confidence in a Labour majority). After the election, the *Daily Mail's* coverage of the results was headlined 'Shock in the Valleys as Welsh Nats surge' (8 May 1999, 8); the *Guardian's* report was headed 'Shocked Labour in Call for Calm', with the main body of the story beginning 'Stunned by the success of Plaid Cymru in denying it an overall majority, Labour in Wales . . .' (8 May 1999, 6).

4. For such contrasting interpretations of the result from within the Welsh Labour party see: Welsh Parliamentary Labour Party (1999); Wales Labour Party (2000); Evans and George (1999); Flynn (2000).

5. Ynys Môn was won from Plaid Cymru by Labour, while Plaid won Carmarthen East and Dinefwr from Labour.

REFERENCES

Evans, C., and George, E. (1999). 'Swings and roundabouts: what really happened on May 6?', *Welsh Labour Action Pamphlet 1*, Cardiff: Welsh Labour Action.

Flynn, P. (2000). *Dragons Led by Poodles*, Bridgend: Seren.

Mungham, G. (2001). 'Labour pains', *Contemporary Wales*, 14, 104–8.

Trystan, D., Scully, R., and Wyn Jones, R. (2003). 'Explaining the quiet earthquake: voting behaviour in the first election to the National Assembly for Wales', *Electoral Studies*.

Wales Labour Party (2000). *Annual Report to Conference.*

Welsh Parliamentary Labour Party (1999). 'Analysis of Labour results in the Welsh Assembly Elections', Report to the WLP Executive Committee.

Wyn Jones, R. (2002). 'New Labour, old heartland', paper presented to conference on 'Business as usual? The 2001 general election in Wales', Aberystwyth.

Wyn Jones, R., and Trystan, D. (2001). 'The 2001 general election in Wales', in Norris, P. (ed.), *Britain Votes, 2001*, Oxford: Oxford University Press.

6. WALES AND WELSHNESS IN MIDDLE CHILDHOOD

Jonathan Scourfield, Andrew Davies and Sally Holland

Fevre and Thompson, in their introduction and conclusion to their collection of theory and research about the nation and identity in Wales (Fevre and Thompson, 1999), summarize very well the different emphases that can be found in sociological writing about Welshness over the last few decades. They observe that a great deal of space has been taken up by commentary on political nationalism and by the asserting of particular positions on the Welsh nation and Welsh culture. Rather than focusing directly on the political realm, this article is concerned with research evidence on the social base of national identities, namely a qualitative study of children's views on national identity. As for asserting any particular version of Wales and Welshness, that is not the primary aim of the article, but we do express some of our own views in concluding it. The research project the article draws on raises a number of important issues that cannot be adequately dealt with here. The purpose of this short journal article is simply to introduced briefly some of our findings and some of the broader issues raised by the project.

In addition to Fevre and Thompson's observations about the limitations of some of the commentary on national identity in Wales, it should be noted that this commentary is overwhelmingly about adults. There is considerable existing research about education and language in Wales in relation to children, but not about children's perspectives on identity, place and nation. This is a gap in current knowledge about Wales and Welshness. Our decision to conduct research on the topic was taken in the context of a growing consensus amongst sociologists that children's perspectives are valid in their own right. This consensus has arisen both out of the recognition of children's rights in the political sphere and from recent developments in the study of childhood, namely the recognition that children should not be understood as partially developed adults, but as social actors and significant authors of their own biographies. Our decision to pursue this study was also taken in recognition that any political vision of the nation has to rely on the co-option of children and their evolving identification with the nation (Stephens, 1997).

It must be acknowledged of course that we are not claiming to be the first to study children's perspectives on national identity. There is emerging work from the disciplines of psychology (Barrett, 2000), geography (Holloway and Valentine, 2000), literature (Meek, 2001) and sociology (Stephens, 1997) that forms the context to our research with children in Wales.

We decided to study the views of children aged between 8 and 11. These ages, between early childhood and adolescence, have been labelled 'middle childhood' (Borland *et al.*, 1998). Although these children are close to becoming young adults capable of taking a full part in social and civic life, it has not traditionally been as commonplace to investigate the opinions of primary-school-age children as has been the case with their older contemporaries. By the later years of primary school children are, however, starting to be considered capable of reflecting upon and evaluating their own life experiences, and are liable to be consulted or interviewed over issues affecting their welfare (Clarke *et al.*, 1996:5). On the other hand, they are not yet subject to the identifications and socialization patterns associated with the cultural categories of youth, teenagerhood and adolescence. Children in middle childhood are also the youngest cohort to be subject to, and potentially conscious of, the current intensified and renewed interest in questions of collective identity in the Welsh public sphere, and as such constitute the first generation to grow up with the consequences of devolution. Researchers have found that even very young children can articulate their views and feelings about a variety of issues if they have an opportunity to do so, and if appropriate methods are used to elicit their views (see, for example, O'Brien *et al.*, 1996).

RESEARCH METHODS

The research was funded by the Social Science Committee of the University of Wales Board of Celtic Studies in 2001–2. We selected six primary schools to take part in the research, chosen to represent a purposive sample of the diversity of life in Wales. These were selected on the basis of information about the socio-economic, ethnic, geographical and linguistic character of their various locations obtained from a variety of sources. The Welsh schools' census provided us some information on the socio-economic make-up of each school (through free school-meal quotas) and the Welsh Index of Multiple Deprivation was also consulted which provides a ward-by-ward breakdown of social and economic deprivation in Wales. Linguistic indicators were obtained from two principal sources; firstly (and more crudely) the schools' census which gives a breakdown of the percentage of pupils taught through the medium of Welsh; secondly, the 1991 census results were consulted, which provide more detailed information about the linguistic character of communities in Wales on a ward-by-ward basis.

We chose three English-medium schools and three Welsh-medium schools: a sample which over-represents the Welsh-medium sector (20.3 per cent of primary school pupils in Wales have at least part of their curriculum delivered through the medium of Welsh (National Assembly for Wales, 2001). This decision was based in part on the centrality of the language to debates about Welshness past and present. For children from monoglot English homes in particular, schooling in the Welsh medium throws up interesting identity choices. The table below briefly describes the research sites. This sample was of course not intended to be wholly representative of

---

The research sites*

1. HIGHFIELDS SCHOOL – an English-medium inner-city Cardiff school with a multi-ethnic intake. The free school-meals quota was close to the Welsh average.

2. PETERSFIELD SCHOOL – English medium, and serving a socially deprived council estate in the eastern valleys of south Wales. More than half of the children in this school receive free school meals.

3. LLWYNIRFON SCHOOL – English medium, in a bilingual area of Powys where between 20 and 35 per cent of the population are able to speak Welsh (1991 census). This school has a very low proportion of children who receive free school meals.

4. YSGOL Y WAUN – Welsh medium and not deprived (in terms of children receiving free school meals) in a largely anglophone area of north-east Wales.

5. YSGOL Y PORTH – Welsh medium, in an area of rural Gwynedd where over 80 per cent of the local population speak Welsh. This school has a low proportion of children receiving free school meals.

6. YSGOL MAESGARW – in a deprived area of the western valleys of south Wales, where large numbers and a significant proportion of the population are able to speak Welsh. The proportion of children on free school meals was well above the Welsh average.

*The names of schools and individual children have been replaced by pseudonyms.

life in Wales: rather it was settled upon in order to take account of regional differences within Wales whilst simultaneously offering us the opportunity to explore diverse, marginalized and contested identities. The sample is also significant in terms of voting results during the 1997 devolution referendum; three being in areas where the majority of the population voted 'yes' and three in areas which voted 'no'.

We spoke to a total of 105 children over three months, conducting a total of eighteen focus groups and fifty-four in-depth interviews. The children were drawn from the 8–11 age bracket, from a range of social classes, ability ranges, ethnicities, nationalities and linguistic identities. Six children from each of year groups 4, 5 and 6 in each school were asked to take part in a focus group, where issues such as nationality, locality, civil identity, language, media, race and cultural difference were discussed.

Our strategy was to combine traditional qualitative interviewing techniques (which Harden *et al.*, 2000, argue should not be dismissed for use with children) with engaging exercises and visual prompts such as are commonly used in research with younger children (see Hill, 1997). We used a card-sorting secret ballot, a video clip, a map of Europe and a sentence-completion exercise. We asked some overt questions about Wales, such as about the Welsh language and media representations of Wales, and some which were less overtly asking about Wales but instead generally enquiring about how the children characterized the place where they lived and what was important to them about it. So, for example, we asked them what a child moving to their school from London would need to know, and we asked them what they would miss about their current life if they had to move to Australia.

We cannot of course on the basis of a small purposive sample quantify children's identities in the way that surveys of national identities attempt to do. We can say something about how the 'work' of identity gets done in social interaction (although this is also limited because participant observation was only a very small part of our strategy) and how children negotiate their ways around the available discourses of the nation.

UNITY AND DIVISION

Unsurprisingly there is unity and division, or commonality and difference, to be found in the children's talk about affiliation to place. To consider first the things that unite, these were the significance of the Welsh language, the importance of accent and sporting affiliations, and the choice of 'Welsh' as the most popular identity label.

There is a general tendency for the children to refer to the Welsh language as a marker of Welshness. Children in Welsh-medium schools, regardless of whether or not they came from Welsh-speaking families, ever used the language outside the classroom, or chose to be interviewed in English, consistently mentioned the importance of their ability to speak Welsh to their self-identification as Welsh. They also spoke of the language as an important marker of difference from other countries, including those within the UK. When we asked if there was any difference between those who attend Welsh-medium and English-medium schools, children from all schools tended to say, however, that there was not any difference beyond language skills, and that children in both types of schools are 'just the same'.

The importance of accent was mentioned across all the schools, and its significance is therefore a point of commonality. What the children share, however, is their perception of accent as a marker of *difference*. This means difference from English people and, as often or more so, difference from other Welsh people. This perception of difference included Andrew, the researcher (brought up in Llanelli), who was thought by children in Ysgol y Waun (north-east Wales) to 'speak funny' and also thought to be more 'Welshy' than the children in Petersfield (eastern Valleys), as shown in the excerpt below. What is interesting is that these children (with Valleys' accents) saw their own voices as within a British mainstream, as represented by *Hollyoaks*, a popular youth soap-opera set in Chester.

Claire:	When I went to Ogmore (. . .) um there (.) all these people was going on the rugby trip and there were two people going from our school and all the other boys that went were like, had the Welsh accent.
Andrew (researcher):	Oh yeah.
Claire:	Different accent.
Andrew:	What different accent?
Aimee:	Well you have got a different accent to us.
Andrew:	Have I? What's my accent then?
Aimee:	Welshy.
Andrew:	Is your accent Welshy?
(General):	No.
Aimee:	It's like on the Holly Oaks.
Andrew:	Holly Oaks. Do you think you've got English accents then?
Child (identity unclear):	No.

(From year 5 focus group in Petersfield)

It might have been expected that accent would be more important for children from English-medium schools, united as they are with English children by language but potentially marked as different by accent. This was the case for some children. It is possible that the perception in the above excerpt is explained by the Petersfield children's relative lack of first-hand exposure to other accents. It is interesting nonetheless that they see themselves as having mainstream British accents, which does perhaps have the effect of making them feel less Welsh, at least in this respect, than Andrew the researcher. Accent can be a powerful marker of social class, of course. The Petersfield children do not feel themselves to be marked as working-class Valleys children by their accent. The children we interviewed in all six schools generally seemed to be unaware of class differences.

Sport unites the children. References to rugby representing Welshness were ubiquitous, even in north Wales, where the social base of the sport is arguably not as strong as in parts of the south. The typical response from both boys and girls when asked about supporting sports teams was that they supported the Welsh national rugby team and an English premier-league football team – usually Manchester United, and when asked they felt comfortable with this combination. We return to sport in the next section of the article. Whilst it is not possible for us to quantify our findings and generalize to a wider population, it is worth noting that 'Welsh' was in fact the most often-cited identity label by the children when we offered them a variety of labels in a 'secret ballot' card-sorting exercise. This does also obscure considerable difference in the meaning of the label of course, and it is to diversity that we now turn.

There are several prominent fault-lines running through the children's perspectives on their identifications with place. All of these were in fact entirely predictable, and we took them into account in designing our research. They are the fault lines of rural–urban environments, social class, ethnicity, Welshness–Englishness, region and language.

There is a noticeable difference in the ways that children talked about their attachment to place according to a combination of environment and social class. Children in Petersfield School (eastern Valleys) and Highfields School (Cardiff), in particular, consistently referred to crime when discussing their affiliations to their local areas. In the case of Petersfield in particular, a school on the edge of a profoundly deprived council estate, concern about crime had a serious impact on their identification with the place. They spoke of liking the place and having family there, and in fact were more localized than children in other schools in their points of reference, perhaps because of social class and lack of mobility, but there was an important proviso that they wished it was a 'nicer place'. Jason thought that the 'nasty people' in the local area would put people off Wales as a whole:

Andrew: What else would you take to show them about the area where you live and what people are like?

Jason: I would take a photo of the nasty people, and I would tell them not to go down Wales.

(Interview with Jason, Petersfield School)

In contrast, the children in Ysgol Y Porth (Gwynedd) spoke of the safety of the area in which they lived, especially, for some children, in contrast to the area of England they had moved from. When asked about London, children in the more rural areas often contrasted positively their home area with London in terms of crime, safety and quality of life. Imagery of Wales varied according to the local environment. So for Siôn, from Highfields School in Cardiff, 'Wales is tightly packed', whereas for Jenny from Llwynirfon in Powys, Wales has 'loads and loads of hills and landscapes and things like that'.

A further aspect of locality was that the point of reference of most children was very local. They tended to refer to their own area within a town, rather than the town itself, or to their own housing estate or village rather than the wider locality. As might be expected, the children offer a child's-eye view of their locality, highlighting facilities and features of an area that might not be prioritized by adults describing the same area.

Andrew: Why do you think I'd settle there?

Joseph: You can go down the field and get lots of friends up there and there's some shops – Lidl is up there.

Andrew: Is there a lot for children to do around here?

Joseph: Go down the field and play football on the farm and a garage quite close to the two of the shops . . . so kids go there to buy sweets and stuff.

(Interview with Joseph, Llwynirfon School)

Melissa: I would show them [visitors] like we used to have a park behind my house but they knocked it down. But we might be having a new one. And I would show them like, the big field we have got, we have got one, one side and then the other side and then I would show them how naughty the kids were . . .

> *David*:   Like show them how quiet it is and all the litter because they tend
> to put it around the back.
> (From year 6 focus group in Petersfield school)

Children's identities were often intertwined with their views of their
localities, and these were dominated by local play-areas, shops and the
presence of 'nasty' people, or bullies, and 'nice' people. There were examples
from all schools of children complaining about criminals or bullies in their
local area, and also of people in their locality being generally nice and
friendly. Perhaps predictably, issues of noise, crime and danger from
drunken adults were more of an urban preoccupation.

Another fault-line is ethnicity. In only one of the schools we selected did
we speak to any children from visible ethnic minorities – Highfields in
Cardiff – and this reflected the ethnicity of the school intakes. The perspectives of the minority ethnic children on identity were very interesting,
and have important implications for attempts in political and cultural life to
construct an inclusive notion of Welshness. The number of minority ethnic
children was small (ten) so caution is of course needed in drawing
conclusions, but it was nonetheless revealing that not one of these children
used the term 'Welsh' as an umbrella identity. One child, Wasim, mentioned
the term Welsh but as an alternative to other identities, such as Pakistani
and Italian. The avoidance of Welsh as an umbrella term might reflect ideas
about alternative nationalities – that you cannot be both Pakistani and
Welsh for example. But some were content to describe themselves as British
(for example 'British Muslim') and refer to 'their country' as Britain. It
might be that the assumption that Welshness can be equated with whiteness
(see Williams, 1995) is alive and well. Bahira, in the excerpt below, indicates
this, with her views of Welsh schools and the Welsh language:

> Because they [children in Welsh school] might be racists or something, I don't
> know and I don't like Welsh. I hate Welsh [. . .] Yeah, because there is
> probably not one person who is Muslim there because not many Muslims are
> fluent in Welsh, like.
> (Interview with Bahira from Highfields School)

There were, however, examples in every school of white children telling us
that of course black people are included in Welshness. The scope of their
stated conception of Welshness is inclusive. There is an interesting exchange
in one of the Highfields focus groups where Nim (Cardiff-born, Chinese

ethnic background) and Edward (Cardiff-born to Scottish mother and Australian father) are in the process of considering inclusive Welshness and negotiating the criteria:

Andrew:	No, right great. What about being Welsh, is that important to anyone?
Nim:	Yes it is.
(Identity unclear):	No.
Edward:	I am not particularly Welsh.
Siôn:	It is important. [to Edward] Where were you born?
Edward:	Cardiff (.) I don't have any Welsh blood.
Siôn:	Yeah you are cos you were born here.
Nim:	Some people say I'm Welsh, some people I'm from Cardiff.
Andrew:	What do you say you are?
Nim:	I say I'm from Cardiff but at the same time I like to think I'm Welsh.

(From year 6 focus group in Highfields School)

Nim seems to be aware of both inclusive and exclusive notions of Welshness. She shows that she can in theory be considered Welsh and is interested in applying this label to herself. Her tentative 'some people say' and 'I like to think' make it clear she knows that this inclusive version of Welshness would also be contested by some.

Of their views on nations, the clearest fault-lines were between Wales and England. It is not the case that the children were generally hostile to England and Englishness. In fact, we interviewed several children of full or partial English origin who were proud of their Englishness. Rather, it was clear that the children were very aware of the border with England and generally had a clearer sense of England than of Britain. Britain was in fact said by some children to be unimportant. Whilst we noted above that the children tended not to comment on social class, the excerpts below show that for the children part of a discourse of distinction between Wales and England is to construct English people (from London in the second excerpt) as both better-off and arrogant.

Siôn:	I just hate England. They just think that they're (.) posh heads or something. They just think (.) they think they're the best, they're the biggest country in the world.
Andrew :	Did you say that your dad was from England?
Siôn:	Yeah.

Andrew: How do you think he would feel about that?
Siôn: He wouldn't mind too much actually. I don't think he
would. He has come to be more Welsh than he is English.
                              (Interview with Siôn in Highfields School)

Eleri: Mae o'n dipyn bach yn wahanol oherwydd (. . .) mae Llundain
              yn dipyn bach mwy posh.
              It's a little bit different because (. . .) London's a little bit more
              posh.
                              (interview with Eleri in Ysgol Y Waun)

For Siôn this is personal; more personal perhaps than most of the children's talk about identities. He is distancing himself from the nationality of his parents. He is clearly backed up in this by his father and in fact may be taking a lead from his father. His language is strong; he hates England. This personal dimension to national identity brings us round to the next section of the article. This next section aims to introduce, with reference to our data, some ideas about the relationship between received ideas about the nation and the response of the individual to these; the relationship between discourse and the subject.

RECEIVED IDEAS AND THE ACTIVE CONSTRUCTION OF IDENTITY

An obvious theoretical consideration that is raised by our research, in fact perhaps the most obvious one, is whether the children are reflexive about national identities or accepting of dominant discourses. Firstly, it is worth noting that we must use plurals here. There is of course not one discourse of Welshness but many. As Dai Smith (1999: 36) puts it: 'Wales is a singular noun but a plural experience.' Andy Thompson observes that in much of the literature on nationalism and national identity 'there is too much reliance on presuppositions about the causal efficacy of a 'common culture' to explain how individuals behave towards each other and how they position themselves in relation to others' (Thompson, 2000: 27). He goes on to assert the importance of considering human agency if we are to understand how national identity works in everyday life. He considers people's active use of categories of nationality to be worthy of study:

Individuals may not be conscious of how they are actively involved in giving life to national identities when they categorise, but they do use these categories to explain, position and make sense. They do not therefore view these categories as their own personal inventions, rather they view them as information that is available for them to use in order to make sense of the actions of others.

(Thompson, 2000: 28)

His insistence on agency in the doing of national identity relates to debates about children as social agents. It has become a given in recent writings about the sociology of childhood that children's agency is denied by traditional social-science approaches, which understand children to be passively socialized into the ways of adulthood. Recent research (see, for example, Prout, 2002) tends to emphasize children's agency.

There are two main points we wish to make here; firstly, that the resources on which children can draw in discussing national identities are few, and, secondly, that we did find some children actively negotiating their identities from the limited resources available.

There are several different aspects of the everyday reproduction of national identities, and we deal with just two of these here. First, there is the daily flagging of the nation that Billig (1995) describes. In the lives of the children we spoke to, this social process is in fact fairly overt, as they sit in classrooms on a daily basis that have wall displays of Wales, Britain, Europe and the world. In all the schools Wales was highlighted in such displays. There were significant differences in emphasis. In the Welsh-medium schools, perhaps unsurprisingly, there was a particular version of Welsh culture, involving the kinds of musical, literary and oral traditions that are displayed in eisteddfodau. In the one genuinely ethnically mixed school you are immediately struck by the word 'welcome' written in at least a dozen languages over the front door, and wall displays reflect the cultural and ethnic diversity of the school.

Another aspect of the everyday reproduction of national identities is the judgements about the nationality of others that we make, mostly unconsciously, on a daily basis; judgements about national *habitus*. Bourdieu's (1986) concept of *habitus* refers to socially-acquired dispositions that are manifested in outlooks, opinions and embodied phenomena, such as deportment, posture, ways of walking, sitting, and so on. This is a process that it is difficult to study without extended participant observation, of course. However, the children we spoke to revealed something of these judgements in their negotiation of identities in focus groups and in their commenting on an imaginary journey taken with the aid of a map through Britain and

Europe. Their comments about both relatively local and foreign others seemed to be generally frank and free from the constraint of politeness or political correctness.

Our research design, dominated as it was by semi-structured talk, was geared in the main towards the children's stated opinions about their identities. These drew on the resources available to them. The two processes described above, banal nationalism and the identification of national *habitus*, are of course, relatively opaque to the children, as they are to most adults, because these processes work by being taken for granted. The children seemed to have a limited repertoire of ideas about Wales and Welshness to draw on. This raises the question of whether children have fewer resources to draw on than adults. We might expect that indeed they would, having had less time and opportunity to be exposed to the resources adults would use as points of reference in discussing nationality. We might also expect children to have fewer resources to draw on than adults because of their stage of cognitive development. It is also true of course that many adults find their resources are limited in discussing national identity. Brian Roberts (1995) found in his research in the eastern Valleys that people tended to use clichés such as chapel, singing and rugby to describe what being Welsh meant to them. Our children also used these images, as well as reference to the Welsh language and, perhaps above all, sport. For many adults, though, there would be little else they could draw on. They may have an opinion on the Assembly, they may be aware of some of the more controversial debates about nationhood that are aired in the Welsh media, but many would not be. For the children we spoke to, cognitive development was an issue, and there was considerable variety in this development that could not simply be categorized by age. For adults too, however, the extent of the ideas they can draw on to describe their national identity and the extent to which they are reflexive about these ideas will depend on, amongst other things, their cognitive skills. These are of course connected with education, which is in turn connected with class. So we need to ask the further question: how reflexive are most adults about their national identities?

The received ideas the children encounter are the school curriculum and school ethos of the nation, the primacy of the Welsh language, the nation as represented in sport and, to a much lesser extent, political rhetoric. As with adults, discourses of nationhood vary according to region. So debates about nationality are more vivid in Gwynedd, for example, than in the eastern Valleys. The children in Ysgol Y Porth (Gwynedd) seemed to reflect the

'Cymuned' debate about language and citizenship that has been centred on localities such as theirs. One child, when asked what he most disliked about Wales wrote 'mae gormod o bobl yn siarad Saesneg' (*too many people speak English*). A few children in this school described the town in which they live as 'Welsh-speaking'. On entering the town, one could not avoid the Cymuned poster stating 'Ardal Gymraeg yw hon' (*this is a Welsh-speaking area*).

Despite the limited resources the children have to draw on, a minority of the children we spoke to can be seen to be active in constructing their national identities, within discursive limits. This is not to say that the majority of the children are merely passive, but simply that given the limits of our research design, agency was observable in the talk of a minority of children. These children made selective and creative use of the resources available to them. One example was of the construction of identity in relation to the school curriculum. In Petersfield school (eastern valleys), the children had been learning about the Second World War shortly before Andrew arrived in the school as a researcher. The war then featured in the children's talk about place and identity in a number of ways. In the secret ballot card-sorting exercise we used a 'you choose' card for children to add anything important to them other than a connection with a place or culture. One of the children wrote on this card 'World War Two':

> *Andrew:* You chose that one. Yeah, why did you, you wrote something else did you, yeah? Do you want to tell?
> *Louise:* I wrote Irish on, because my bampa was Irish.
> *Andrew:* Right okay, so that's important to you.
> *Melissa:* I wrote World War Two on it because my mother's father was in World War Two.
> (From year 6 focus group in Petersfield School)

Melissa is selectively using this particular discourse of the *British* nation since she can see a connection to her own family history – a connection that, no doubt, her teacher has encouraged her to make. The recent influence on this choice of identity illustrates the very contingent nature of identity and the dependence of identity on performance in specific contexts of interaction (Goffman, 1959). The same child would not necessarily have made the same choice a year or even a month later. We expand on this issue of the contingent nature of identity in a separate paper (Scourfield and Davies, 2002).

Rowland, in Maesgarw School, also draws on twentieth-century history to argue his point about self-determination. Throughout the focus group he made Welsh nationalist arguments, about, for example, the need for the Assembly to have more power than it currently has. Then in the context of a discussion about who should decide on a new road through the local area, he argues that local people, including children, should take the decision, by overtly drawing on nationalist history and imagery in referencing Tryweryn:

Rowland: If someone wanted to turn Maes Garw into a reservoir like (.)
Dafydd: Whoa!–
Rowland: – And build a dam –
Dafydd: No way! –
Rowland: If we went up to a Member of Parliament and said like 'we don't want the village to turn into a, like, water, cause we can't bring your kids back and say this was going to be yours, but now they've topped it up and 'sorry son it's all gone'.

(from year 6 focus group in Ysgol Maesgarw)

It may be of course that Rowland is repeating parental arguments here. He may have heard one or more of his family members talking about Wales in these terms. Nonetheless, he is active in making creative and selective use of the knowledge he has to display his political and national identity to his peers.

A final example of agency is to do with sport. The children repeatedly talked about supporting the Welsh rugby team and English premier-league football teams. We made a point of asking them what they thought about this, and varying degrees of reflexivity can be found in their responses. It seemed almost to take more of an active decision to support a local football team than to support Manchester United, which was by far the most popular option. To support a local team was to reject the powerful force of the dominant peer-group culture. Some children did seem to have thought through the possible conflict. One girl in Petersfield, Emma, had clearly done so, and was proud of her decision to maintain support for both Welsh nation and English football club.

Yes it is OK because I have got (.) most of my bedroom is stars and moons but then I have got a massive poster of Manchester United. And I've got a postcard and the [Welsh] national anthem . . .   Most people support Man United in Wales, I can tell you now that there is more than fifty people in this school that support Manchester United.

(Interview with Emma from Petersfield School)

As we have explained, then, for most of the children, their talk about Welsh national identity was limited in its points of reference. For the minority ethnic children and for any children with parents of mixed nationalities, the more general topic of identification with places and cultures was much more open (Scourfield and Davies, 2002), but for these children too, the topic of Welshness had its limits. Agency could be seen in some children's talk about Wales, and the active negotiation of identities was certainly going on in the focus groups. In terms of agency, there is much more to say from our data across a range of different aspects of identity, place and culture. One major issue is how children manage the relationship between individual and collective identities; what Richard Jenkins (1996) calls the 'internal–external dialectic of identification'. This topic will be explored in a future paper. This article is simply intended, however, to introduce our research on children in Wales, so we cannot take the discussion further at this point.

TO CONCLUDE

In this article we have reported on a project which explored children's local and national identities in a purposive sample from within Wales. We have attempted to give an overview of the main themes emerging from the research, some of which will be expanded on in future papers. We have described some of the main points of commonality and difference in the children's descriptions of their own and others' identities. Children from a range of linguistic, social and regional backgrounds highlighted the import- ance of language, regional accent and sport as aspects of identity, and the main label chosen by the majority of children to describe themselves was 'Welsh'. Aspects that highlighted issues of difference included ethnicity, the local environment and distinctions between England and Wales. We have also noted that the children's freedom to actively construct their own visions of national identity was limited, at least within the context of research interviews. Like adults, children have a limited repertoire of received ideas about nationality and identity.

We hope that our findings may be viewed as both interesting and rather encouraging in some respects. Most children displayed an inclusive notion of what it is to be Welsh, for example by correcting their peers within focus groups who had stated that they themselves were not really Welsh due to the nationality of their parents. There was also minimal hostility spoken of between children who attend English-medium and Welsh-medium schools. These were simply seen as children like them, often friends and neighbours, who happed to attend a different type of school. This is not meant to imply that the Welsh language was not important to Welsh-speaking children. For these children, the language was almost universally spoken of as an important aspect of Welsh identity, even for those who chose to converse with the researcher in English. Some children could be seen to be absorbing and interpreting debates about the language and community change prevalent in the Welsh media and political arena.

There are some aspects of our findings that may be of interest to policymakers and educators. These centre around an inclusive Welshness, encouraging children's agency in constructing their own creative visions of Wales, and incorporating a child's-eye vision within our adult understandings of our communities.

Although, as is stated above, most children displayed an inclusive notion of Welshness, we note that within our small sample of minority ethnic children, none labelled him- or herself as Welsh. Whilst we would not wish to impose a compulsory Welsh identity on all children who move to Wales from elsewhere, or whose parents are not Welsh, we believe that it is important that this identification remains an *option* for all living in Wales. A more vigorous promotion of diverse Welsh identities in the media and educational materials might be one step forward. Welsh-medium schools and Mudiad Ysgolion Meithrin might wish to ensure that their facilities are promoted amongst minority ethnic communities. Promoting an inclusive notion that incorporates many ways of being Welsh is important not only for visibly minority ethnic children, but also for children whose families have migrated from other parts of the UK and for monoglot English-speaking children in Wales.

We do not wish to suggest that children should be simply expected passively to incorporate an adult-driven expanded vision of Welshness. Instead, we suggest that we encourage children's agency in constructing their own creative visions of Wales and what it means to be Welsh citizens. Drawing on the evidence from this particular sample it is likely that there will continue to be elements of children's identities that will be widespread across Wales, as well as many variations. Aspects such as family and friendship networks, the local environment and, for Welsh speakers, language, were aspects of identity placed to the fore by the children in this study.

Our final point relates to local markers of identity. Whilst many children spoke of large public Welsh landmarks, particularly the Millennium Stadium, when exploring the relationship between identity and place, they were also likely to identify with small local markers, some of which would be almost invisible to adult eyes, such as informal play areas. We were struck by the children's descriptions of their local environments in the midst of conversations about their identities. The children were particularly affected by issues such as crime, play space and family networks. Policy-makers and politicians may well be advised to incorporate local children's viewpoints when considering community developments. Children's particular and specialist knowledge can be insightful and of much use.

Acknowledgements

The research reported in the paper was dependent on the funding of the University of Wales Board of Celtic Studies' Social Science Committee. Other members of the research team were Bella Dicks and Mark Drakeford. Maire Messenger-Davies and Catherine Maclean gave valuable help on research design.

REFERENCES

Barrett, M. (2000). 'The development of national identity in childhood and adolescence', inaugural lecture, 22 March, University of Surrey, Guildford.

Billig, M. (1995). *Banal Nationalism*, London: Sage.

Borland, M., Laybourn, A., Hill, M. and Brown, J. (1998). *Middle Childhood: The Perspectives of Children and Parents*, London: Jessica Kingsley.

Bourdieu, P. (1986). *Distinction*, London: Routledge.

Clarke, K., Craig, G., and Glendinning, C. (1996). *Children's Views on Child Support*, London: The Children's Society.

Fevre, R., and Thompson, A. (eds.) (1999). *Nation, Identity and Social Theory: Perspectives from Wales*, Cardiff: University of Wales Press.

Goffman, E. (1959/1990). *The Presentation of Self in Everyday Life*, London: Penguin.

Harden, J., Scott, S., Backett-Milburn, K., and Jackson, S. (2000). 'Can't talk, won't talk?: methodological issues in researching children', *Sociological Research Online*, 5, 2: *http://www.socresonline.org.uk/5/2/harden.html*

Hill, M. (1997). 'Research review: participatory research with children', *Child and Family Social Work*, 2, 171–83.

Holloway, S. and Valentine, G. (2000). 'Corked hats and Coronation Street: British and New Zealand children's imaginative geographies of the other', *Childhood*, 7, 3, 335–57.

Jenkins, R. (1996). *Social Identity*, London: Routledge.

Meek, M. (ed.) (2001). *Children's Literature and National Identity*, London: Trentham Books.

National Assembly for Wales (2001). *Welsh in School*, Cardiff: National Assembly for Wales.

O'Brien, M., Alldred, P., and Jones, D. (1996). 'Children's construction of family and kinship', in Brannen, J., and O'Brien, M. (eds), *Children in Families: Research and Policy*, London: The Falmer Press.

Prout, A. (ed.) (2002). *Children and Society*, special issue on the ESRC Children 5–16 programme, 16, 2.

Roberts, B. (1995). 'Welsh identity in a former mining valley: social images and imagined communities', *Contemporary Wales*, 7, 77–95.

Scourfield, J. and Davies, A. (2002). 'Children's negotiation of national identities', paper presented at the British Sociological Association's Annual Conference in Leicester.

Smith, D. (1999). *Wales: A Question for History*, Bridgend: Seren.

Stephens, S. (1997). Editorial introduction: 'Children and nationalism', *Childhood*, 4, 1, 5–17.

Thompson, A. (2000). 'Nations, national identities and human agency: putting people back in to nations', *Sociological Review*, 49, 1, 18–32.

Williams, C. (1995). 'Race and racism: some reflections on the Welsh context', *Contemporary Wales*, 8, 113–31.

7. CIVIL SOCIETY AND OBJECTIVE 1

Elin Royles

INTRODUCTION

In March 1999, West Wales and the Valleys was given Objective 1 designation for the 2000–6 Structural Funds programming period. Within three months, the Economic Development Committee of the National Assembly met for the first time on 16 June and discussed Objective 1. Since that first meeting, Objective 1 has been an issue of the greatest importance for the new Assembly. Internally, disputes over the implementation of the programme have led to some of the more dramatic moments in the institution's otherwise rather prosaic existence – most notably as the issue which led to the replacement of Alun Michael as First Secretary of the National Assembly. Beyond Cardiff Bay, it may be confidently asserted that the ability of devolved government to deliver on the (often unrealistic) expectations surrounding Objective 1 is of immense symbolic importance in determining public perceptions of the fledgling body. This article seeks to use the Objective 1 programme as a prism through which to view one particular aspect of the devolution experience in Wales, namely the role of civil society organizations in the 'new Welsh politics'.

In political rhetoric at least, establishing the National Assembly for Wales was heralded as more than an important institutional innovation. It was hailed as ushering in a new participative political culture to Wales, characterized by partnership, inclusiveness and openness. More than any other sector perhaps, it was civil society organizations that were to be the main beneficiaries and motors of this new dawn. Given the immense practical and symbolic importance of the Objective 1 programme for West Wales and the Valleys, the extent of civil society involvement in the programme provides a good test of the degree to which the rhetoric is reflected in reality. This article will therefore examine the extent of the involvement of civil society actors in the different stages of the Objective 1 process between 1998 and 2002. Crucially, an attempt will be made to identify and estimate the relative weight of those factors – including devolution – influencing the extent of civil society involvement in the programme.

The article proceeds in five sections. The first section outlines the context of this study of the role of civil society organizations in the Objective programme. Following from this, the article concentrates in turn on different stages of the Objective 1 policy-making. Section two focuses on the drafting of the Objective 1 document, section three on decision making, and section four on the implementation of the programme. The discussion in all of these sections is based on an analysis of primary and secondary sources, as well as evidence from a series of qualitative semi-structured interviews conducted in order to ascertain the views of a broad cross-section of those involved in the policy process. In the fifth and concluding section, an assessment is made of the relative weight of those factors that influence civil society engagement, in particular, the experience of civil society involvement in previous Structural Funding programmes in Wales in the 1994–9 programming period, the impact of European Commission regulations 2000–6, and devolution.

To what extent has devolution lived up to the rhetoric? To what extent has devolution actually furthered civil society involvement in the governance of Welsh society? Has policy-making become more inclusive since devolution? These are some of the questions on which this attempt to use Objective 1 policy-making as an index of democratic development in post-devolution Wales seeks to shed light.

1. CIVIL SOCIETY: DEFINITIONS AND CONTEXT

For over a decade, the concept of civil society has been extensively used on a global scale both in political rhetoric and across academic disciplines. However, it continues to be problematic due to its ambiguity and competing perceptions of civil society. While this article aims to contribute to empirical understandings of the role of civil society in post-devolution Wales and, as such, contemporary debates surrounding the theory of civil society lie beyond its purview, a number of issues of more general import emerged from the research, of which some brief mention might be made. Firstly, the interviews conducted for this study highlighted the ambiguities and contra-dictions surrounding the meaning of 'civil society'. While the term is widely used, there is little of consensus or consistency about its usage. Secondly, and relatedly, much of the confusion stems from the 'fuzziness' of boundaries in modern liberal, capitalist democracies: put simply, civil society, state and economy all overlap and interact. One impact of this is that categorizing different actors is difficult – to what extent, for example, should the Third Sector, co-operatives and trade unions, be viewed as forming part of 'civil society'? In this context it should be noted that Commission regulations and documentation for Structural Fund programmes in Wales do not refer directly to civil society per se. These documents do however refer to voluntary and community sector organizations, both of which are almost universally considered important parts of civil society. In part in order to sidestep disputes over the exact boundaries of civil society, this article concentrates on the interrelationship between these faces of civil society – that is, voluntary and community sector organizations – and the Objective 1 programme.

Civil society and devolution
In the immediate post-referendum period 'civil society' became a buzzword of the New Welsh Politics and part of political rhetoric. Civil society was viewed as integral to changing political culture in post-devolution Wales by promoting active citizenship, contributing to a new participatory democracy and achieving a new inclusive society (Hain, 1999: 14–5; Davies 1999: 7). Consequently, civil society was central to addressing devolution's greatest challenge namely, 'to develop a new political culture which replaces dogma with a new constructive approach, one that places a value on consultation and partnership' (Davies, 1999: 15). Ironically, pre-devolution, civil society in Wales was characterized as underdeveloped and weak, but it was anticipated that constitutional change could lead to its revitalization (Wyn Jones and Paterson, 1999).

The structures of the National Assembly for Wales (NAW) suggest a concerted attempt to open up policy-making and present channels for civil society input, particularly in relation to Objective 1. The European Structural Fund reforms in 1989 made partnership in Structural Fund policy-making a key requirement, but the Welsh Office was accused of being too bureaucratic and seeking to control relationships between local government and the Commission. Morgan states, 'indeed it was at this time that the local authority partners acidly described the Welsh Office style as "Raj style of management" on account of its hierarchical and imperious attitude towards others' (Morgan, 2002: 1). This resulted in the shifting of the main administration of

Structural Funds in Wales from the European Affairs Division (EAD) of the Welsh Office to an independent secretariat, the Wales European Programme Executive (WEPE) in 1997. Following devolution, aspects of WEPE and EAD were combined in the Welsh European Funding Office (WEFO), an executive body of the Assembly established in 2000.

The 1998 Government of Wales Act established a new constitutional settlement with the National Assembly inheriting those powers previously exercised by the Welsh Office and the Secretary of State for Wales. One of the implications of this development was, of course, that rather than a small group of Welsh Office ministers there were now sixty Assembly Members (AMs) who could be held to account. In theory at least, this provides greatly increased opportunities for civil society to seek influence through lobbying and briefing Assembly Members. Furthermore, the committee structure of the Assembly with its subject committees, cross-cutting and regional committees, also facilitates civil society involvement. (Chaney *et al.*, 2001)

The main official channel for civil society engagement in the Assembly's work is the Voluntary Sector Partnership Council, but as the partnership's first meeting was not until October 2000, it did not have an opportunity to contribute to Objective 1 policy-making. A more powerful channel in relation to Objective 1 is civil society's direct contacts with the Civil Service by participating in consultations, task forces and as advisers and this is considered in section two. Furthermore, the commitment to open government resulted in the National Assembly's website which provides civil society organizations with information on its work. With regard to Structural Funds, the WEFO website is a communication and information tool promoting accessibility to European programmes.

2. DRAFTING THE PROGRAMME – EXPERTISE AND CAPACITY

The Task Force
Following Labour's victory in the 1997 general election, concerted political efforts under the leadership of Ron Davies to gain Objective 1 designation for West Wales and the Valleys for 2000–6 commenced. Lobbying to secure Objective 1 was previously undertaken mainly by local government and Welsh Office officials.[1] However, the academic case for Objective One made by Kevin Morgan and Adam Price in the Institute of Welsh Affairs publication *The Other Wales: The Case for Objective One Funding Post 1999* (1998), played an important role. It generated public debate about Objective 1, and thus reinforced the political case.

Prior to the designation of West Wales and the Valleys as Objective 1 in March 1999, the then Secretary of State, Ron Davies, set up the European Task Force in October 1998. It was to advise the Secretary of State on the new Structural Funds Regulations and to develop strategies and programmes to implement the funds in Wales post-2000.[2] The Task Force comprised a range of actors and civil society organizations including the Wales Council for Voluntary Action (WCVA) and Disability Wales. Its membership partly reflected efforts to encourage better relations between government and spheres such as voluntary organizations and trade unions.

TABLE 7.1
European Task Force membership

	October 1998	May 1999
Politicians	1 – MEP	2 – AM/MP, MEP
Government actors	5	8
Government agencies	6	13
Regional agencies	1[1]	4[3]
Local authorities	2	5
Private and third sector	5 – Federation of Small Businesses (FSB), Confederation of British Industry (CBI), National Farmers Union in Wales (NFU), Farmers Union of Wales (FUW), Wales Trades Union Congress (WTUC)	5 – FSB, CBI, NFU in Wales, FUW, WTUC
Higher education	2	2
Voluntary sector	1 – WCVA	2 – WCVA, Disability Wales
Other	1[2]	1[2]
Total	24	42

Notes: [1] This is the North Wales Economic Forum on behalf of all regional fora.
[2] Hywel Ceri Jones was European adviser to Ron Davies, the Secretary of State for Wales.
[3] These are the four Regional Economic Fora.
Source: North Wales Economic Forum – minutes European Task Force meeting 16 October 1998 and minutes of European Task Force meeting 14 May 1999 ETF (99).

The European Task Force's work continued after the National Assembly for Wales was established, and during the preliminary policy stages it was the main body responsible for preparing the Objective 1 Single Programming Document (SPD). The Secretariat for the European Task Force was provided by the EAD of the Welsh Office and the Assembly, and it was responsible for editing the SPD. Sub-regional task forces and lead bodies compiled different parts of the document and developed the

Programme Complement.³ Local authorities dominated the sub-regional task forces, and civil society's input depended on relationships with local authorities. However, civil society was directly represented on the drafting team of the SPD. The lead body in drafting Priority 3 of the SPD (Community Development) was the WCVA, and Chwarae Teg also played a central role in drafting the cross-cutting theme of equal opportunities within the programme.⁴

Between July and September 1999, there was a consultation on a draft of the SPD that offered opportunities for civil society more broadly to input on Objective 1. The consultation document was widely distributed and it generated public awareness of the programme. However, the potential impact of organizations on the programme through the consultation can be questioned. Firstly, the sheer volume of responses received is indicative of difficulties in absorbing disparate viewpoints and dangers of consultation overload. Furthermore, the delayed timing of the consultation suggests that it was more a means of generating greater awareness and disseminating information about the Objective 1 programme.

Despite the key part the European Task Force played in the preliminary stages of Objective 1, the Assembly Director of Economic Affairs announced its termination in September 1999, meaning that it was only in existence for only just under a year – from October 1998 to September 1999 (McAllister, 2000: 46). Respondents provided different explanations of this committee's brief lifespan. To many, the setting up of a Shadow Monitoring Committee rendered the Task Force superfluous. Others highlighted various shortcomings, in that it could not effectively develop a strategic approach as its membership was too large and continuously expanding, reaching over thirty. As one interviewee commented, it was 'too big, too unwieldy and too wide and had done its work and what we now needed to do was push the thing on and to reconstruct the partnership later' (interview, public sector, NAW). In reality, the sub-regional Task Forces undertook the majority of the detailed work and the Task Force did not engage in the programme to the same extent. Despite its size, the Task Force did not significantly widen and extend the representativeness of actors involved in the partnership. Civil society organizations' representation was limited, and the Task Force's composition was overwhelmingly public sector dominated, largely including the 'usual suspects'. This composition resembles the 1994–9 Structural Fund programmes and is indicative of the Task Force's establishment during the pre-devolution period according to the Welsh Office's conception of partnership.

Why engage civil society in Objective 1 drafting?

Despite the relatively narrow representation of 'partnership' on the European Task force, organizations such as WCVA and Chwarae Teg were key players in drafting Objective 1. This highlights key factors in civil society's involvement in the programme. During previous programmes, drafting was predominantly the domain of civil servants and local authority officers. As these programmes progressed, some civil society organizations had a greater role in drafting. In particular in the context of the Objective 2 programme between 1997 and 1999, WCVA and the Community Development Foundation Wales were members of the working group that assisted in preparing the SPD (WEPE, 1997: 227). Although Chwarae Teg had had only a limited role in previous programmes, they had developed considerable expertise on equality and gender issues that was important for Objective 1. The expertise explanation for the role of organizations is suggested in the SPD (WEFO, 2000e: 157).

With regard to the impact of European Commission regulations on the role of civil society in Objective 1, the general definition of partnership had not changed significantly between 1994–9 and 2000–6. However the 2000–6 regulations extended the composition of partnership to include 'the regional and local authorities, including those responsible for the environment and for the promotion of equality between men and women, the economic and social partners and other competent bodies' (European Commission, 2000: 36). This promoted greater engagement and consultation with partners in different stages of the programme (European Commission, 2000: 26). The Commission's greatest influence on the role of civil society organizations in drafting Objective 1 was the shift in agenda for 2000–6 from 'hard' measures of infrastructure to 'softer' measures such as community development, and cross-cutting issues of sustainable development and equal opportunities.

A deeper explanation for WCVA and Chwarae Teg's involvement is evident in examining the effects of devolution. Juxtaposed to the expertise that some civil society organizations brought to drafting the SPD was the lack of capacity within the Welsh Office to write aspects of the SPD such as 'Community Development'. This reflects a broader capacity problem within the Welsh Office. In the early stages, the overload generated by the coincidence of establishing the Assembly and developing Objective 1 was serious. In parallel to formulating Objective 1, the European Affairs Division had to conclude the 1994–9 programmes and agree other Structural Funding programmes for 2000–6. As a result, the Welsh Office and subsequently the National Assembly were significantly under-resourced for Objective 1. In addition, Civil Service working practices exacerbated these difficulties. Welsh Office turnover and staffing policy in transferring staff between departments constrained learning and organizational memory in policy development. One interviewee remarked,

> one of the problems in the Assembly is because of their staff turnover and staffing policy people never learn . . . I can remember being there in 1999 talking about how we had done things in 1994 . . . officials looking at you completely blankly, so as an organization the Assembly doesn't learn.
>
> (interview, public sector, Local Authorities)

Furthermore, previously the Welsh Office had been dependent upon Whitehall for policy direction, and consequently its policy-making capacities were weak. This exacerbated the difficulties of developing Objective 1 and increased the importance of assistance by external actors such as civil society organizations. One interviewee explained:

> the devolution vote gave the legitimacy . . . for the Assembly and it exposed bigger and bigger gaps in the skills base and knowledge base within the Assembly and the Welsh Office because they had been used to essentially administering and tailoring London programmes. And suddenly they had to look for the answers and the answers were coming forward to a certain extent from civil society.
>
> (interview, public sector, NAW)

Consequently, one of the unexpected results of devolution is that the lack of capacity within the Civil Service generated a need for civil society actors' engagement and expertise in Objective 1.

Another impact of devolution evident in drafting Objective 1 was the opening-up of political engagement. The arrival of sixty Assembly Members transformed the channels by which organizations could increase pressure on particular points. Members were often willing to attempt to influence civil servants on organizations' behalf. According to one respondent,

> if you're in a reasonable partnership yourself it takes nothing to get in touch with an AM and say . . . what are you going to do about it? And I suspect that there is quite a lot of that type of lobbying going on as well.
>
> (interview, voluntary / community sector)

The backgrounds of many AMs make them particularly sympathetic to civil society. For example, the Minister Jane Hutt, prior to devolution, was Director of Chwarae Teg and a Chair of the Economic Development Committee; the late Val Feld was Head of the Equal Opportunities Commission in Wales. That these individuals had been selected, elected and appointed to the Cabinet demonstrates the changed political climate in Wales and the potential influence of civil society actors through prominent AMs. It is clear that the Assembly is predisposed to being much more sympathetic to civil society interests than was the case under the old Welsh Office system.

The lack of continuity in political leadership after 1997 was problematic to the development of Objective 1. In the first eighteen months of the devolution process there were three different leaders; Ron Davies, Alun Michael and the current First Minister, Rhodri Morgan. While this negatively affected Objective 1 policy-making, it could be argued that it provided opportunities for civil society involvement. Consequently, the drafting stage was a real partnership process with various sectors such as civil society leading on different aspects of the programme.

3. DECISION-MAKING IN OBJECTIVE 1

New inclusive structures?

A Shadow Monitoring Committee (SMC) for Objective 1 was initially convened in March 2000 and became the Programme Monitoring Committee (PMC) proper once the Commission agreed on the SPD in July 2000. In May 2000, a Structural Funds Working Group was established by the Assembly that in many ways superseded the European Task Force (McAllister, 2000: 46). There was some duplication of membership with the Task Force; but it was more broadly based due to reduced public sector and increased voluntary and private sector representation. Civil society's representation included WCVA, Chwarae Teg, Groundwork Wales, LEADER Network, Valleys Partnership and Wales Wildlife Trust. This particular combination reflected efforts to be more inclusive and develop a broader partnership in the post-devolution period. That the Structural Funds Working Group advised the Monitoring Committee gave support to representatives from civil society organizations with less experience of Structural Funds.

The Structural Funds Working Group also advised on negotiating the SPD with the Commission. A small delegation went to Brussels to

TABLE 7.2
Shadow Monitoring Committee

Politicians	2 AMs
Government actors	4
Government agencies	7[1]
Local authorities	2
Social partners	6 – British Telecom, Federation of Small Businesses, North Wales Chamber, Transport and General Workers Union, NFU Cymru, Wales Co-operative Centre
Higher education	1
Voluntary sector	6 – WCVA × 2, Chwarae Teg, Wales Wildlife Trust, Groundwork Wales, Cymad
Total	28

Note: [1] One was from the European Programme Executive. Some of these were included as specialist statutory bodies.
Source: WEFO website: minutes meeting Shadow Monitoring Committee, 7 March 2000.

Structural Funds Working Group

Government actors	1 – NAW
Public sector	6 – 3 local authorities, 2– government agencies, 1 higher education
Social partners	6 – FSB, CBI, Chamber Wales, Wales TUC, NFU Wales, FUW
Voluntary/community	6 – WCVA × 2, Chwarae Teg, Wales Wildlife Trust, LEADER, Groundwork
Specialist statutory bodies	8
Total	27

Source: WEFO website: minutes of Shadow Monitoring Committee, June 2000.

participate in negotiations with the Commission. It was led by the NAW and other bodies included the Welsh Local Government Association and WCVA (WEFO, 2000a). That WCVA was involved on such a high level of interaction with the Commission is indicative of the expertise and status of the voluntary sector in Objective 1.

The 'one-third principle'

The Shadow Monitoring Committee made important decisions relating to the operation of Objective 1 that directly affected civil society's role in the programme. A key decision was PMC membership – this was to be constituted on the basis of equal representation from each of the three sectors of the partnership. That is, one-third public or statutory sector, one-third private sector and social partners, and one-third community and voluntary sector, the so-called 'one-third' principle. On the Shadow Monitoring Committee, the 'one-third' voluntary sector membership comprised the WCVA,

TABLE 7.3

Programme Monitoring Committee: membership of the 1994–9 programmes

	Rural Wales Objective 5b 1994–9	ISW Objective 2 1997–9
Commission	4	2
Government actors	3[1]	3
Government agencies	6	10 – 6 + 4 WEPE
Local authorities	6	5
Private sector		1
Third sector	1 – TGWU	1 – Wales Co-operative Development & Training
Higher education	2	3
Voluntary sector	3 – WCVA, Disability Wales, CYMAD	2 – WCVA + Disability Wales
Total	25	27

Note: [1] Two of these are central state actors – Department for Education and Employment and Department of Trade and Industry.
Source: WEFO. These numbers are based on membership lists of 1998–9.

Objective 1 Programme Monitoring Committee membership

Government actors	8 – 2 AMs, 6 WEFO officials
Public sector	5 – 2 local authorities, 2 Government agencies, 1 higher education
Social partners	4 – FSB, CBI Wales, Chamber Wales, NFU Cymru
Voluntary/community	6 – WCVA x 2, Chwarae Teg, Wales Wildlife Trust, LEADER, Groundwork
Specialist statutory bodies	7[1]
Total	30

Note: [1] These include three European Commission officials.
Source: WEFO website: minutes of PMC meeting, 22 June 2001.

British Trust of Conservation Volunteers, Groundwork Wales and the LEADER network (WEFO, 2000b).[5]

The Shadow Monitoring Committee elaborated upon the delivery structures of the programme that further enhanced civil society involvement in Objective 1 (WEFO, 2000c). To overcome the lack of strategic approach of the 1994–9 programmes, packages of programmes were to be implemented by local and regional partnerships in the form of Local and Regional Action Plans. Local government raised concerns about the practicability of implementing the 'one-third' principle at all partnership levels and argued for some flexibility (WEFO, 2000a). Nevertheless, the Shadow Monitoring Committee decreed that 'the clear view of the Committee was that the "one-third" principle should be adhered to in all partnership groups' (WEFO,

2000a). This confirmed that the 'one-third' was to be reproduced at all levels of Objective One implementation, and transformed civil society's participation in Structural Funds.

In terms of decision-making, there had been some increase in the engagement of civil society during the 1994–9 programmes. WCVA's Director represented community and voluntary organizations on WEPE's Board of Directors and numerous organizations sat on the Programme Monitoring Committees (Ecotec, 1999: 71; Pieda plc, 1997: 112). Civil society organizations were also involved in groups to which ranking and selecting projects had been delegated. For example, on the technical group for Objective 5b, three out of twenty-four members were voluntary sector, while two represented the education sector (Pieda plc, 1997: 114–15). Nevertheless, the drastic increase in the representation of civil society organizations on various Objective 1 groups is significant.

How did the 'one-third principle' come to Objective 1?
The decision-making stage therefore transformed the extent of civil society involvement in Objective 1. That civil society organizations had been represented on the SMC and the PMC both reflected and contributed to conscious efforts to expand civil society involvement throughout the programme. According to one interviewee, 'no doubt that the process has been much more inclusive of civic Wales . . . no doubt at all that the thirds principle really helped the Third Sector, the voluntary sector, to get seats at the top table where they'd never had seats before' (interview, public sector, higher education). Other aspects of devolution shed light on how the 'one-third' principle became a pivotal characteristic of the West Wales and the Valleys Objective 1 programme.

Politicians actively promoted the opening up of the SF structures to engage partners and increase civil society input. The Economic Development Committee was particularly supportive and numerous respondents identified the role of the late Val Feld (then Chair of the Economic Development Committee) in advocating the integration of the 'one-third' principle and gender balance in Objective 1. Indeed, some argued that the 'one-third' principle would not have been implemented at all had it not been for active endorsement of influential politicians. As one interviewee explains, 'In terms of partnership that would not have happened, that was ultimately a political decision probably in the early euphoric days in the Assembly which simply would not have happened had it still been left to the Welsh Office' (interview, voluntary/ community sector). An affirmation of partnership and inclusiveness permeated the work of the Assembly as a whole. This was partly due to the rhetorical expectations of 'partnership' and a 'team Wales' approach surrounding devolution, and the political results of the National Assembly's first election in 1999, that left the Labour party without an overall majority in the Assembly. As one respondent explained: 'there are clearly demands from parts of the Assembly especially in a period where you haven't got overall control of government for partnerships and a clear direction that this should be a more meaningful approach than was before' (interview, public sector, NAW).

While some Assembly politicians therefore strongly advocated partnership in Objective 1 policy-making, there was some frustration among other politicians that the Objective 1 Partnership had a greater role in developing the SPD than the Assembly itself. This was particularly a concern as Objective 1 was seen as the Assembly's first test, and the impression was that the new institution would be judged by its success. Some politicians attempted to gain greater control on the Objective 1 decision-making structures. One interviewee rationalized the situation as follows:

> In particular Val Feld . . . countered the worst excesses and actually encouraged a participative way of working but that wasn't the way across the board. I think it's inevitable . . . it was one of the first issues on the Assembly's desk and it was a really difficult one for them. They were bound to want to get hold and put their mark on it.
>
> (interview, public sector, NAW)

Increased political engagement in Structural Funds is emphasized by an AM chairing the Objective 1 Programme Monitoring Committee. Bachtler argues, 'with the exception of Northern Ireland, no other UK programme experiences this degree of "politicisation" of the Structural Funds' (2002: 36). However, this goes hand-in-hand with the 'one-third' principle that promotes civil society's involvement in Objective One.

The 'one-third' principle coupled with the desire for a more strategic approach to the programme, has provided civil society organizations with a direct role in decision-making and implementation at all levels. Indeed, the extent of their involvement is greater than ever before and far exceeds the requirements of Commission regulations. This is confirmed by a Commission official's view on the positive aspects of Objective 1 management. Manfred Beschel stated, 'there is a very powerful and well functioning partnership situation, it is something that I found impressive at the beginning' (Select Committee on Welsh Affairs (2002), question 157). It could be argued that the creation of extensive partnerships following devolution has led to a greater democratization of the Structural Fund process. The significance of the 'one-third' principle for civil society participation in Objective 1 underlines the importance of political will within the Assembly and demonstrates an important effect of devolution. But how has this been played out in the implementation of Objective 1?

4. IMPLEMENTING OBJECTIVE 1 AND CIVIL SOCIETY

Objective 1 structures

The Single Programming Document was submitted to the Commission in April 2000 and finally adopted in July 2000. Local and regional partnerships had already been developing projects, but Commission approval allowed for the Programme Monitoring Committee to be established and set Objective 1 implementation into action.

Due to the programme structure and the 'one-third principle', civil society input into Objective 1 implementation has been extensive. Committees at all levels face a heavy workload, as responsibilities for management, implementation and monitoring are delegated to partnerships. This has been time-consuming as, while the PMC meets twice annually, regional and local partnerships and sub-groups meet monthly. To encourage their participation, voluntary sector representatives are entitled to claim travel and subsistence expenses (WEFO, 2000d).

The degree to which civil society organizations can contribute to partnerships is dependent upon their resources and capacities. Larger civil society organizations and national bodies often employ full-time staff dedicated to European issues and have similar levels of expertise to the public sector. As a result, they have contributed constructively to partnerships. Partnerships are more difficult for smaller or grassroots civil society organizations. These have predominantly sat on local partnerships and some possess little previous Structural Fund experience. Ensuring regular attendance at meetings is an issue for smaller organizations, a problem shared with the private sector. In addition, these organizations are often volunteer-based or have a limited number of staff. The proliferation of paperwork and technical discussions in meetings can create feelings of frustration.

In many ways, it has been simply assumed that all civil society organizations can participate effectively and disparities in experience, skills and resources have been disregarded. Not all civil society organizations know how to take advantage of their potential role in Objective 1. One interviewee remarked, 'the door was open for them, there was a seat round the table for them, but nobody trained them or prepared them for the role' (interview, public sector, WEFO). Training provision to promote effective engagement was available to the Shadow Monitoring Committee, but since then this seems to have been left to individual local partnerships (WEFO, 2000b). For both larger and smaller organizations, the lack of capacity to deal with the pressures of partnerships means that they feel overstretched. One interviewee expressed this clearly: 'I think what has happened is that all of us who are partners who do not have the wherewithal to support the demands that are being put on us in the last two, three years, we're really starting to buckle under the weight a bit' (interview, voluntary/community sector).

Despite the pressures, civil society participation in Objective 1 has broadened perspectives and expertise within policy-making, thus improving the relevance and legitimacy of the programme. Some respondents pinpointed the role of civil society in the context of economic development; its particular expertise in community regeneration makes it extremely important, given the high rate of economic inactivity in Wales. Furthermore, its presence has counterbalanced an over-concentrated business approach to the economy.

However, there is some disagreement over whether the 'one-third' principle is beneficial to the delivery of the developmental goals of the Objective 1 programme. To some public sector representatives, the 'thirds' principle is too rigid. It has left the public sector, the main drivers of European funding, under-represented, and the expectations of civil society's contributions are too high. The Task and Finish Group that was established due to concerns about Objective 1 implementation and reported in December 2000 pinpointed that a lack of expertise and informed guidance has impacted upon Objective 1 (Benfield *et al.*, 2000: 7). It also stated that while 'decision-making has been at best based on inclusivity', nevertheless 'the working groups from the European Task Force onwards have tended to be representative rather than capable of taking strategic decisions' (Benfield *et al.*, 2000: 26). Thus despite the apparent advantages arising from civil society involvement, some sectors are yet to be persuaded that this has improved the effectiveness of Objective 1.

Civil society in Objective 1 projects

The Objective 1 programme is divided according to broad areas of activity priorities, and civil society is most heavily involved in the implementation of

Priority 3, Community Economic Development.[6] The SPD recognized the effectiveness of community and grassroots groups in developing projects targeting social exclusion and promoting bottom-up community development (WEFO, 2000e: 19, 245). The WCVA is lead body for the regional level Community Economic Regeneration Partnership related to Priority 3. As previously noted, the emphasis in the SPD on community development partly related to the shift in Commission guidance and regulations towards developing local capacity during the 2000–6 period.

As with Objective 1, during the 1994–9 programming period civil society was most involved in implementing community development projects (WEPE, 1997; Welsh Office, n.d.). But both Objective 5b and Objective 2 programmes found fully involving community and voluntary organizations difficult. The complexities of the process, problems deterring application submission, match-funding and cash-flow difficulties frustrated civil society engagement (Pieda plc, 1997: 70, 120, 127, 138; Ecotec, 1999: 37).

Objective 1 programme implementation has highlighted that civil society organizations face similar problems to those encountered with the 1994–9 programmes. From the start, funding problems were evident and the Assembly agreed a 'gap-funding' mechanism to alleviate funding difficulties between the expiry of the 1994–9 programme and Objective 1 (WEFO, 2000b).[7] In relation to Priority 3, a sub-group of the Community Assets Partnership examined those aspects that were impeding civil society organizations seeking to propose projects in 2002. It reported that a lack of match-funding availability inhibited project development, but that greater match funding was becoming available through other programmes (WEFO, 2002). In this regard, the PMC has been responsive to the problems facing civil society and this can partly be attributed to the representative nature of committees. Unfortunately, the provision of key funds, allowing simplified access to European funding to local communities with the public sector bearing accountability, has occurred in only a few local partnerships.

The Task and Finish Group reported a number of difficulties with Objective 1 implementation. It identified that the complexity of the application process frustrated civil society involvement, particularly in relation to Priority 3. Complexity, jargon, delays and uncertainty surrounded the Objective 1 application process. That the different levels of partnership in the programme are involved in deciding on applications has further exacerbated the difficulties encountered. In the light of the obstacles serving to prevent some organizations from taking full advantage of the opportunities that Objective 1 was meant to open up, the Task and Finish

Group called for 'simple, flexible and customer friendly' first contact with the European funding system (Benfield *et al.*, 2000: 10). It recommended that Technical Assistance be made available to support a Voluntary Sector Support Unit to ameliorate the situation (WEFO, 2001). The Unit was set up in WCVA and offers guidance, information, counselling sessions and training on European funding, with teams in different regions of Wales.

The complexity of the application process presents many ironies. Firstly, while Priority 3 is mostly aimed at small grassroots organizations, the application process makes Objective 1 a turn-off for them particularly as accessing funds from other sources is easier for example, from Communities First or the National Lottery. Secondly, the complexity and bureaucracy implicit in Structural Funds dissuades grassroots organizations from getting involved. However, the bureaucracy surrounding Objective 1 arises primarily from EU requirements for sound management of public money – an eminently sensible requirement that, nonetheless, seems to stand in contradiction to the Commission's stated desire to involve grassroots organizations. Bachtler concurs that 'bureaucracy is endemic to Structural Fund implementation, especially in Objective One areas' (2002: 37). Thirdly, the 'one-third' principle and the structure of the programme have boosted civil society involvement in Objective 1, but this negates the ability of organizations to contribute to implementing projects under Objective 1. So while Commission regulations and devolution promote democracy and greater participation in Objective One, the bureaucracy involved in implementing the programme detracts from achieving these democratic aims.

Due to the key importance of capacity and experience in ensuring civil society involvement in Objective 1, it is not surprising that the main civil society actor not only in implementation but throughout the process, has been the WCVA. This may also reflect, that in the early stages of Objective 1, transition pressures meant that the Welsh Office and Assembly remained dependent on previously existing relationships. Furthermore, most of civil society was inexperienced, lacked capacity, and was simply not geared up for devolution or Objective 1. In the five years before the Assembly's establishment, the WCVA played an increasingly prominent role, as exemplified with regard to Structural Funding programmes. Following Labour's accession in 1997 the organization became an influential voice. It has good working links with the Welsh Assembly Government and the broader public sector in Wales. Capacity building within civil society is a long process and partly explains why WCVA has been so influential in the Objective 1 policy process. The WCVA provided the Assembly with one dependable organization that produced a high-quality and consistent contribution, and could present itself as the voice of the voluntary sector in Wales.

As Objective 1 has developed, other voices from civic Wales, such as the British Trust of Conservation Volunteers, Chwarae Teg and Groundwork Wales, have become increasingly prominent in the Objective 1 process. In the current situation WCVA, 'are seen more as first among equals and a number of other quite significant players involved . . . It's ended up with the range of voluntary sector bodies you've got on the Structural Funds Monitoring Committee' (interview, public sector, NAW). Some interviewees argued that, had the Voluntary Sector Partnership Council been founded earlier, civil society's contribution to policy-making would have involved a broader range of groups, thus being more representative from the start. However, the WCVA's pivotal role in developing Objective 1 has reflected not only the constraints on the Assembly but also the weakness and underdevelopment of civil society actors in the pre-devolution era.

5. CONCLUSION – ASSESSING THE IMPACT OF DEVOLUTION

This article has identified that civil society organizations have played a key part in the Objective 1 policy process, a greater role than ever before in Structural Funds in Wales. A number of factors have contributed to this situation. It could be argued that greater civil society involvement in Objective 1 was itself simply a natural extension of the process that had already begun to characterize Structural Fund policy-making in Wales. During the 1994–9 programming period, some civil society organizations had a greater role than previously in drafting and decision-making, even if implementation remained the main focus of civil society involvement. However, their involvement in this earlier period is simply not comparable to the very extensive role that civil society has played in the context of Objective 1. This is not merely a difference of degree – civil society actors now play a qualitatively different role than they did in the past across the whole range of the Objective 1 process.

European Commission Regulations have also contributed, as the 2000–6 Structural Fund Regulations encourage greater involvement of all partners, including sectors of civil society, in areas such as community development, equal opportunities and sustainable development (even if, as we have noted, the bureaucracy implicit in the same regulations serves to frustrate the involvement of grassroots civil society organizations). Again, however, the very significant enhancement of civil society engagement witnessed in the current Objective 1 programme cannot be adequately explained simply by reference to the impact of Commission Regulations, not least because the breadth and depth of civil society involvement in the West Wales and the Valleys programme has far exceeded Commission requirements.

Different aspects of devolution have been central to promoting civil society's involvement in Objective 1. Contributory factors include the lack of capacity within the Civil Service administration for policy development. This was due partly to the Welsh Office's previous dependence upon Whitehall for policy direction, but more importantly to the shortfall in staff resources owing to the establishment of the National Assembly. Devolution has also opened up the process of Structural Fund policy-making in Wales to greater political influence. This relates to the concerted political attempts to foster partnership and inclusivity, and the role of AMs and their accessibility to civil society actors. That devolution has created a new context is confirmed by Commission official Manfred Beschel's views on the implementation of Objective 1. He states: 'I do think that devolution creates a different kind of visibility for people. Partnerships in a devolved region, where the link to political representation is much closer, does make a difference, I can quite clearly say that' (Select Committee on Welsh Affairs, question 162).

Devolution has therefore encouraged the deep involvement of civil society in the Objective 1 policy process. However, the relative effectiveness of those organizations seeking to be engaged varies greatly due to imbalances in resources and organizational capacities. As one interviewee stated,

> they are creating opportunities and whether those opportunities are exploited depends on the capacity of civic organizations to have the time and the resources and the expertise to make use of some of those opportunities. So if you're not tooled up in the new Wales, however inclusive and transparent it is, you can't participate in it.
>
> (interview, public sector higher education)

Civil society's engagement demonstrates greater partnership-working than ever before in Objective 1 and that the concept is ingrained in Welsh policy-making. The development of the 'one-third' principle in Objective 1 most particularly has extended to be a guiding factor in other Structural Fund and National Assembly programmes, such as Communities First.

Whatever the influence of European regulations and other factors, it is the devolution process in Wales which has been the main driver for more intensive involvement of civil society in all aspects of Objective 1. This reflects sincere efforts on the part of the National Assembly for Wales to develop more inclusive structures and, hence, democratize the policy process in post-devolution Wales. There remains however a significant problem, arising from the lack of capacity that characterizes many, if not most, civil society organizations. 'Tooling up' civil society to play its part in the 'new Wales' is crucial if we are to create a real change in the political and policy culture of post-devolution Wales.

NOTES

1. Securing Objective 1 funding entailed working with the Office of National Statistics to make the case to the European Commission for redrawing the NUTS 2 boundaries in Wales, following the 1996 local government reorganization. This led to creating a new region of 'West Wales and the Valleys' that would qualify for Objective 1 under the criterion of GDP a head being less than 75 per cent of the European Union average.
2. The Objective 1 programme is worth 1.8 bn. euros to West Wales and the Valleys between 2000–6 (excluding match funding).
3. The sub-regional task forces for Objective 1 were West Wales, and the Valleys.
4. Chwarae Teg is an organization formed to promote and increase economic participation by females, and represented the European Equality Partnership.
5. Different terms utilized in the interviews to refer to this were the 'three-thirds' principle, the 'thirds' principle.
6. Priorities are subsequently divided into measures that provide further detail on how the aims of the programme are to be implemented. Priority 3 includes Measure 1: Community Action for Social Inclusion, Measure 2: Partnership and Capacity Building, Measure 3: Regeneration of Deprived Areas through Community-led Initiatives and Measure 4: Support for the Social Economy.
7. Though there were difficulties in delivering advance ERDF payments to the voluntary sector this was possible under ESF.

REFERENCES

Bachtler, J. (2002). 'Objective 1: a comparative assessment', *Contemporary Wales*, 15.
Benfield, G., Davies, G., Davies, N., Jackson, G., Johnes, C., Morgan, K., and Sommer, T. (2000). *Task and Finish Group Report on the Implementation of Objective One Structural Funds*, WEFO.
Chaney, P., Hall, T., and Pithouse, A. (eds.) (2001). *New Governance: New Democracy?*, Cardiff: University of Wales Press.
Davies, R. (1999). *Devolution: A Process Not an Event*, The Gregynog Papers, 2 (2), Cardiff: Institute of Welsh Affairs.
Ecotec Research and Consulting Ltd (1999). *Interim Evaluation of the ISW Objective 2 Programme 1997–99 and Ex-post Evaluation of the ISW Objective 2 Programme 1994–96, Final Report on the Ex-Post Evaluation of the 1994–96 Programme*, Birmingham: Ecotec.

European Commission (2000). *Structural Actions 2000–2006 Commentary and Regulations*, Luxembourg: OOPEC.

Hain, P. (1999). 'A Welsh third way?', *Tribune Pamphlet*, London: Tribune Publications.

McAllister, L. (2000). 'Devolution and the new context for public policy-making: lessons from the EU Structural Funds in Wales', *Public Policy and Administration*, 15, 2.

Morgan, K. and Price, A. (1998), *The Other Wales: The Case for Objective One Funding Post 1999*, Cardiff: Institute of Welsh Affairs,

Morgan, K. (2002).'The two worlds of Objective One', *Agenda: Journal of the Institute of Welsh Affairs*, Cardiff: IWA (Summer).

Pieda plc (1997). *Interim Evaluation of the Rural Wales Single Programming Document 1994–1999*, Cardiff: Welsh Office.

Select Committee on Welsh Affairs (2002). *Welsh Affairs – Minutes of Evidence*, *http://www.publications.parliament.uk/pa/cm200102/cmselect/cmwelaf/520/2012801 .htm*, 22 June 2002.

Wales European Programme Executive Limited (WEPE) (1997). *ISW SPD 1997–99 Industrial South Wales Single Programme Document Objective 2* (n.p).

Welsh European Funding Office (WEFO) (2000a). *Minutes of the Shadow Monitoring Committee*, 3 May 2000, *www.WEFO.wales.gov.uk/newprogs/objective1/Obj1-minutes/(2000-05-03)*

Welsh European Funding Office (2000b). *Minutes of the Shadow Monitoring Committee*, 7 March 2000, *www.WEFO.wales.gov.uk/newprogs/objective1/Obj1-minutes/2000-03-07*

Welsh European Funding Office (2000c). *Minutes of the Shadow Monitoring Committee*, 29 June 2000, *www.WEFO.wales.gov.uk/newprogs/objective1/Obj1-minutes/2000-06-29*

Welsh European Funding Office (2000d). *Minutes of the Programme Monitoring Committee*, 15 December 2000, *www.WEFO.wales.gov.uk/newprogs/objective1/Obj1-minutes/2001-02-05*

Welsh European Funding Office (2000e).*West Wales and the Valleys Objective One Single Programming Document (SPD) 2000–2006*, Cardiff: National Assembly for Wales.

Welsh European Funding Office (2001). *Minutes of the Programme Monitoring Committee*, 5 February 2001, *www.WEFO.wales.gov.uk/newprogs/objective1/Obj1-minutes/2001-03-19*

Welsh European Funding Office (2002). *Minutes of the Programme Monitoring Committee*, 18 March 2002, *www.WEFO.wales.gov.uk/newprogs/objective1/Obj1-minutes/2002-06-21*

Welsh Office (n.d.). *Rural Wales Objective 5b Single Programming Document*, Cardiff: Welsh Office.

Wyn Jones, R., and Paterson, L. (1999). 'Does civil society drive constitutional change?', in Taylor, B., and Thomson, K. (eds.), *Scotland and Wales: Nations Again?*, Cardiff: University of Wales Press.

8. WALES: HOME RULE OR HALF-RULE?

(The 2002 Hallstatt Lecture[1])

Simon Jenkins

I have been asked to talk about governing Wales. But let us clear one matter away at the start. An iron law of self-esteem holds that you may criticize another person in almost all respects, but not their nationality or place of origin. You certainly may not crack jokes at its expense. Only natives may do that. Only Jews may tell Jewish jokes. Only blacks may satirize blacks. Only citizens of Wolverhampton may be unkind about Wolverhampton.

I am as bad. In England I may be almost a republican. But abroad, if I hear someone attack the royal family, some weird tribal DNA has me galloping forth as Queen's Champion. I sometimes do *Any Questions?* It doesn't matter where we are, or how notoriously dull or ugly is the place. Be it Swindon or St Helen's, Handsworth or Hull, never be rude about the venue. You are an outsider and they will tear you to pieces.

Many visitors to this part of Wales come from Birmingham, a metropolis, some say, that keeps its physical virtues well hidden and wears its blemishes on its sleeve. Dare I list the blemishes? Certainly not. It is rude. Leave that to a Brummie. But wait. It so happens that, by a quirk of parental fate, I was born in Selly Oak General Hospital, Birmingham. Ah, says Birmingham, that's all right. You're one of us. Tell us what you think of Birmingham. I have a licence to comment.

I noticed that all commentators at the Commonwealth Games were under instructions to 'be very nice about Manchester'. Listening to the sugary coverage, I wondered if Manchester had just lost a war or suffered some terrible natural disaster. The schmoozing was relentless. 'We're having these glorious games in MANCHESTER . . . What lovely people they are in MANCHESTER . . . What an ideal place MANCHESTER is for athletics, hockey, cross-country, synchronized swimming or whatever'. Manchester seemed unable to stand any criticism. It had to take pre-emptive action to protect its feelings.

I am afraid Wales is no different. Any passing jibe, by commentator, quizmaster or a certain quizmistress, and the Welsh howl with indignation. Bruised by history, they take refuge in hypersensitivity. So, what's my licence? Like probably many in this room, I am half Welsh. And since all Britons have a fear of sinking into that ultimate ethnic anonymity of being English, I cling to that half. I regard myself as Welsh. I do so even when that half is Glamorgan. The horrible truth is that anyone from Glamorgan with a Norman-root name is probably English, or at best of wholly anonymous ancestry. From the French 'Jean' comes John, Jones, John's-kin, Jenkin, Jenkins and so on. Likewise Davies, Richards and Michaels. With a name like Jenkins you must come from Wales, I am told. No, I reply, with a name like Jenkins I must come from England. How we longed for that precious initial P, the 'ap' prefix as in Pugh, Price, Powell, Parry. Instead we had the Anglo-Saxon mark of Cain, the suffix 's' for son.

So I am half-Welsh, live in London most of the year and have holidayed in Wales for fifty years. How Welsh am I? And what is the strength of my licence to criticize? My mother, fiercely English, rather resented my supporting Wales in matches between the two countries. A rough compromise was reached that we cheered England for the first half, and Wales for the second. Welsh-born or even Welsh-descended Londoners may have no Welsh home, no vote, no family, no link with the place, yet feel a duty to defend Wales, and a licence to attack. On the other hand, English with no Welsh ancestry who live in Wales, work in Wales, spend in Wales, uphold Welsh culture, are denied that licence. They are not even English, they are *Saeson*, Saxons. They are outsiders, especially those with second homes in Wales. It is all most confusing.

- This question of group identity is no light affair. In America it is called the New Politics. Native Americans, American Indians to you and me, used to suppress that ethnicity. They now boast it. They can claim membership of a reservation, and the right to astonishing gambling concessions that it brings. They need prove only one-sixteenth Indian blood to qualify. It is as if the English had long overwhelmed Montgomeryshire and any lingering indigenous Welsh were suddenly granted, say, Caersws as a tribal Reservation – where they decided to build Britain's biggest casino. That is what the virtually extinct Pequot Indians have done in rural Connecticut. Jan Morris's satirical novel, *Our First Leader*, has all Welsh Wales, *Y Fro Gymraeg*, as just such a reservation – a sort of asylum camp for

Welsh-speakers. In Spain, group politics is more serious. Those of Basque ancestry apparently have a particular DNA marker in their blood, not possessed by other Europeans. Extremist Basque politicians are proposing that only Basques with this marker be allowed to vote in local elections.

I have spent so much time on this matter of identity because it underpins any discussion of self-government in Wales. Group identity is what defines not just a nation but a sub-nation, a region, a neighbourhood. Who you think you are and where you live defines how and by whom you want to be governed. Thus when Britons go to distant continents, most of us if asked where we are from will say 'from Britain', not 'from Europe'. Britain is therefore our prime focus of sovereignty. When in Europe, we may be more specific. We may say we are from England, Scotland, Wales. Speaking to someone else from Britain, however, it gets more interesting. Cities are easy. We come from London, Birmingham, Manchester, Bristol. Smaller places require not one but two points of reference. King's Lynn in Norfolk, Evesham in Worcestershire, Ludlow in Shropshire. And what of Wales? You may refer to Cardiff or perhaps Swansea. But usually you first mention Wales. You will say Wales, then Aberystwyth, or Wales, then Bangor. When asked where we went on holiday, we have to produce the mouthful: 'a village in Wales called Pennal, that's near a place called Machynlleth in Montgomeryshire, er, in mid-Wales'. One thing you never leave out is the reference to Wales.

These terms define the geographical entities within which we wish to be governed. They define self-rule. But of course self-rule is not simple. Nobody rules themselves. The only true home rule is parental, and few parents enjoy much sovereignty even there. As soon as we form communities, we admit to tiers of government. Those tiers reflect a hierarchy of groups to which we feel we belong. I believe that to work and enjoy support, these tiers must be based on the geographical areas with which we identify. Of late, they have been remorselessly removed from what I call 'home', and therefore from true self-government.

Let me talk a while about the quayside railings in Aberdyfi. They are a fine set of railings, of the post and chain variety. They would have been installed in the nineteenth century by the local vestry, paid for perhaps by a local sea captain or slate merchant or from the local rate precept. Either way they would have been Aberdyfi's business. Today there is no vestry and no specifically local rate. The so-called community council is purely consultative. Recently the relevant authority, in Caernarfon, decided on the basis of a health and safety report to replace the railings with fixed bars of an appropriately municipal design. It claimed the decision for itself, possibly in league with an even more distant body, the National Park Authority in Penrhyndeudraeth. That decision, of the Gwynedd Unitary Authority, will then be conditional on a budget and a rate approved in Cardiff. That rate will be based on targets and performance indicators, quite detailed ones, drawn up by the Treasury and Audit Commission in London. Aberdyfi's railings are a tiny cog in the gigantic computerized model of the public sector fashioned by the Treasury. Somewhere they are on its scanner.

Now quayside railings are not a matter of national defence, which I happily defer to London. They are not a matter of international trade or tariff, which I might even defer to Brussels. This is not a question of the price of lamb or even a subsidy to the late-lamented Cambrian Coast Express. It is a railing in Aberdyfi. It is a lump of iron on the seafront. Nor is the decision even in the hands of some neighbouring centre of democratic authority, such as Tywyn or Dolgellau or Machynlleth. It is in Caernarfon, Cardiff, London. These decisions go ever upwards, as if British local government was striving to imitate the Roman Catholic Church. It is ironic that the nearest outpost of government to modern Aberdyfi should be the military headquarters of a medieval English king, Edward I, in Caernarfon. Local government in the Dyfi Valley has taken seven centuries to come full circle. Except that I bet even Edward I might have delegated decisions on Aberdyfi railings to his constable closer to hand at Harlech.

Local government has always been a matter of tiers; in Wales's recent experience, blood, sweat and tiers. The Tudor monarchs ended the medieval division of Wales between Principality in the north and west and Marches in the south and east. They gave Wales the same structure as in England, thirteen counties with parishes and sheriffs. In 1889, this structure was replaced by democracy, by elected councillors. To the thirteen counties were added 164 municipal, rural and urban districts. Liberals won every county except Brecon – and did so until the rise of Labour. But Wales never became a political entity. The Labour party and its trade-union allies dominated the industrial south-east. The rural counties remained mostly Liberal. Even at its zenith, the Welsh Liberal party was divided into a South Wales Federation and a North Wales Federation. Lloyd George's attempts to merge the two always foundered. As a Cardiff aldermen said, 'the cosmopolitan population from Swansea to Newport will never bow to the domination of Welsh ideas'.

As Gladstone who lived in Wales pointed out, Wales never had a constitution or independent legal institutions, like Scotland. Historically, geographically and emotionally, the so-called principality was split many ways. There was its Cymru *Cymraeg*, Jan Morris's Wales, a Ruritania of myth and magic in the north west. (In her latest novel, she shrinks Wales from that of her delightful *Machynlleth Triad*, when all Wales was ruled from Maengwyn Street.) Now only Welsh-speaking Wales is so ruled. She still places the historical capital, after Glyndwr, here in Machynlleth, not farther north. She has foreign embassies overlooking Derwen-las. She has an international airport, God help us, on Borth Bog and container ships lying at anchor off the tax haven of Aberdyfi. That is one Wales, that of the Old Principality.

Then there is Wales of the northern coastal strip, an extension of Granadaland from Manchester. Then there is the great inland sweep of Powys, with Machynlleth as Morris's Danzig, its outlet to the sea. There is the Little England Beyond Wales, Pembrokeshire and its hinterland. And there is the industrial south-east, Glamorgan and Monmouth.

Plenty of fully-fledged countries have a similar diversity; and plenty of smaller ones. Estonia is half the size of Wales and has a United Nations seat. But they have a political history on their side. The Welsh seem rather to fit the description of Marx's friend, Engels, who called them a 'remnant people, mercilessly crushed by the course of history'. The precursor of Plaid Cymru's nationalism was the Victorian cultural movement, Cymru Fydd. It was essentially romantic, giving rise to the eisteddfodau launched at a Bardic Gorsedd on, of all places, Primrose Hill in London. Cymru Fydd spoke in 1886 of the voices of England and Wales as 'united not in unison but in harmony'. Nationalism was a song. Both Lloyd George and the Liberal MP for Merioneth, Tom Ellis, called themselves Welsh Nationalists. But they meant something different. To Ellis, Welshness was united in Nonconformity and its related cultural life, not in a constitution.

My father was an ardent expatriate Welshman. But like those early cultural nationalists he held firmly to the view that Wales was a culture, not a country. Nor was that culture synonymous with the Welsh language. Though he could read and, on occasions, even speak Welsh, he found bilingualism a patronizing imposition. A language, he thought, was not living if it had to be propped up by the state and ham-fisted positive discrimination. It might be studied and celebrated, but if it had to be made a bureaucratic job-requirement, a linguistic closed shop, it was dead. Welshness was rather embedded in religion, education, literature, song, but not in linguistic politics.

As a result of all this, Welsh political distinctiveness has been on a hiding to nothing throughout history. In the nineteenth century, Wales at

Westminster was noted only in such matters as Sunday Abstinence, introduced in 1881, or Church Disestablishment. With the rise of Labour, Welsh industrial power in Glamorgan and Monmouth was based on nationalized industries, whose strength lay in keeping close to Westminster. It lay in national trade unions, whose strength lay in unity. And Glamorgan was always the bugbear. Sixty per cent of the Welsh population live in Cardiff, Swansea and their immediate hinterland. They always behaved as a Wales apart, what some call rugby Wales.

The history of Welsh devolution has been dire. In 1892 a proposal for a Welsh assembly collapsed when Glamorgan demanded twenty-five seats and proposed just two for Merioneth. Another conference on Welsh devolution in 1922 – held in Shrewsbury of all places – was boycotted by Glamorgan. The 1920s did see a revival of cultural nationalism in the form of Plaid Cymru. Its founder, Saunders Lewis, declared that protecting the language was more important than self-government. This shut the Plaid off from the potential support of the eighty per cent of the Welsh population with no command of the language. Plaid Cymru is no longer so exclusive.

Not until 1964 did the Labour Government introduce even a Welsh Secretary and a Welsh Office. But its powers were administrative, like those of a present-day regional office of Whitehall. All legislation – and statistics – retained that fell rubric 'England and Wales'. A proposal to make the Welsh Office subject to a devolved assembly was massively defeated by a Welsh referendum in 1979 – by eighty per cent to twenty per cent. A statement from the anti-devolution campaign in Clwyd was explicit: 'People in South Wales are very charming', it said, 'but as a crowd they are loud and coarse. We do not want to be governed by Cardiff. It would be a dictatorship.'

Over the past two decades, the Westminster Government treated Wales much as it treated Scotland, subject to ever more London-based centralization. It was staffed by ministers appointed by the British prime minister and officials employed by a London civil service. Few ministers even sat for Welsh seats – for fear, someone said sarcastically, of pro-Welsh bias. The Welsh Office became a place of political exile, a political Siberia. Peter Walker could pretend to be a viceroy. John Redwood could pretend to be right-wing. William Hague could find a local bride, to his credit a Machynlleth girl.

Wales was never left in peace. In 1974 it lost its historic thirteen counties to eight super-counties. Its 164 districts became just thirty-six. Big was said to be beautiful in local government. A sop to the Welsh was to give the new counties the names of ancient kingdoms. The princes of Gwynedd, Dyfed and Powys again walked the Cambrian Mountains – as if the Welsh were hobbits and local government a theme park.

That structure lasted barely two decades. In 1996 the centralizing Tories decided that the reduction of Wales from 177 democratic authorities to forty-four was still too much for them to handle centrally. Anyway, two-tier was boring. The number of democratic bodies was slashed to twenty-two, the new-fangled unitary authorities we have today. I would bet that Wales has the fewest elected officials per thousand citizens, and thus the least democratic and most bureaucratized local government of anywhere in Europe.

New Labour's consolation prize, of course, was a revival of a devolved assembly. Devolution only just squeaked through in Wales – by 7,000 votes out of a million who voted, and that was just half of the electorate. Only a quarter of Welsh adults voted for devolution. Indeed, it is hard to believe there would have been any Welsh Assembly had the pressure for a Scottish Parliament not been so strong. Wales had humiliatingly to climb on Scotland's back to be allowed any home rule.

Nor was it home rule: the power of the Assembly is notoriously limited. It is probably the most impotent national assembly in the free world. A central government Secretary of State remains in being. The Assembly cannot pass legislation and cannot raise taxes. Even London's Ken Livingstone can do the latter. All it does is administer powers allowed it from London, and criticize the exercise of those powers. And it can talk. It can talk about anything it likes.

This is nothing remotely approaching the powers enjoyed by the Scottish Parliament or of provinces elsewhere in Europe. Germany's Bavarian assembly can pass laws and raise taxes. So can Italy's Val d'Aosta, Venezia and Sardinia. So can Spain's Catalonia, Andalucia and Galicia. The Basques, with their own history and culture and mining tradition, not unlike Wales, are virtually autonomous. They set their own taxes and decide what to remit to Madrid. Wales is simply not on the same constitutional planet.

Indeed I would say the Welsh Assembly has probably less discretion than Merionethshire County Council had prior to 1974. With rate-capping, fixed business-rates, standard spending assessments and a formidable battery of performance targets, audits and controls, Westminster leaves local democracy in Wales with far less discretion than it had twenty-five years ago. Counties then could fix their own rates. They could plan their schools and what to teach in them. They ran their own police. I remember there was always a policeman in Pennal. They could build their roads and clinics. They could decide their Sunday drink-laws. All that local freedom has gone.

In this important respect, the advent of the Welsh Assembly has been neither here nor there. By taking power away from properly local government, central government has diminished, not increased, the amount of devolution in Wales – and indeed in England. The Assembly has been a cosmetic device, a sop and a distraction.

On this analysis, Wales has neither home rule nor subsidiary local democracy nor even the half-rule enjoyed by Scotland. No observer of Welsh politics, after two years of devolution, can sense the blood of a new regional autonomy coursing through the arteries and veins of the land. There is no north–south transport network. A Scottish energy minister can decide to turn mid-Wales into an upland turbine park to pretend he is meeting some international treaty on non-fossil fuel. There is no Welsh motorway remotely on the scale of that enjoyed by, say, Tyneside, the Midlands or the north-west. Wales's transcontinental highway is the A470, Heaven help us, on which you cannot overtake a hay truck for fifty miles. Wales's answer to the Canadian Pacific Railway, Y Cymro, pretends to run a service from Anglesey to Cardiff by way of Crewe. As for the Welsh media, it is the south Welsh media. On BBC Wales, Swansea cat stuck in Swansea tree is headline news. In Bangor you have to murder ten grannies in their beds to get the same attention.

Meanwhile what I call proper self-government has drifted ever farther from the grassroots of consent. It is absurd to claim that what now exists in Cardiff is a substitute for what has been taken away in the past quarter-century from towns and districts the length and breadth of Wales. Communities as coherent and as proud as Machynlleth, Dolgellau, Llanidloes, Newtown or Aberystwyth, in no sense enjoy civic power. Machynlleth's grand town hall has been demolished. Similar municipalities in Germany or France or Switzerland would elect their mayors, raise their rates, decide for themselves how to run their libraries, museums, police stations and sports centres. They would install their own railings. And I am afraid they are better run that way. Britain's centralization, this lack of local 'freedom to lead', is the most glaring reason for the poor performance of British public services.

Let me return to where I began. Wales does have a national identity. It is reflected in more than 'culture'. It is reflected in the loyalty of those who live here or originate here. A nation is a house built of many rooms, of accent and dialect as well as language, of literature, of religion, of history and of geography. Wales may never have enjoyed anything that could be called statehood. But neither really did Ireland. Nor did the Isle of Man – way outranking Wales in the autonomy stakes. Places such as Flanders, Alsace, Luxembourg, Latvia, Slovenia, Monaco, Andorra, Sicily or Slovakia have all slipped in and out of independence over history. Far more now enjoy it than did, say, a century ago. Only in Britain has the trend been the other way. All these places, some no bigger than Powys or Clwyd, enjoy some degree of autonomy. None has as little as Wales.

I am in favour of granting more powers to the Cardiff Assembly, at least as much as enjoyed by Scotland. And let's look for a moment on the bright side. If asked, I would still rather have a Welsh Assembly than not. Unlike regional England, Wales does have a local means of holding its administrators to public account. Those who execute London policy in Wales are now accountable to representatives elected by the Welsh, not appointed by a British prime minister. They may have to do what they are told by Whitehall, but they must answer for it in public. And they do. There must be far more coverage in the *Western Mail* and BBC of Welsh government than there was five years ago. This is an advance on nothing. Even a talking shop is better than no shop at all. And the Assembly is more than a talking shop. It is at least an answering shop.

I would go further. Through its Assembly and First Minister Wales has an identity it did not have before. I have watched the evolution of the Mayor of London. One thing even Ken Livingstone cannot pretend is that he is just a party leader. He is the leader of a whole city and, curiously, he behaves like one. Rhodri Morgan, whatever his background, is the leader of Wales, not of the Labour party in Wales. We can insult south Welsh politics as corrupt, aged, venal and costly. But it is at least now more open and democratic. The Assembly can make a stink. Through what I call the power of noise, it can embarrass. It can thus undermine the party institutions on which even Westminster ultimately depends.

But Cardiff government will never be self-government. That has to be local. Some time ago I came across a Plaid Cymru policy statement which made a good point. It took its cue from the old maxim, 'small is beautiful'. The party, it said, should concentrate on local identity rather than national. It should stress the continuity and vitality of Welsh communities, not the Welsh nation. It was in local communities that historical Welshness resided, not in institutions established in Cardiff.

There is nothing archaic or perverse in this. It is in the nature of a community to want to make its decision for itself, even to protect itself from over-rapid change. In Devon planning permission is being used, apparently legally, to restrict new housing to people of five years' residence. Village preservation is a fierce issue in Cornwall, the Lake District and the Yorkshire Moors. The slogan, 'No new outsiders' is alive and well in Kent, Sussex and the Home Counties. Nimbyism is not a Welsh word. The phenomenon is potent across Europe. Switzerland, a confederation of self-governing communes, has all but shut its borders to newcomers. This can seem intolerant, even racist. Cosmopolitans may deplore it. But we must beware the hypocrite. The outsiders who claim the right to buy property in the Celtic fringe are the same as fiercely oppose newcomers, asylum seekers, executive estates or skyscraper flats anywhere near their principal home.

I am now in danger of alienating everyone. This is dangerous territory. I long to see more autonomy devolved to the lowest tiers of government – even if it does mean three tiers of government in Wales. I want town and parish councils given back many of the powers long taken from them. They should be permitted some control over their appearance, their development and even the protection of their old character. I like the French custom of local elected mayors and councils. They would fight, subject to appeal, over every planning permission, every new estate, every traffic scheme.

Above them, the old counties made sense. They reflected historic patterns of regional loyalty. They still do. Their capitals are where markets are held, schools and colleges flourish. They are the centre of the revived arts festival. I accept that this localism must come, warts and all. If the people of Ceredigion prefer wind turbines to tourism, that must be their decision. In the long run they will be the poorer. If farmers want to kill off bed-and-breakfast ramblers by planting acres of sitka spruce, that too is their decision. If local residents want to imitate Devon and use the planning system to keep out outsiders, so be it. Wales's population is static. No immigration is bad for an economy. A booming, confident place would welcome newcomers. But if Wales, or Merioneth, or even Machynlleth is scared of immigrants or cannot accommodate them without destroying the local environment, so be it.

Of course protection must be accorded to civil and human rights. There are limits to regulatory discrimination, as to racism. There are property rights and employment rights and nationally-agreed rules on nature and architectural conservation. You cannot make a local democracy omelette without breaking eggs. People, democrats, want to influence the changing character of where they live.

This is the other side of so-called globalization. More people care about 'local'. More are retired. More are educated. More have money to spend. One of the things on which they will spend it is on their immediate surroundings. This includes re-empowering them to decide how far and how fast those surroundings change.

Somewhere in this I find a composite of a new Wales. It is not Jan Morris's Ruritania, much though I admire her ideology of Simplicity and Locality. It contrives to embrace in one polity entity the Wales to which most Welsh people now do feel some sense of loyalty and identity. I think devolution is an idea that has yet to be developed. But I think true devolution lies closer to home. It lies in the streets of Machynlleth. It renders unto the Caesars of Cardiff and London the functions that are properly theirs. But it renders unto the gods of home and hearth what is properly local. So bring back Machynlleth's parliament, call it what you will. This is the Wales that needs home rule, not half-rule. Recapture that and Wales really will be forever. *Cymru am byth.*

NOTE

1. This lecture was delivered at the Tabernacle, Machynlleth, 21 August 2002.

9. DEMOCRATIZING LOCAL GOVERNMENT IN WALES

Angharad Closs Stephens

On 3 July 2002, the Commission on Local Government Electoral Arrangements in Wales published its report on improving local democracy in Wales.
The Commission was established by the Labour and Liberal Democrat
coalition government in the National Assembly, and was charged with,
among other tasks, identifying the objectives of an electoral system for local
government in Wales. The Commission was chaired by Professor Eric
Sunderland, and during its year's work, sought evidence from councils,
politicians, pressure groups, civic groups and individuals across Wales. One of
the Commission's thirty-three recommendations was to introduce a
proportional representation voting system, the Single Transferable Vote
(STV) in time for the 2008 local council elections in Wales. Angharad Closs
Stephens was one of the members of the Commission. Here are her
reflections on the Commission's work and its conclusions.

In many ways, Wales is a newborn democratic country. Since 1999, we have
had a government based in Wales charged with the task of assembling a
Welsh democratic political community. With the establishment of the
National Assembly, the people of Wales have had to think anew about the
following themes and what they want them to mean: representation,
equality, elections, government function, delegation of political powers,
coalitions, political parties, and electoral systems. The number of women
members, the less formal political style and accessibility of the Assembly are
all testaments to the benefits of being able to design a new democracy. Local
government in Wales is however, more a reflection of the old-style politics
and forms of rule that governed Wales for most of the twentieth century. It
displays many of the values that are important and special to Wales, such as
the close contact between a representative and his or her community, but

also the less amenable qualities, like the fact that Wales has for a long time been ruled more or less by one party.

At the first National Assembly election, the new electoral system, combined with Plaid Cymru's unexpected electoral success, meant that the Labour party's hegemonic rule in Wales was shattered. With the largest number of seats but lacking an overall majority, the minority Labour government eventually gave way to the form of government that a more proportional system of voting often brings: coalition, in this case between Labour and the Liberal Democrats. The programme of the new administration was outlined in *Putting Wales First: A Partnership for the People of Wales*, and included a pledge to establish an independent commission to review the electoral system used for local government in Wales. The appointment of such a Commission was one of the Liberal Democrats' key conditions for a partnership coalition:

> We will initiate a full independent review into possible voting systems for Local Government elections in Wales, including those which would achieve greater proportionality in the representation of political parties. We will press the UK Government to bring forward Assembly sponsored legislation to implement the Assembly's conclusions from the review.
>
> (*Putting Wales First: A Partnership for the People of Wales*)

The establishment of the Commission and its membership was quietly announced by the Finance, Local Government and Communities Minister, Edwina Hart, to the Local Government and Housing Committee, to try to avoid causing a storm in the Labour ranks in the run-up to the 2001 general election. However, thunderous cries promptly followed, and before the first meeting the Commission had already been dubbed 'the ticking bomb which could destroy the Assembly coalition' (Betts, 2001).

WHO CARES?

Although the issue of electoral systems raises strong passions among some members of political parties and interested groups, it by passes the majority of the Welsh and British public as more or less irrelevant. It is first and foremost an issue of technicality and mechanics, and for that reason, is not something that generally provokes strong emotions: 'Interest in electoral systems among the public is generally low. The mechanics of different electoral systems are seen as being an abstract and boring subject with little relevance to the majority of the voting public' (White, Hedges and Seyd, 1999: 6). However, it is an issue with which the British political agenda has flirted throughout most of the twentieth century. In 1917, the all-party Speaker's Conference unanimously recommended a change to the Single Transferable Vote and Alternative Vote, but the proposition foundered. In 1931, the Labour government introduced a bill proposing a change to the Alternative Vote but it was defeated by the Lords. Again, after the 1974 general election, when the Conservatives received more votes but fewer seats than Labour, about a hundred Conservative MPs became advocates of electoral reform (Jenkins Report, 1998). In the moves toward democratization across Mediterranean Europe in the 1970s, across Latin America and most recently Eastern Europe, several countries have had to discuss and decide upon a suitable electoral system. (only one of which, and very briefly, decided on the British first-past-the-post model (Farrell, 2001: 2)). In the 1990s, Italy, Japan and New Zealand have all moved to change their electoral systems, and in Britain a new electoral system was recently introduced for the National Assembly for Wales, the Scottish Parliament and the Greater London Authority, as well as for the European Parliament elections in 1999. Consequently, although the subject of electoral systems might not be a popular political issue, it clearly has been important for many people across many countries for many years. One reason why the electoral system has always held a place on the political agenda is that the issue does not end with mechanics; the electoral system raises fundamental issues about what we want politics and democracy to mean.

Although the Commission was immediately labelled 'the PR commission', our brief in identifying the objectives of an electoral system for local government in Wales stretched much wider. We were asked to give due consideration to five particular factors:

- the level of participation in local government elections;
- the capacity of each elected member to represent his or her electors in ways that reflect the expectations of electors;
- the capacity of the whole council to reflect the diversity of interests and values in the local community;
- the capacity of the council to provide effective and transparent leadership which reflects the electoral choices of the electorate;
- the capacity of the council to provide effective arrangements for scrutinizing and holding its leadership to account.
  (For a full account of the Terms of Reference for the Commission, turn to Appendix 2 of the Final Report (Report of the Commission on Local Government Electoral Arrangements in Wales, Sunderland report, 2002).)

It was agreed at the first meeting that we should take our research and consultation as wide as possible, and that principle remained important to all involved throughout the working period. That was partly as a result of the membership of the Commission, because we all came to the topic from different backgrounds and looked at local government from different angles. However, it was also to do with the basic fact that any discussion on electoral systems is inherently tied to broader debates about representation, equality, democracy and so forth. We therefore, partly inevitably, looked at a range of different issues including: turnout, the voting age, uncontested seats, the frequency of elections, the demographic make-up of councillors, the voting process, councillor pay and voter education. On one hand, the electoral system is only one factor among many more which could possibly serve to revitalize local democracy. On the other hand, it is a crucial factor, one which the majority of us came to believe would better enable local councils to tackle some of the other issues mentioned above. Those issues, I will argue, are intrinsically related to the electoral system.

A PICTURE OF LOCAL GOVERNMENT IN WALES

The typical county and county borough councillor in Wales is white, male and retired. To be precise, 99 per cent of councillors in Wales are white, 81 per cent are male and 48 per cent are retired (for a statistical profile of local councils in Wales, see chapter 2 of the Commission's Report). In terms of age, the picture seems grim for ensuring a new generation of councillors; the average age of a councillor in Wales is 59, 2 per cent are under 35 years of age, 11 per cent are under 45, while 37 per cent are over 65. When we revealed those statistics in meetings with councillors across Wales, who reflected the facts exactly, the majority said that it did worry them that nobody seemed to be taking their place. Wales has fewer female councillors than England or Scotland, and, unlike those two nations the figure for Wales is not rising. Only 13 of 1,270 councillors in Wales described themselves as 'non-white'. Overall, county councils in Wales do not reflect the society that they represent, nor do they reflect the diversity of backgrounds and experiences in Wales's local communities. After being presented with those figures at the first meeting, it was agreed that we would add another factor to consider in assessing electoral systems: the capacity of an electoral system to secure the involvement of more female candidates, and members of so-called ethnic minorities.

In terms of participation, an indicator of any healthy democracy, Wales has a high level of uncontested seats in county and county borough councils; 17 per cent of councillors in the 1999 local government election were elected unopposed. Nobody was nominated to stand against them so there was no competition for the job, and effectively the voters in those constituencies had no choice. In Scotland, by contrast, fewer than 5 per cent were returned unopposed. A reason given by certain councillors, who had repeatedly not faced competition, was that it was a signal that they were doing a good job and that nobody wanted to get rid of them. Others viewed the situation with concern, and believed, as we as a Commission did, that lack of competition cannot be regarded as indicative of healthy democratic politics. Similarly, in terms of turnout, we viewed the fact that only 47 per cent had voted in the 1999 elections, and only 41 per cent when account is taken of uncontested seats, as a poor reflection of county councils' ability to engage with the electorate. Although turnout for local government elections in Wales is slightly higher than in England (ERS), it remains well below that for comparable EU countries (White, Hedges and Seyd, 1999: 3).

PRESENTING THE CASE

Those figures who vehemently opposed the establishment of the Commission were unsurprisingly also the key advocates of retaining the status quo in terms of electoral system. The main body of proponents of the first-past-the-post system consisted of the Labour party, the Welsh Local Government Association (WLGA) and the Conservative party. The main arguments espoused were that the system is tried and tested, easy to understand, that the boundaries of electoral divisions reflect 'natural' communities, that there is a clear link between a councillor and his or her electors, and that unlike more proportional systems, first-past-the-post produces 'strong and stable' government. The main argument against the current system is the discrepancy between the share of the votes received and the share of political power that a party wins overall. The system can give parties exaggerated majorities, leading to single-party dominated councils which lack effective opposition. For example, in 1999 in Blaenau Gwent, Labour won 46 per cent of the vote and 81 per cent of the seats; in 1999 in Caerphilly, Plaid Cymru won 41 per cent of the vote compared with Labour's 37 per cent, yet Plaid Cymru won 53 per cent of the seats and Labour 38 per cent; in 1999 in Newport, Labour won 45 per cent of the vote and 85 per cent of the seats, while the Conservatives won 26 per cent of the vote and 11 per cent of the seats (Local Elections Handbook, 1999). With less representation of different viewpoints, political debate is curtailed, and there cannot be effective scrutiny of the decisions that council takes. The impression that the result might be a foregone conclusion, as it seemed in many of the south Wales valleys for most of the twentieth century, can also deter candidates from other parties from standing, leaving seats uncontested. Often, it can either seem pointless to vote for a different party who do not stand much chance of gaining sufficient representation, or the voter is not offered a choice at all.

The simplicity of the system is often quoted as one of its main values. That simplicity is said to lie with the facts that voters only vote for one candidate (although only roughly half of the electoral divisions in Wales are single-member), and that a single government is formed by the winning party (although again, not always). The system encourages 'a politics of centralism' by proclaiming the myth that everyone in the community decided on one candidate and one government (Farrell, 2001: 65). In truth, because the first-past-the-post system is a plurality and not a majority system, the winning candidate can be, and is often, returned without having an overall majority of the votes. Also, as first-past-the-post gives greatly exaggerated majorities to the winning parties, smaller parties are often left with little representation, often less than the share of the vote they received. For example, in 1999 in Torfaen, the Liberal Democrats won 16 per cent of the vote, and 2 per cent of the seats (Local Elections Handbook, 1999). The *simplicity* then, in fact works by minimizing competition and abating diversity, and presenting itself as the only means towards a politics of unity.

Those who wanted to retain the status quo in terms of system, however, were equally concerned about turnout and 'modernizing' local government. The WLGA's evidence, quite rightly, pointed to a crisis of participation across UK political culture. However, the crucial difference between the camp who want to retain first-past-the-post and those who favour reform is that the former group do not accept any relationship between current problems in local councils and the electoral system. The WLGA's submission adopted the Labour government's line in the white paper, *Modern Local Government: In Touch with the People* (HMSO, 1998), that 'reforms to the political, management and consultation arrangements are of greater importance and urgency' in addressing the current weaknesses in local government. There is no doubt that there are better management and consultation arrangements which could be introduced to local government, but such arrangements cannot address the disproportional and dominating rule that some parties, invariably Labour in Wales, practise over many local councils. The WLGA also argued that, 'it is politics and issues which engage the electorate and not voting systems'. Again, I would agree. The problem arises however, when it is a single party that dominates the politics and issues to be discussed and, more seriously, the way in which they should be addressed. Under the recent changes to local government management structures, outlined in the Local Government Acts of 1999 and 2000, there is a potential sea-change in what being a councillor is thought to be. As part of the modernization agenda, the vast majority of councils have moved to a 'leader and cabinet' model of government which discharge most functions, with the remainder under politically balanced council boards for decision-making purposes. With power held in fewer hands, more emphasis will come to rest on the role of scrutiny, and perhaps on a councillor's representative responsibilities. As part of our terms of references we were asked to bear such changes in mind. Moreover, the current flux in local government structures provided the scope for us to think more widely about the fundamental role of local councils: what is local government for, and why is it important?

VIEWS ON REPRESENTATION

Underlying the arguments by those who favour simple majority systems such as first-past-the-post, and those who believe that elections should be held under proportionally-representative systems, is a different conception of what 'representation' means. Political scientists have generally differentiated between two different types of 'representation'; 'microcosm' and 'principal – agent' (McLean, 1991). Microcosm representation is the theory that an elected body should reflect as far as possible the society it represents. It should be a 'microcosm' of society, in respect of gender, 'race', age, employment backgrounds and so on. The 'principal-agent' theory of representation, on the other hand, holds that voters choose one agent to represent their interests and values. That elected member will be able to represent all the interests in his or her locality, regardless of the background or values of the individual member. According to the 'principal-agent' theory, therefore, if the elected body consists of a substantial majority of white, retired males, it is representative if the members are making decisions on behalf of those that they represent.

There was a strong caucus of us on the Commission who argued that an elected body that is not representative of society cannot be as effective in representing the diversity of interests and values in a community. I often focused on the importance of representation of and for women, and Charlotte Williams was a very strong voice for the representation of ethnic minorities. However, the 'microcosm' theory of representation has its difficulties theoretically. I would not be willing to argue that a man cannot represent a woman nor a woman a man, if only for the simple reason that no one has experienced the exact same background or has the exact same set of values as anybody else, regardless of gender. The difficulty rests with the fact that any argument that more women should be members of an elected body has to rest on the uncomfortable notion that women are somehow *different* from men. In arguing for an increase in women's representation, the most common response as to how to tackle the problem was to build a crèche. Despite the merits of such an idea, it assumes that all women are mothers and that the only obstacle in the way of women standing as councillors is care of children. In asserting the importance of the representation of any group, it is crucial to recognize the differences within that group, such as 'race', age, ideology, values and so on; that there is no such thing as a 'woman's point of view'. Rather, the argument for increasing the number of women in an elected body may perhaps rest with the fact that to do so would essentially entail including people who are not currently, as a group, in positions of power in society. This might, but not necessarily, lead to new issues being placed on the political agenda, topics that Mansbridge has called 'uncrystallized interests' (1999). By increasing the diversity of experiences and characteristics embodied by elected representatives, one can widen what constitutes 'politics'. The fundamental principle is that there is strength in diversity, and that variety enriches democracy.

One of our terms of reference in identifying the objectives of an electoral system was to consider 'the capacity of the whole council to reflect the diversity of interests and values in the local community'. I have mentioned how the first-past-the-post system works to elect one candidate and a single-party government, who are said to work, after the election, to represent all the different views in that society. Under a more proportional system, however, 'the election is an end in itself . . . and not . . . a means to the end of forming a single party government' (Rose in Bogdanor and Butler, 1983: 34). Those who are against a proportional representation system often point to the 'instability' of coalition government. We were asked by the WLGA to look to Italy and Israel as 'proof' of such instability, and even told that the Israeli elder statesman Shimon Peres had recently called for the adoption of a first-past-the-post system to end political instability in that state! There was certainly an overlap between those who pointed to the weaknesses of coalition government and those who believed that the Labour–Liberal Democrat coalition at the Assembly was 'proof' of the failure of joint government. In a country where one party has ruled without much competition for most of the last century, and where coalition government has not been part of the political culture, the responsibility of shared power is obviously proving difficult for some: 'The Labour administration in the Assembly is constrained by a deal produced as a result of PR' (WLGA, 2001). The National Assembly Member for Neath even suggested that the Assembly should change to use the first-past-the-post electoral system, presumably in order for Labour to 'get on with the job'. In essence, however, views towards coalition government are underwritten by assumptions about what elections, and indeed politics are about. Should elections work to reflect the diversity of interests in a society, or are elections about choosing a government which voters can then hold to account? (See Curtice, Seyd, Park and Thomson, 2000: 5.)

Data are now increasingly collected as to the views of the people of Wales towards the new system of voting and its resultant effects as seen in the National Assembly (see Curtice, Seyd, Park, and Thomson, 2000). There is no spectacular support for coalition government, but neither is there a surging belief that one-party government in the Assembly would be better.

Which do you think would be generally better for Wales nowadays?

To have a government in Cardiff formed by one political party on its own	48%
To have a government in Cardiff formed by two political parties together – in coalition	47%

In response to the common argument that coalition government, a product of the new voting system, leads to unstable government, there is hardly any support. If anything, more people tended to positively disagree with that statement.

The new voting system will lead to unstable government

Agree strongly / Agree	16%
Neither agree nor Disagree	29%
Disagree strongly / Disagree	36%
Can't choose	18%

In general, it seems that the people of Wales are content with the new system of voting used in the National Assembly elections. Those who identified themselves as Liberal Democrat and Plaid Cymru supporters were the ones mostly in favour of the new electoral system. Perhaps this support is somewhat influenced by the fact that the new electoral system undoubtedly benefited Plaid Cymru and the Liberal Democrat party. However, despite the fact that using proportional representation for the National Assembly elections had to be foisted on the Welsh Labour party by their British leadership, the majority of Labour supporters are also in favour of keeping to the new system.

Some people prefer the new way of voting for the Welsh Assembly, as they say it means all parties are fairly represented. Others say that the old way of voting for elections to the House of Commons is better as it produces effective government. Which comes closer to your own view?

	Overall %	Con %	Lab %	Lib %	PC %
Keep to the new way of voting	56	39	56	68	76
Use the old way of voting	33	53	34	20	19

When asked if the new electoral system should also be applied to local council elections, again there is no swell of support for change, with 45 per cent in favour. However, it is a much stronger call than the voice against any change. Nevertheless, in reading such statistics, we have to bear in mind how unpopular the issue of electoral systems is outside political studies and, perhaps, the low level of information that people generally have about the subject.

Should the new way of voting (i.e. that used for the Welsh Assembly) be used in future local council elections in Wales?

Agree strongly / Agree	45%
Neither agree nor Disagree	21%
Disagree strongly / Disagree	17%
Can't choose	15%

THE PRACTICE OF PUBLIC CONSULTATION

I have touched on the issue of the popularity – or rather, the lack of popularity with regard to electoral systems as a subject. Electoral systems don't cut waiting lists or reduce class sizes and do not generally constitute a 'hot' political topic. This proved to be a difficulty for the Commission in two ways. First, nobody can dispute the WLGA's argument that 'there is no surging popular agitation for change'. It follows presumably that something is only important if it is popular. Secondly, conducting any sort of consult-ation exercise with the general public, to secure the legitimacy of our eventual conclusions, was always going to be difficult. Unsurprisingly, not many people wanted to come to the local council chamber on a winter evening to discuss the comparative merits of STV, AV+, SV, AV and so forth. This lack of interest is linked to a lack of general knowledge about the subject: 'The subject of electoral systems is too dry to arouse much spontaneous interest . . . and voters generally have little existing knowledge to build on' (White, Hedges and Seyd, 1999: 2). It was difficult to discuss the merits of different systems when many people had never before been introduced to the different arguments. I am not implying that the subject of electoral systems is a difficult one, but simply that an hour or two's meeting was probably only enough to *introduce* the issues under scrutiny. Moreover it is important to note that qualitative research has suggested also that opinions on the subject change as voters learn (Curtice, Seyd, Park and, Thomson, 2000: 4). Looking back, our 'consultation exercise' probably served more as a means of beginning the process of educating and disseminating information on the subject, rather than 'discovering' the people of Wales's views on changing the electoral system for local government.

Once again, I would emphasize that I am not suggesting that electoral systems are difficult to understand. In fact, every member of the Commission was determined that we never dismissed an electoral system as being 'too complicated', as we believed that every voter was capable of learning how to express a preference in different ways. My concern is with the somewhat unthinking manner with which bodies such as ours, and other public and private bodies, sometimes approach the task of 'consulting' with the public. The main critique that I, and certain other members of the Commission, expressed at the end of our work was that of our own methodology in this regard. Perhaps we replicated the traditional forms and means of 'reaching out' to the public, such as public meetings, letter-writing, advertisements in local papers and the still-limited-in-access form of the website. They are strategies that have not been particularly successful in the past, nor were they especially successful for us. Although the academic groups and individuals, politicians and political parties, and pressure groups that had a clear interest all responded enthusiastically, the public meetings were generally not well attended. Recent evidence has suggested that response rates to consultation exercises on new council structures can be as low as 1 per cent (Public Administration Select Committee of the House of Commons, sixth Report, 2001). Such strategies for 'consultation' continue to be used time and time again, mainly because they are easy. However, they are not faulty strategies in themselves, nor would I suggest that they should be dispensed with. The main issue in my view lies with the fact that the burden still lies with the public to make the effort to take part. In the course of our work, we criticized many councils for failing to take, as one member put it, the mountain to Muhammad rather than waiting for Muhammad to come to the mountain. All the councils were interested in getting more women, young people and different ethnic communities involved, but generally approached the subject as if they were the 'hosts' inviting selected others in as 'guests', strictly on the terms that they had laid out. (This was not true of all councils, some of which were very proactive and imaginative in setting up youth councils and so on.) In realizing that we had also perhaps been guilty in some instances of the same outlook, we became more proactive in targeting certain under-represented groups. We visited certain schools and youth councils, and, at the other end of the spectrum, Age Concern, and went back to make contact with various equality bodies once again. In looking at the practices of many councils, we came to realize that in our own work also we needed to be more organic and creative in 'bringing people in'. Going into schools to *tell* young people about councils totally ignored the basic issue that councillors are *accountable* to those young people.

APATHY AND ANTIPATHY

The issue of falling turnout, apathy and perceived decline of interest in 'politics' is today an issue of concern across political parties, across different tiers of government, and throughout western democracies more generally. The concern was shared across the vast majority of local councils in Wales, but strikingly few had actually begun to engage with the deeper issues involved in the debate. Fewer still had considered that their own methods of 'doing politics' might be contributing to the problem. The most popular response by far with regard to how to deal with falling turnout was to look at electoral laws, that is, extending postal votes, extending voting times, voting in supermarkets, lowering the voting age and, the most popular panacea of all – voting through the internet. There is no doubt that mechanisms to ease the process of voting in hectic post-modern schedules are necessary. However, it seems to me that such issues of mechanics also provide a convenient diversion to politicians and many political scientists from having to engage with more fundamental questions about the increasing divide between 'the people' and structures of power.

A crucial point which many working in formal politics fail or refuse to recognize is that the decline in interest is not with 'politics' in general, but with the formal political process. In researching the background and views of non-voters at the 2001 general election, the Hansard Society found that the participants in their focus groups contradicted many of the reasons for not voting quoted in the press at the time. None of the non-voters spontaneously gave 'the foregone conclusion of the result' or the *process* of voting as a reason for not voting. Rather, 'not voting was something that most of them had consciously chosen to do; a positive abstention' (Hansard Society Briefing, 2001). Some of these respondents quoted lack of knowledge, no credible alternative, a negative view about the political system and the distance of politicians as reasons why they did not vote. Of particular interest, however, is the fact that 24 per cent of 18–24 year-olds who did not vote considered themselves to be active citizens (attending a political or interest group meeting, taking part in a demonstration, presenting their views to a local or national politician). One of the reasons this group of activist non-voters gave for not voting was that 'other activities offer opportunities to affect real change' (Hansard Society Briefing, 2001). There is further evidence that, while traditional political activity declines, selective participation in wider political movements is on the increase (Public Administration Select Committee, 6th Report, 2001). The key challenge for councils is how to translate that interest and activity in local campaigns into formal involvement with the local council.

Our Report makes several recommendations as to how under-represented groups might become more involved in local politics, or of ways in which our councils can become more representative of the general community at large. One such recommendation was that the age of entitlement to vote should be lowered to 16 years, and that the minimum age for candidates should also be lowered from 21 to 18 years. However, such recommendations are not presented as having a direct or positive correlation to turnout. Again, making it easier to vote will not necessarily make people, and young people especially, *want* to vote. The young people that I met with often stated lack of understanding of politics as a reason why they shouldn't 'have the right to vote'. Although the lack of education on the *technical* aspects of voting in schools and in the different media is of concern, this uncertainty seems to me to stem more from a conception that politics is somehow 'over there', quite separate from their everyday lives. Such a perception could either derive from policy – a sense that politicians rarely discuss what are considered important issues for young people. Or, it could also be a consequence of the *presentation* of 'politics' as a difficult, stuffy, white, male, middle-class-dominated establishment, a conception that reaffirms the belief that it is not relevant to certain groups of people:

There is a sense that 'politics' is familiar (not least because of national media coverage) but at the same time it is seen as being distant and having little direct relevance to, and impact on, people's day-to-day lives. Younger non-voters tend to associate 'politics' with Westminster and Prime Minister's Question Time, which is viewed negatively.

(Hansard Society Briefing, 2001: 5)

Similarly, with regards to the recommendation that the Single Transferable Vote system (STV) represents a more suitable electoral system for local government in Wales, I feel confident in claiming that no member who proposed this change felt it would serve as a panacea for turnout, apathy or uncontested seats. The case for change to a proportional-representation system is made by stating that every vote would count; that it would increase competition which *might* improve turnout; that it would better reflect a diversity of views; and that presenting a 'slate' of candidates would offer voters more choice and pressure political parties to present a diversity of candidates. The arguments of increased *choice* and more power to the *voter*- were crucial in persuading certain members who never before thought that they would come to favour STV. I have argued throughout that, in essence, arguments in favour or against proportional representation are underwritten by different views as to what purpose elections serve, and what we mean by equality, democracy and, more generally, politics. The tension between both views is articulated in what Chantal Mouffe has phrased the 'democratic paradox': between liberalism and democracy, or put another way, between freedom and equality (2000). Should a single political party be given the freedom to rule the electorate equally, or is freedom the equal representation of different political views? Mouffe attacks the current British consensus of Tony Blair's 'Third Way' that politics is a centre-ground compromise, and that there are solutions which can satisfy everybody. Rather, she argues, such compromise works against the political, by marginalizing dissent and failing to provide a legitimate space for different viewpoints:

The specificity of modern democracy lies in the recognition and the legitimation of conflict and the refusal to suppress it through the imposition of an authoritarian order. A well-functioning democracy calls for a confrontation between democratic political positions, and this requires a real debate about possible alternatives. Consensus is indeed necessary but it must be accompanied by dissent.

(Mouffe, 2000: 113)

Her analysis may, in my view, be extended to the electoral system currently used in local government that ensures the completely disproportionate dominance of one party, and also to the claim that this dominant ruling party has the capability (and the political will) to represent the diversity of interests in a community. This 'smoothing out' of political representation depends on the exclusion of other voices and other interests from positions of political authority. It is also a hollowing out of the democratic process. 'In a democratic polity, conflicts and confrontations, far from being a sign of imperfection, indicate that democracy is alive and inhabited by pluralism' (Mouffe, 2000: 34). Mouffe goes on to argue that failure to provide a democratic outlet for political confrontation may, at the extreme, lead to the political in its antagonistic dimensions manifesting itself through other channels, perhaps through violent nationalism or religious fundamentalism. Perhaps the greatest mistake of those who favour the presumed consensus of dominant single-party politics is to succumb to the illusion that antagonisms disappear after elections. It is senseless to think so and, consequently, surely preferable to give such antagonisms a political outlet within a pluralistic democratic system (Mouffe, 2000: 114). Our recommendations, including those on the electoral system and many others, were concerned with extending competition and increasing diversity in local councils. But rather than believing in some facile way that such an outcome would instantly counteract the downward trend in turnout and the upsurge of so-called apathy, it was our conviction that infusing the political process with a plethora of different values and experience would serve to enliven politics and broaden debate in local councils. This has a value in and of itself, above and beyond any impact that such a development might eventually have in rekindling public interest in representative politics.

WHAT HAPPENS NEXT?

I have tried to explore different understandings of what we mean by 'politics'. However, it is 'politics', in its most crude sense of power politics that holds the future of local government reform in its hands. On 24 September 2002, the Scottish Parliament Executive announced that a draft bill to introduce the Single Transferable Vote for local elections in Scotland would be published in 2003. The Scottish Executive had also commissioned an independent Commission, called the Renewing Local Democracy Working Group, chaired by Richard Kerley, to look at, among other tasks, an appropriate proportional system for local government. Its conclusions included the recommendation of the Single Transferable Vote, which looks increasingly likely to be at the heart of local government modernization in Scotland (Kerley Report, 2000). In Wales, we have now come to the end of a further consultation period on the conclusions of our Report. As with the Kerley Report, two members dissented from our recommendation of a change in the electoral system, as one Labour and one Conservative member joined forces to write their own 'minority view'. A few of us on the Commission argued relatively hard to ensure that the dissenting section was named 'minority view' and not 'minority report', and that it was included as part of the views on the electoral system rather than as a separate chapter on its own. It seems now like a petty argument, but, from a political perspective, we wanted to ensure that the 'minority view' was awarded minimal status so as not to undermine the legitimacy of our arguments for the single transferable vote. Such tactics, however, did not make much difference once the media seized on the 'splits' within the group. It also misrepresented how united we all were on the other thirty-one recommendations on how to work to revitalize local democracy and overcome some of the current weaknesses in local government. However, what happens next in Wales depends on the political will and political make-up of the Welsh government. I mentioned that it was part of the Liberal Democrats' terms of agreement for coalition that secured the establishment of the Commission. It is likely that what happens next depends on their presence or power in any future Assembly government, to be elected in May 2003.

As I have said, there is no simple answer to the question of which electoral system would work best for local government in Wales. Rather, the broader debate about what one wants representation and politics to mean will, to a large degree, determine which system one prefers: 'Ultimately, it is a normative judgement call' (Farrell, 2001: 11). Nevertheless, I have also tried to show that such a judgement call does not necessarily have to be a trade-off between one principle and another: 'an electoral system can allow for maximum representation of minority interests without necessarily threatening the stability of government' (Farrell, 2001: 10). It will, however, mean rethinking the traditional 'tried and tested' ways in which we have perceived the typical councillor, the ways in which decisions are and have been taken, and, more widely, what we have thought local councils and councillors are *for*. It will take much more than any one electoral system can offer to re-engage the electorate in local politics, to make local councils more dynamic and more relevant. Perhaps the current Assembly government will decide that changing the electoral system would in no way work towards such goals. However, the very establishment of the Commission on Local Government

Electoral Arrangements in Wales has secured the issue of electoral systems a place on Wales's political agenda. Our recommendation of a more proportionally representative electoral system in time for the 2008 local council elections can and well may be ignored. Nevertheless, the debate has been sparked, views have been expressed and arguments have now been aired *outside* of the usual suspects or political elite. Whatever the present government decide to do (or not do), those recommendations now *exist* for future governments, coalitions and leaders; for politicians who have the courage and political will to develop a creative democracy in Wales.

REFERENCES

Betts, Clive (2001). 'Voting reform squad named but treading softly on PR trail', *Western Mail.*

Bogdanor, V., and Butler, D. (1983). *Democracy and Elections,* Cambridge: Cambridge University Press.

Curtice, J., Seyd, B., Park, A., and Thomson, K. (2000). *Wise After the Event? Attitudes to Voting Reform Following the 1999 Scottish and Welsh Elections, CREST,* London: The Constitution Unit.

Farrell, D. (2001). *Electoral Systems: A Comparative Introduction,* Basingstoke: Palgrave.

Hansard Society Briefing (2001). 'None of the above: non-voters and the 2001 election', *www.hansard-society.org.uk*

HMSO (1998). *Modern Local Government: In Touch with the People,* London: The Stationery Office.

Jenkins Report (1998). *Report of the Independent Commission on the Voting System, http://www.official-documents.co.uk/document/cm40/4090/ chap-7b.htm*

Kerley Report (2000). *Report of the Renewing Local Democracy Working Group,* see *http://www.scotland.gov.uk/library2/doc16/rldw-00.asp*

Local Elections Handbook (1999). London: LGC Communications.

Mansbridge, J. (1999). 'Should blacks represent blacks and women represent women? A contingent "Yes"', *The Journal of Politics,* 61, 3, 628–57.

McLean, I. (1991). 'Forms of representation and systems of voting', in Held, D. (ed.), *Political Theory Today,* Oxford: Polity Press.

Mouffe, C. (2000). *The Democratic Paradox,* London: Verso.

Public Administration Select Committee, Sixth Report (2001). 'Public participation: issues and innovations', House of Commons, London: The Stationery Office.

Putting Wales First: A Partnership for the People of Wales (2000), see *http://www.wales.gov.uk/organicabinet/content/putting.html#top*

Sunderland Report (2002). Report of the Commission on Local Government Electoral Arrangements in Wales, Available at *www.cologea.com*

White, C., Hedges, A., and Seyd, B. (1999). *New Electoral Systems: What Voters Need to Know,* SCPR, London: The Constitution Unit.

WLGA (2001). 'Response of the WLGA to the Commission on Local Government Electoral Arrangements in Wales', available at *www.cologea.com,* September.

10. AN OVERVIEW OF THE WELSH LABOUR MARKET

Melanie K. Jones, Richard J. Jones and Peter J. Sloane

INTRODUCTION

This article paints a portrait of the Welsh labour market over the last decade. Several data sources are used to describe important aspects of the labour market, namely employment, unemployment, inactivity, earnings, vacancies, and education and training in Wales. As well as inter-temporal comparisons, the paper also compares the labour market in Wales to those in the rest of the UK, and considers variations across areas within Wales. In this article we assume that there is an entity that we can describe as 'the' Welsh labour market. In practice, it may be more accurate to talk of Welsh labour markets, given natural barriers between north and south Wales and close links between parts of east Wales and parts of England. The awarding of Objective 1 funding for West Wales and the Valleys has emphasized such distinctions. Similarly, there are important economic and labour market differences between urban and rural Wales.

THE WORKFORCE

One of the most important features of any labour market is the number and quality of people in the workforce. The 2001 census reported that the population of Wales was 2.9 million, of whom nearly 60 per cent were of working age, similar to the proportion in 1991, but less than the corresponding figure for England (61.5 per cent). Calculations presented in the National Assembly's 'National Economic Development Strategy' suggest that having a smaller proportion of the population of working age accounts for 2.5 of the 20 percentage-points' gap between Wales and the UK average per capita GDP (National Assembly for Wales, 2002a). Cross-border commuting to work also lowers the effective working population to some extent. For example, in 2001, 75,000 Welsh residents worked outside Wales, whilst only 42,000 non-residents made the opposite journey.

The amount a workforce produces also depends, in part, on their skills and abilities. An absence of skilled workers can hamper the expansion of indigenous firms and deter other firms from relocating into Wales. One in five firms who responded to a survey conducted by Future Skills Wales reported that they felt that the skills of their employees were 'not high enough to meet their current business objectives' (Future Skills Wales, 1998). Moreover, a quarter of these firms felt that this had restricted the development of their business. The same survey also found that 30 per cent of firms had 'hard-to-fill vacancies', that is, vacancies that had been hard to fill in the twelve months prior to the survey. Employers suggested that half of these vacancies were difficult to fill because there were not enough suitably skilled people in the area (compared to 42 per cent in the UK as a whole) and 20 per cent because the applicants lacked the qualifications required.

The skills gap is also reflected in the lack of formal qualifications held by workers in Wales. Data from the labour-force survey suggest that around 40 per cent of working people in Wales held qualifications at NVQ level 3 or above, compared to 48 per cent in Scotland and 43 per cent in England. This represents an improvement since 1993, when 29 per cent of working-age people in Wales were qualified to NVQ level 3 or above. The disparity is smaller at NVQ level 4, where 27 per cent of the working-age population in Wales were qualified to this level, compared to 28 per cent in England and 33 per cent in Scotland in 2002. In 2002, the proportion of Welsh workers with A levels (or equivalent) and GCSE passes was relatively similar to England. However, 12 per cent of Welsh workers held degrees compared to 15 per cent in England. Moreover, the proportion in Wales with no qualifications (19 per cent) is high than in England (16 per cent).

Part of the explanation for the gap in formal qualifications between Wales and the rest of the UK may stem from a failure to acquire basic skills. The Basic Skills Agency (2001) reports a plethora of figures that highlight the shortfall in the acquisition of basic skills in Wales. For example, at the end of primary school, 22 per cent of Welsh children are below the required level in English, and 26 per cent in maths. At key stage three, 38 per cent of 14 year-olds fail to attain the expected standard in English and the same proportion are below the target in maths (National Assembly for Wales, 2001a). The cumulative effect of under-attainment is highlighted by figures produced by the Wales National Assembly and Basic Skills Agency (2001), which estimate that over three-quarters of a million people in Wales have literacy and numeracy problems. Figures from the International Literacy Survey (ONS, 1997) reveal that Wales performs badly when compared with other industrialized countries, since a quarter of people of working age within Wales have poor basic skills compared with 22 per cent in England, 12 per cent in Germany and 7 per cent in Sweden. Another survey, conducted by the Basic Skills Agency between 1996 and 1999, revealed variations in the basic skills problem within Wales, the most acute basic skills problem being in areas with high unemployment and high levels of social housing, such as Blaenau Gwent, Torfaen and Merthyr Tydfil (Basic Skills Agency, 2001). Tables 10.1 and 10.2 show the qualification attainments in areas with different European Objective funding status.

TABLE **10.1**
NVQ level 3 qualifications by Objective 1 area.
Number of working age qualified to NVQ level 3 or above in Wales

Area		1998	1999	2000	2001	2002	% change 1998–2000	% change 2000–2
Objective 1	Number ('000s)	371	392	382	382	413	2.96	8.12
	Percentage	33.8	35.2	34.6	34.9	37.0	2.37	6.94
Objective 3	Number ('000s)	267	245	260	289	280	–2.62	7.69
	Percentage	41.8	39	40.3	43.4	43.1	–3.59	6.95

Source: QLFS, NOMIS. All data refer to the quarter ending in February of each year.

TABLE **10.2**
NVQ Level 4 Qualifications by Objective 1 area.
Number of working age qualified to NVQ level 4 or above in Wales

	Area	1998	1999	2000	2001	2002	% change 1998–2000	% change 2000–2
Objective 1	Number (000s)	191	204	197	209	207	3.14	5.08
	Percentage	17.4	18.3	17.8	19.1	18.6	2.30	4.49
Objective 3	Number (000s)	145	140	155	182	153	6.90	–1.29
	Percentage	22.7	22.4	24.0	27.3	23.6	5.73	–1.67

Source: QLFS NOMIS. All data refer to the quarter ending in February of each year.

Between 1998 and 2002, educational attainments, for those of working age were lower at NVQ level 5.3 and 4 in the Welsh Objective 1 area. The proportions with NVQ level 5.3 and 4 have increased over the period, and the rate of increase in the Objective 1 area (since 2000) was greater, closing the gap on the Objective 3 area.[1]

Information on the distribution of broad skills is available in the Work Skills in Britain study (Felstead *et al.*, 2002). This estimates a required-qualifications index, based on the qualification required to get the current job held by respondents to the survey. In Wales this was 1.95 compared to 2.41 in London and 2.30 in the South East. Only the East Midlands and Eastern Regions had (slightly) lower figures than Wales. A training-time index, based on the time taken in training for the type of work currently done, showed a lower figure in Wales than in any other region apart from the East Midlands, though the learning-type index, based on time taken to become fully proficient at the job, suggests that the complexity of job is not very different in Wales from that elsewhere. Data from the same survey on the regional distribution of generic skills show that Wales is above average in the requirement for physical and horizontal communication skills, but below average in high-level communication skills. The labour-force survey reports that in August 2002, 11.8 per cent of working-age people in Wales had received some form of job-related training in the previous month, lower than the proportion in England (13 per cent) but higher than the rate in Scotland (10 per cent). There were differences in the provision for males and females. In Wales, 14 per cent of working-age women received job-related training, higher than the rates in England (13 per cent) and Scotland (11 per cent). In contrast, less than 10 per cent of working-age males in Wales received job-related training, the same rate as in Scotland but lower than the rate in England (12 per cent).

ACTIVITY AND INACTIVITY

An area of increasing concern for policy-makers in Wales is the relatively high rate of economic inactivity amongst working-age people. Using the strong assumption that those who are inactive are potentially as productive as those who are employed, the National Assembly (2002a) estimates that a higher inactivity rate accounts for 5.3 per centage points of the GDP gap; less than 1 percentage point is ascribed to differences in the unemployment rate, and 12 percentage points are due to differences in productivity between Wales and the rest of the UK. Though this may overstate the importance of inactivity, since it may be that those who are inactive are potentially less productive, the resulting lack of opportunities available to them is part of the reason why they withdraw from the labour market.

The economically inactive can be divided broadly into two groups. The first group consists of those who are forced to become inactive, including those who are unable to work due to long-term sickness or disability. O'Leary *et al.* (2002) note that one of the reasons for high levels of inactivity in Wales is the relatively high percentage who describe themselves as long-term sick. Between the late 1970s and the mid-1990s the number of incapacity/invalidity benefit claimants more than doubled in Wales. In 1991, this figure was a third higher than in England. For example, there are 440,000 disabled people in Wales, accounting for nearly 23 per cent of the working population, compared with an average of only 18 per cent for Britain as a whole.[2] The second group consists of those for whom inactivity is the outcome of rational economic decision-making. This includes those who are retired, those in full-time education, and those who choose not to work because they are looking after family or have become discouraged from searching for work and are classified as economically inactive. Job-search theory suggests that unemployed individuals may choose to withdraw from the labour market and become inactive when the expected value of search activity is lower than the costs associated with undertaking that search. This may be particularly true for older workers, who have less time to reap the benefits of job search than young workers. More specifically, for older workers the discounted value of a wage received until retirement will be lower than the same wage received until retirement for younger workers. Therefore, other things being equal, the older worker is more likely to find that the cost of search exceeds the benefits of search. Evidence presented by Manning and Burdett (1996) suggests that this does happen in the UK. The local labour-force survey indicates that in 2001, Wales had the highest proportion of inactive workers, who 'do not want to work', at nearly 75 per cent compared with 73 per cent for England and 65 per cent for Scotland.

Over the decade, total inactivity rates remained relatively stable as shown in Table 10.3, a pattern replicated in the rest of Britain. Inactivity rates differ by standard statistical region; in 1991 inactivity was highest in Wales, at 26 per cent and lowest in the South East, at 17.5 per cent. In 2002, the rates were 25.3 per cent and 16.6 per cent respectively, showing no tendency for convergence. Areas of high inactivity and unemployment tend to coincide, suggesting inactivity is not solely determined by supply-side factors.

TABLE 10.3
Activity rates

Country	Total activity rates (%)		Male activity rates (%)		Female activity rates (%)	
	August 1992	August 2002	August 1992	August 2002	August 1992	August 2002
Wales	73.6	74.7	80.6	80.3	65.8	68.5
Scotland	79.2	79.6	86.6	83.3	71.3	75.7
England	80.1	79.8	87.9	85.2	71.6	73.8

Source: QLFS, NOMIS.

There are important gender differences in the dynamics of inactivity over time. Between 1991 and 2002 male inactivity rose across the UK, though by the smallest percentage in Wales. Female inactivity fell during the decade, consistent with increased participation, narrowing the gap in activity rates between genders. Blackaby *et al.* (2001) suggest increased female earnings, improvements in household technology and changes in work preferences contributed to increasing female participation. Both male and female inactivity rates remained above the UK average in August 2002, at 19.7 per cent and 31.5 per cent respectively.

Inactivity in Wales exceeds the British average in each of the 16 to 24, 25 to 49 and 50 year-old to retirement-age groups. In the 16 to 24 year-old group, inactivity rose by 12 per cent in Wales, whereas for Britain the rate remained fairly stable. Higher inactivity rates in Wales are also partly attributable to higher participation rates in full-time education amongst 16 to 19 year olds. In contrast, inactivity in the 25 to 49 year-old age group fell within Wales to 17.1 per cent, bringing it closer to the rate in England of 15 per cent, which was also relatively stable over the period. Inactivity rates for the 50 year-old to retirement age-group, although declining over the period, were substantially above rates for the UK as a whole, at 37.7 per cent compared with 29 per cent, in August 2002.

The level of inactivity varies between unitary authorities in Wales. In May 1994, the percentage of working-age people classified as inactive was highest in Rhondda Cynon Taff at 37.1 per cent and lowest in Powys at 14.6 per cent. In May 2002, inactivity varied between 13.6 per cent in the Vale of Glamorgan and 41.2 per cent in Ceredigion. Thus, intra-regional inactivity has shown no tendency to converge over the decade. Although for Wales as a whole total inactivity remained relatively stable through the 1990s, unitary authorities experience greater variability over time. For example, Torfaen exhibited a 40 per cent rise and the Vale of Glamorgan a 40 per cent fall between May 1994 and May 2002. Activity rates are consistently higher in the areas eligible for Objective 3 area as shown in Table 10.4. Between, 1996 and 2000, the level of economic activity rose in the Objective 3 area, but fell slightly in the Objective 1 area. In contrast, between 2000 and 2002 the number economically active fell in the Objective 3 area, but not in the Objective 1 area.

TABLE **10.4**
Economic activity in different European Objective funding areas.
Economic activity in Wales

Area		1996	1997	1998	1999	2000	2001	2002	% change 1996–2000	% change 2000–2
Objective 1	Number									
	('000s)	797	800	790	816	791	777	798	–0.75	0.88
	Rate	72.4	72.7	72.0	73.2	71.6	71.0	71.5	–1.10	–0.14
Objective 3	Number									
	('000s)	473	491	479	481	510	520	489	7.82	–4.12
	Rate	75.9	78.0	75.0	76.7	79.0	78.0	75.1	4.08	–4.94

Source: QLFS, NOMIS. All data refer to the quarter ending in February of each year.

EMPLOYMENT STRUCTURE

Since the late 1970s, one of the defining characteristics of the Welsh economy has been a structural change away from heavy industries, such as coalmining and steel production, toward a more service-based economy. In 1992, almost a quarter of million people, one in five of the working population, were employed in manufacturing, but by 2002, this had fallen to 210,000 people or 16 per cent of the workforce. Conversely, over the same period, the number employed in the service sector increased by 130,000 to 913,000, with the largest part of this rise taking place in the public administration sector, where 88,000 more people are employed now than a decade ago. In 2002, Wales had a higher proportion of the workforce employed in public administration than the rest of Britain (31 per cent compared with 24 per cent in England and 28 per cent in Scotland). In contrast, despite a rise of 26,000 employees over the decade, the proportion in banking and finance, a high wage industry, remains low at 9 per cent, compared with the British average of 16 per cent.

A notable feature of the Welsh economy has been its ability to attract investment from overseas. At the turn of the millennium, nearly 74,000

TABLE **10.5a**
Occupational structure of employment in the UK (%s)

Occupational group (SOC90)	August 1992			August 1996			August 2000		
	England	Scotland	Wales	England	Scotland	Wales	England	Scotland	Wales
Managers & administrators	15.6	12.0	15.7	16.1	12.8	15.4	16.5	14.2	13.5
Professional	9.9	9.8	8.8	10.5	10.3	8.6	10.9	10.3	10.6
Associate professional & technical	9.1	8.7	7.8	9.7	9.9	8.7	10.9	10.1	9.3
Clerical	15.6	14.1	14.0	15.0	14.4	12.6	14.7	14.4	14.4
Craft & related	13.8	14.9	13.3	12.3	13.0	13.2	11.6	12.1	12.4
Personal & protective services	9.7	10.2	10.9	10.7	11.7	11.6	10.8	12.1	11.1
Selling	7.8	8.1	7.4	7.8	8.3	8.6	8.2	8.7	8.2
Plant & machine operative	9.2	10.1	11.1	9.4	9.5	11.1	8.6	8.8	11.0
Other occupations	8.7	11.3	10.4	8.0	9.6	9.6	7.4	9.0	9.1

Source: QLFS NOMIS

TABLE **10.5b**
Occupational structure of employment in the UK (%s)

Occupational group (SOC2000)	August 2002		
	England	Scotland	Wales
Managers & senior officials	14.7	12.4	11.2
Professional	11.5	12.1	12.2
Associate professional & technical	13.7	12.8	12.6
Administrative and secretarial	13.2	13.2	11.2
Skilled trades	11.5	12.2	13.5
Personal service	7.1	7.2	8.0
Sales and customer service	7.7	8.2	9.1
Process, plant & machine operatives	8.2	8.6	9.6
Employment in elementary occupations	12.1	12.9	12.5

Source: QLFS, NOMIS.

people were employed in the 356 foreign-owned manufacturing plants in Wales, representing a third of the manufacturing workforce (National Assembly for Wales, 2000a). In 2000, just under 11 per cent of the workforce in Wales (135,000 people), were employed in hi-tech industries, with 8 per cent in hi-tech manufacturing and 3 per cent in hi-tech services (National Assembly for Wales, 2000b). This compared with a total of 14 per cent in Germany, 13 per cent in Sweden and the UK average of 12 per cent.

The occupational structure of employment in Wales has also changed in the last decade as evidenced by the information in Tables 10.5a and 10.5b. There are 4,000 fewer workers in unskilled occupations and 18,000 fewer in clerical occupations, though the percentage share of clerical jobs has risen slightly. In contrast, there are 38,000 more professionals and 28,000 more associate professionals than a decade ago. A corollary of this is that, by 2002, Wales had a higher proportion of both professional and unskilled workers than the rest of the UK, but a smaller proportion of employees in managerial or senior administrative roles.

In 1992, 61 per cent of people aged between 16 and 24 in Wales were in employment, lower than the corresponding rates for England (62 per cent) and Scotland (64 per cent). This difference is partly due to the higher participation rates in further education in Wales noted earlier. Over the decade, the employment rate in this group fell more quickly in Wales than the rest of the UK, resulting in wider differences by 2001, when the corresponding figures were 53 per cent for Wales, 62 per cent for England and 63 per cent for Scotland.[3] During the 1990s, employment in the 25 to 49 year-old group increased in all countries, but the regional differences remained in 2001. In 1992 in Wales, 75 per cent of this group were employed, compared to 78 per cent in England and 77 per cent in Scotland. In 2001 the corresponding figures were 78 per cent, 82 per cent and 80 per cent. The proportion of people aged over 50 years in employment is significantly less than for the other age groups. However, over the period, this proportion rose, by around 15 per cent in all areas. Again, Wales had the lowest figures throughout the decade, at 27 per cent in 1992 and 31 per cent in 2001, compared with 32 per cent and 37 per cent for England and 31 per cent and 33 per cent in Scotland. Even though employment rates were lower in this group, the concentration of population aged over 50 in Wales meant that, in 2001, Wales had the highest proportion of its workforce aged over 50 in Britain. Moreover, population projections suggest that by 2005 approximately 50 per cent of the working-age population in Wales will be over the age of 40.

The proportion of working-age females in employment was lower than males, for all countries over the entire decade. In Wales in 1992, 72 per cent of males were employed and 63 per cent of females; the corresponding figures for 2001 were 74 per cent and 63 per cent (below the rates for England). The proportion of females in total employment has been relatively stable over the period, at around 44 per cent for Wales and England. However, differences between sectors emerged: in the first quarter of 2002 19 per cent of working males were employed in the public sector and for working females the figure was 39 per cent. Indeed, since 1994 women in Wales have become increasingly reliant on the public sector for employment.

The ratio of full-time to part-time workers, for both the UK and Wales, has been fairly consistent throughout the decade at three to one. However, substantial gender differences remained. In 2001, 51 per cent of females worked part-time compared to only 15 per cent of males (ONS, 2001). O'Leary *et al.* (2002) suggest that increased demand in female-dominated sectors has resulted in the growth in the number of part-time jobs, to attract women with family commitments.

It has been suggested that one of the reasons for the lower GDP and employment rate in Wales is the lack of entrepreneurial spirit. Wales has a lower business start-up rate than the rest of the UK and the European average. However, as a proportion of total employment, the rate of self-employment in Wales is similar to that in England, at around 12 per cent, and higher than the rate in Scotland (10 per cent). A decade ago Wales was the leader in the UK, with 14 per cent of all employed workers being self-employed compared with 13 per cent in England and 9 per cent in Scotland. There are gender differences in self-employment rates, with working men twice as likely to work for themselves as working women, throughout the UK.

In 1993, employment rates ranged from 59.5 per cent in Bridgend to 80.6 per cent in Powys. By 2001 Ceredigion had the lowest employment rate, at 55.6 per cent, and Monmouthshire the highest, at 77.3 per cent. Employment in the Objective 3 area, in both 1993 (70.6 per cent) and 2001 (73 per cent), is higher than similar figures for the Objective 1 area (64.5 per cent and 67.3 per cent). [4]

In November 1993, Neath and Port Talbot had the lowest ratio in Wales of self-employed workers to total workers at 3 per cent. At the other extreme, 43.9 per cent of workers in Powys were self-employed. By May 2002, Bridgend had the lowest proportion of self-employed workers (4.4 per cent), and Powys still had the highest with 27.4 per cent. Between 1993 and 2000, self-employment accounted for a larger proportion of employment in the Objective 1 area than in the Objective 3 area. By August 2002, the proportion in self-employment was 13 per cent in the Objective 3 area and 11 per cent in the Objective 1 area. The proportion of full-time employment also varied, from 83.2 per cent in Caerphilly to 67 per cent in Conwy in 1993. By 2001, the growth in full-time employment in Conwy meant the rate rose to 82.1 per cent, the highest of any unitary authority in Wales; whilst a decline in Pembrokeshire resulted in only 67 per cent being employed full-time. Employment comprises a slightly greater amount of full-time work in the Objective 3 area (75 per cent compared with 73.4 per cent in the Objective 1 area in 2001), and this remained relatively stable over time. The Objective 3 area had greater proportions employed in managerial, professional, and associate professional and technical groups. In contrast, employment is concentrated more in craft, plant- and machine-operative, and unskilled groups in the Objective 1 area.

EARNINGS

In 2001, employees in Wales had the lowest average (mean) gross weekly earnings for full-time workers in Britain. The low average is the result of both a high proportion at the bottom end of the pay distribution and a low proportion at the upper end of the pay distribution. In Wales, 26.5 per cent of workers earned less than £250 per week and only 27 per cent earned more than £460, the corresponding figures for England being 19.8 per cent and 34.8 per cent. Between 1997 and 2001, average earnings rose in Great Britain by 20.9 per cent but the growth was slowest in Wales, at 15.7 per cent.

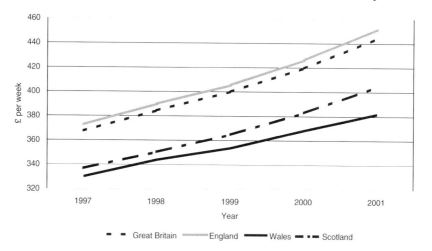

Source: NES Office for National Statistics.

Figure 10.1
Average weekly earnings in Great Britain 1997–2001 – all workers

Therefore, average earnings in Wales exhibited no tendency to converge with the UK as illustrated in Figure 10.1 and are consistent with the findings of Cameron *et al.* (2002), who, for the period 1975 and 1995, identify a decline in relative earnings in Wales. Low earnings may contribute to a high level of inactivity since they reduce the incentive to seek employment.

Although nominal wages are lowest in Wales, regional price differences may explain part of this differential. In January 2002 average prices in Wales were estimated to be 3.8 per cent below the UK average (Baran and O'Donoghue, 2002). The nominal average wages discussed above can be adjusted using the relative price-levels to calculate real wages. In 2001, average nominal earnings in Wales were £382, 14 per cent below the UK average of £442. When price-level differences are taken into account the real earnings differential is reduced to 10 per cent.

Over time, earnings inequality in Wales has narrowed slightly, in contrast to the widening earnings inequality in Britain for the period 1975–96 identified by Dickey (2001). Part of the decreasing wage inequality may be due to introduction of the minimum wage, since low-paid workers are over-represented in Wales and thus the effect on the distribution of earnings may be greater in Wales. Robinson (2001) reports that the proportion of low-paid men fell by 64 per cent in Wales between 1998 and 1999, similarly by 45 per cent for females, exceeding national effects.

A number of factors may contribute to Wales's lower average earnings than the rest of the UK. One set of explanations focuses on the occupational structure of the Welsh labour market, notably the relative dearth of well-paying, senior managerial and administrative posts compared to the rest of the UK. Moreover, public sector employment, which is relatively important in Wales, is associated with a compressed earnings distribution (Blackaby *et al.*, 1999). Human capital theory suggests that the wages of an individual depend on their educational attainments and accumulated work experience. It was noted above that Welsh workers have lower educational attainments than do workers in the rest of the UK. Moreover, individuals who do have high qualifications are often attracted out of Wales to places where there are more suitable employment opportunities (Forsythe, 1995).

Average weekly earnings for full-time workers differ considerably by gender throughout the UK, with the female average consistently below the male. In 2002, average female earnings in Wales were £345 per week, £88 less than the male average. The 25 per cent raw wage gap is lower than in either Scotland or England. Blackaby *et al.* (2001) suggest that between a quarter and a half of the raw gender pay-gap in Wales may be due to discrimination;

however, the under-representation of women at senior levels is also important (Blackaby *et al.*, 1999). In 1997, average earnings were lowest in Conwy, at £284, and highest in Neath and Port Talbot, at £351. In 2001, Flintshire had the highest mean average earnings, at £421, just above Neath and Port Talbot (£417), and Conwy still exhibited the lowest average, at £326. The high average wage in Neath and Port Talbot in part reflects the concentration of employment in manufacturing. The decline of manufacturing with relatively high-paid jobs (for example Corus) is a concern to the whole economy, but since the effects are spatially concentrated, sub-regional disparities may widen. In 1999, the average earnings in the non-Objective 1 area were £313, substantially higher than the £289 average in the Objective 1 area. Although average earnings have risen, in 2002 the gap remains, with similar figures of £356 and £320 respectively. [5]

UNIONIZATION

In 2001, the labour-force survey reported that 35 per cent of workers in Wales belonged to a trade union or staff association, a higher proportion than any other region in Britain. The corresponding rates were 25 per cent for England and 33 per cent for Scotland. Union membership has declined over time, particularly for males. For example in 1994, around 40 per cent workers in Wales were union members. The effect on earnings may depend on union recognition rather than membership; individuals who are not union members may be covered by collective agreements. In 2001, the percentage affected by union pay agreements in Wales (41.6 per cent for males and 41.5 per cent for females) is higher than in England (32.8 per cent and 34.9 per cent), but similar to Scotland (41.6 per cent and 45.5 per cent). The decline in union membership has coincided with a fall in union militancy. In 1990, there were 85 days lost per 1,000 employees because of industrial stoppages, this fell to 6 days per 1,000 employees in 2000. These members are almost insignificant compared to the early 1980s when 2,903 days were lost per 1,000 employees (National Assembly for Wales, 2002b).

VACANCIES

Vacancy statistics are based on administration information supplied by job centres. The basic count used indicates the current number of unfilled vacancies that have been notified by employers. [6] There are several reasons why regional vacancy statistics may be less reliable than other labour-market indicators. The most serious drawback is that not all vacancies are notified to job centres; many are advertised by different means. Another complication is that vacancies are allocated to job centres, which may not coincide with the area where the vacancy occurs.

TABLE **10.6**
Number of vacancies by country

| | Vacancies notified to job centres 1991–2000 | | |
	1991 average	2000 average	% change
Wales	10,640	13,070	+22.84
Scotland	21,396	25,527	+19.31
England	136,226	183,890	+34.99
GB	168,262	222,487	+32.23

Source: NOMIS.

As illustrated by Table 10.6, between 1991 and 2001 there was an increase in the number of vacancies notified to job centres. In Wales the number of vacancies increased by 20 per cent over the period, less than the corresponding figures in England. The type of vacancy also differs between countries with the per centage of full-time vacancies in Wales is less than England or Scotland throughout the period. In July 2000, full-time vacancies represented 63.6 per cent of all vacancies in Wales but 69.8 per cent in England. Analysis of vacancies by industry shows that, when compared to England, the proportion of vacancies in manufacturing and particularly in public administration, education and health was greater in Wales. In April 2001, the proportion of vacancies in public administration, education and health in Wales (29.6 per cent) was double that of England (14.2 per cent). A similar breakdown by occupation reveals a higher proportion of vacancies in personal/protective services in Wales (21.3 per cent in October 2002), but a lower proportion of vacancies in distribution, hotels and restaurants and financial services. The structure of vacancies indicates a continuation of the trends identified in the employment structure, a higher concentration in the public sector at the expense of sectors such as banking and finance compared with the rest of the UK. Vacancies are distributed unevenly across Wales. WEFO (2001) notes that there are 'hot-spots', notably in east Wales, where filling vacancies appears to be a significant problem for certain employers. The localized nature of labour markets, together with a degree of geographical immobility of labour, means that labour shortages could constrain the growth of certain areas.

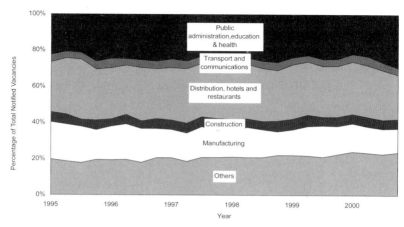

Source: NOMIS.

FIGURE 10.2
Notified vacancies in Wales, by industry, 1995–2001

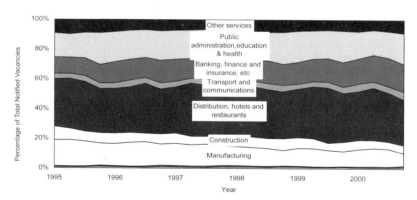

Source: NOMIS.

FIGURE 10.3
Notified vacancies in Great Britain, by industry, 1995–2001

UNEMPLOYMENT

According to the claimant-count measure of unemployment, in September 2002 there were 46,400 people unemployed in Wales, representing 3.6 per cent of the workforce.[7] Claimant-count unemployment has gradually fallen, from over 10 per cent at the trough of the last recession, to be lower in 2002 than at any other time in the last quarter of a century. The International Labour Organization (ILO) measure of unemployment provides an unemployment rate in Wales of 5.3 per cent, which equates to over 71,000 people. Figure 10.4 illustrates that the ILO measure has been almost uniformly higher than the claimant count over the last decade, and that the gap between the two measures has grown from less than one percentage point in the early 1990s to two percentage points around the turn of the millennium.

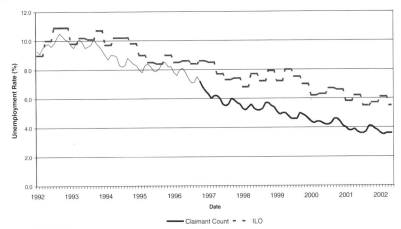

Source: NOMIS.

FIGURE 10.4
Claimant count and ILO unemployment in Wales, 1992–2002

Typically, three age categories are considered when looking at the age profile of unemployment – 16–24, 25–44 and over 45. The proportion of the unemployed who are aged between 16 and 24 has fallen since 1991 throughout the UK, but by a smaller per centage in Wales. Thus, relative to the UK, claimant-count unemployment in Wales has become more concentrated in the 16–24 age-group – 31.4 per cent in September 2002, compared to 27.4 per cent in England. In contrast, the proportion aged between 25 and 44 has fallen in Wales, whilst remaining fairly stable for Britain as a whole. In Wales this proportion (44.3 per cent in September 2002) remains below England (48 per cent) and Scotland (46.4 per cent). The proportion of the unemployed aged 45 or over in Wales rose from 17.6 per cent in January 1991 to 24.7 per cent in January 2002. The increase in Wales has been greater than in the rest of the UK, contributing to convergence in the proportion unemployed in the eldest group among countries within the UK.

Figure 10.5 shows that throughout the 1990s, the male unemployment rate exceeded its female counterpart, a feature common to the rest of the UK. For example, in Wales the male unemployment rate was 10.6 per cent in January 1991, more than double the female rate of 4.0 per cent. Similar to other parts of the UK, total unemployment has halved over the period, but female unemployment has experienced a slightly greater decline than its male counterpart (falling to 6 per cent for males and 1.9 per cent for females, respectively, in January 2002). Thus, unemployment gender differentials have increased slightly in Wales, similar to England and Scotland. However, the gender difference in unemployment rates is greater in Wales throughout the period (the ratio of male to female unemployment was 3.16 in Wales, 2.65 in England and 2.95 in Scotland in January 2002). Part of the explanation for the unemployment differential may lie with structural changes mentioned earlier, notably the decline in manufacturing industry, traditionally associated with male employment, and the rise in employment in the services sector, where females have greater representation.

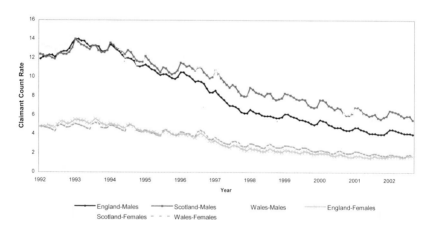

Source: NOMIS.

FIGURE 10.5
Gender differences in claimant count unemployment in the UK, 1992–2002

The problem of long-term unemployment has received a great deal of attention because of the costs associated with having individuals without work for long periods. Unemployed workers are unproductive and this represents a waste of scarce resources. Paying welfare benefits is a burden on taxpayers. Bivand (2001) estimates that the cost to the Treasury (and therefore ultimately the tax payer) is over £10,000 per unemployed person per year. Moreover, long-term unemployment may be self-perpetuating because human capital might depreciate whilst the worker is unemployed (see Roed, 1997, for an overview). Of the 46,000 people unemployed in Wales in September 2002, 30 per cent had been without work for over six months and just under half of these had been unemployed for over a year. These proportions are broadly similar to those for the rest of the UK. However, they have changed dramatically over time. In the ten years up to the summer of 1997, typically half of the unemployed had been without work for over six months and half of these again were unemployed for over a year, the actual proportions varying counter-cyclically. The proportion of the workforce who are long-term unemployed (for more than twelve months) has been declining throughout the UK since 1992. After 1992 and up to the end of 1996, the proportion of long-term unemployed declined faster in Wales than in the rest of the UK. From 1997 onwards, although the proportion continued to fall, it did so more slowly, so that the rest of the regions in the UK were able to 'catch up', giving the similarity of long-term unemployment rates currently observed. It should be noted that extended spells of unemployment might have beneficial effects. Individuals may voluntarily choose jobs that are characterized by frequent lay-offs but have an associated compensating wage-differential (Feldstein, 1978). Alternatively, extended periods of job search lead to more efficient matching, so that workers are able to find jobs in which they are more productive and receive higher wages (Alchian, 1969; Boheim and Taylor, 2002).

Except for brief periods in 1993 and 1994, the unemployment rate in Wales has been higher than that in the rest of the UK, especially England, for the last two decades. This is consistent with the analyses of Brown and Sessions (1997) who find, after controlling for many demographic characteristics, there are significant regional disparities in unemployment risk, with individuals in areas such as Wales facing a higher risk of unemployment, all else being equal. In the 1990s the gap narrowed considerably, reflecting a convergence in unemployment rates across the UK, continuing the trend identified after the recession of the early 1990s (Evans and McCormick, 1994). For example, in late 2002, unemployment rates in the UK ranged from 5 per cent in the North East to 1.7 per cent in the South East. In the late 1980s, the differential between these two regions was over 8 percentage points, though with higher absolute levels of unemployment. At the time of writing, only the South East, Eastern England and the East Midlands have lower claimant-count unemployment rates than Wales. The unemployment rate in Wales has tended to be similar to that in Scotland, with the difference between the claimant-count rates in the two countries not exceeding one percentage point over the last decade.

The convergence of regional unemployment across the UK has raised the significance of intra-regional differences. The unemployment claimant count is reported by Unitary Authority areas within Wales for males, females and overall in Table 10.7. Unemployment in each unitary authority exhibits a downward trend from 1996, as identified for Wales as a whole. However, the percentage fall in unemployment differs between areas, and substantial intra-regional differences remain. Unemployment is prevalent in three main areas: the former mining and steelmaking areas in the south Wales valleys, rural west Wales and north-west Wales. In contrast, urban centres such as Cardiff, commuter areas such as the Vale of Glamorgan and areas neighbouring England (such as Flintshire, Wrexham, Powys and Monmouthshire) have lower claimant-count unemployment rates. In 1996, for example, the male unemployment rate ranged between 17 per cent in Blaenau Gwent and 5.6 per cent in Powys, whereas in 2002 the corresponding figures were 10.2 per cent and 2.6 per cent for the same areas, indicating persistence in the relative position of areas. Indeed, Blaenau Gwent, the area with the highest unemployment rate, exhibited the smallest percentage decrease in unemployment from 1991 to 2002, for both males and females. Intra-regional dispersion was also evident for females, but to a lesser extent. Anglesey had the highest female claimant count rate, 7 per cent in 1996 and 3.6 per cent in 2002. In 1996, Torfaen had the lowest unemployment at 2.8 per cent, but by 2002 the relative positions changed, with Monmouthshire having the lowest claimant count rate of 1.1 per cent. The figures confirm a continuation of an east/west divide identified in the 1980s by Morris and Wilkinson (1989, 1993) and more recently discussed, with respect to north Wales, by Minford and Stoney (2001). In 2002, unemployment rates in Anglesey, Gwynedd, Pembrokeshire and Carmarthenshire all exceeded the Welsh average, with Flintshire, Wrexham, Powys and Monmouthshire below it. Location, particularly distance from and access to large urban markets and infrastructural endowments, seems to be important in determining the investment decisions of companies and thus economic success of areas.

Growth in south Wales, particularly in Cardiff, has been concentrated along the M4, which has attracted significant inward investment. In north Wales, growth again stems from the east (along the A55), resulting in lower unemployment and higher GDP in these areas.

TABLE **10.7**
Unemployment by unitary authority

	Total unemployment claimant-count year averages for unitary authorities in Wales					% number change 1991–2002	% rate change 1996–2002
	1991 Number	1996 Number	%	2002 Number	%		
Anglesey	3326	3182	12.5	1629	6.6	–51.02	–47.20
Blaenau Gwent	3137	2889	12.7	1768	7.2	–43.64	–43.31
Bridgend	5466	3775	6.8	1887	3.5	–65.48	–48.53
Caerphilly	7180	6288	11.3	3017	5.1	–57.98	–54.87
Cardiff	13761	12756	7.0	5522	2.9	–59.87	–58.57
Carmarthenshire	5700	5459	7.1	2651	4.5	–53.49	–36.62
Ceredigion	1887	2011	5.9	900	2.7	–52.31	–54.24
Conwy	3467	3929	8.2	1684	3.8	–51.43	–53.66
Denbighshire	2971	3217	7.5	1230	2.8	–58.60	–62.67
Flintshire	3938	3884	5.9	1861	2.6	–52.74	–55.93
Gwynedd	5021	5383	9.3	2413	4.6	–51.94	–50.54
Merthyr Tydfil	2895	2521	11.0	1217	5.8	–57.96	–47.27
Monmouthshire	2229	2124	5.7	885	2.2	–60.30	–61.40
Neath Port Talbot	4857	4280	7.7	2408	4.9	–50.42	–36.36
Newport	6440	5762	8.5	2936	3.6	–54.41	–57.65
Pembrokeshire	4960	5083	10.9	2290	5.3	–53.83	–51.38
Powys	2919	2665	4.4	1380	2.1	–52.72	–52.27
Rhondda Cynon Taff	10722	8331	9.5	3618	4.3	–66.26	–54.74
Swansea	9660	8089	8.1	4066	3.9	–57.91	–51.85
Torfaen	4000	3071	6.0	1509	3.7	–62.28	–38.33
Vale of Glamorgan	4279	4120	8.2	1930	3.8	–54.90	–53.66
Wrexham	4355	3848	6.5	1696	2.8	–61.06	–56.92

Note: The rate change could be calculated only from 1996. Figures are based on an average of the monthly observations.

The housing market has also been found to contribute to regional unemployment disparities because of its influence on labour mobility (Henley, 1998). Economic theory postulates that if labour is perfectly mobile, then differences in unemployment rates between areas should result in workers in the high unemployment areas looking for work in the low unemployment areas. Thus, with perfect labour mobility, regional disparities in unemployment rates should be only a temporary phenomenon. However, council housing and other forms of social housing can impede the geographical mobility of labour by 'locking' council-house tenants into the labour market in their immediate travel-to-work area. This can be accentuated by subsidized rents in the social housing sector, that make council-house tenants reluctant to move to find work in another locality (Hughes and McCormick, 1981). In 2001, almost one-fifth of the housing stock in Wales was rented from local authorities, new-town corporations or registered social landlords, similar to the proportion in 1991, though very different from 1981 when the figure was almost 30 per cent (National Assembly for Wales, 2001b). Higher concentrations of social housing are associated with high unemployment areas. For example, in Blaenau Gwent 30 per cent of dwellings are socially owned. Similarly in Torfaen the figure is 28 per cent, and in Merthyr Tydfil, 26 per cent. In contrast, low unemployment areas such as the Vale of Glamorgan, Ceredigion and Monmouthshire have low concentrations of social housing (13 per cent, 11 per cent and 15 per cent respectively). The growth of owner occupation and associated increased transaction costs when moving, limits search location and increases commuting distances (Oswald, 1996). Migration between areas within Wales and between Wales and the rest of the UK is hindered by house-price differentials. For example, between April and June 2002 the average price of a house in Cardiff was £111,083, compared with £41,726 in Blaenau Gwent.[8]

The monetary and personal costs associated with commuting mean the majority of people work within the local authority where they reside. For example, in 2001, 73 per cent of all working residents in Wales worked and resided in the same local authority. Cardiff had the largest net commuting inflow (42,000) with the majority of the corresponding gross inflows coming from the surrounding areas of the Vale of Glamorgan (19,000), Rhondda Cynon Taff (17,000) and Caerphilly (12,000). Areas near England also had large net outflows of workers, with 18 per cent of workers from Monmouthshire and 26 per cent from Flintshire working outside Wales.

Access to transport is also important in determining the area in which people are able to work. Typically, those living in rural areas have more limited access to public transport. For example, according to the labour-force survey, in Powys only 2.6 per cent use public transport to get to work, compared to 16.5 per cent in Cardiff and 14.6 per cent in Newport. Compared with those in England, people in Wales are more heavily dependent on car transport to get to work, with 77.9 per cent of people in Wales travelling to work by car, in 2001, compared with 69.3 per cent in England. Access to a car is higher in low unemployment areas. For example, in 1991, 43 per cent of households had no car in Merthyr Tydfil and Blaenau Gwent, compared with 21 per cent in Monmouthshire (National Assembly for Wales, 2002c). As with many other social problems associated with unemployment, there is a question over the direction of causation. For example, are workers unemployed because they lack access to cars or do they not have access to cars because they are unemployed?

The Objective 1 area has a higher unemployment rate than the Objective 3 area. In January 1996 the unemployment rate for the Objective 1 area was 9.3 per cent, compared with 7.3 per cent in the non-Objective 1 area. Since then the rates have fallen in both areas, so that by January 2002 the respective figures were 4.8 per cent and 3.0 per cent. Unemployment fell proportionally more in the non-Objective 1 area until 2000, since when the Objective 1 area has experienced a faster decrease in the unemployment rate. These results are in line with the improvement in economic activity in the Objective 1 area after 2000. Since 2000, the Objective 1 area has out-performed the Objective 3 area, in that unemployment and inactivity have fallen more quickly, a reversal of trends in the end of the last century.

The proportion classified as long-term unemployed, that is unemployed for more than a year, also exhibits geographical variations. In 1991, Merthyr Tydfil had the highest proportion of long-term unemployed, with one in three of unemployed men being unemployed for over twelve months. Powys had the lowest proportion in long-term unemployment (14.4 per cent). By 2002, the situation had changed considerably; Anglesey had the largest proportion (38.7 per cent) and Rhondda Cynon Taff the lowest (9.8 per cent). For females, the long-term unemployment rate was highest in Anglesey in both 1991 and 2002. In 1991 Powys had the lowest proportion of females in long-term unemployment, but in 2002 this changed to Wrexham. Unlike unemployment, which fell over the period for all areas, the proportion of males in long-term unemployment rose in seven, predomin-antly rural areas, where long-term unemployment, although reduced since the early recession, was still above its 1991 level. In contrast, areas such as Rhondda Cynon Taff, Caerphilly, Cardiff and Merthyr Tydfil experienced substantial falls in the proportion of long-term unemployed (between 45 and 65 per cent). The most significant change for all areas over the period is the rise in the proportion of unemployed aged 45 or above. Significant intra-regional differences emerge, with particularly high unemployment growth rates for males in the previously heavily industrialized areas of Merthyr Tydfil (71.03 per cent) and Neath and Port Talbot (63.57 per cent). However, for females, the greatest rise is experienced in the rural areas of Anglesey,

Monmouthshire and Ceredigion. It is these rural areas that have the largest proportions of unemployed aged 45 or above, consistent with the decline of agriculture, combined with geographical and occupational immobility of labour.

Traditionally, policy-makers have been concerned with high levels of unemployment amongst young people, because the usual costs of unemployment are accentuated by the detrimental impact on future labour-market prospects (Gregg, 2001). There has been a 67 per cent fall in youth Job Seeker Allowance claimants since the launch of the New Deal programmes in Wales. Since its launch, 24,800 young Welsh people have secured jobs through the New Deal and 80 per cent of those have retained their jobs for thirteen weeks or more (Hansard, 2002). The New Deal may also have had beneficial effects for other groups. For example, between July 1998 and March 2002, 24,700 long-term unemployed people joined the New Deal scheme. Of these, 2,400 were still participating at the end of June 2002, whilst 6,300 secured jobs, either on or when leaving, any stage of the New Deal process. This included 5,300 (84 per cent) who had entered jobs that lasted for at least thirteen weeks. In October 1998, the New Deal was extended to lone parents, and by June 2002 the uptake reached 23,700. Half of these (11,900) had gained employment since joining the programme. Of course, those who found jobs after participating in the New Deal might have found work anyway (the deadweight effect). Furthermore, the recruitment of New Deal participants may be at the expense of people employers would have recruited anyway (substitution effect) or may be at the expense of workers already in the firm (displacement effects).

Falling unemployment and regional unemployment convergence suggest labour-market conditions have improved over the decade. However, recently, some authors have criticized the definitions of unemployment, arguing that joblessness remains, but has become 'hidden', undetected by traditional measures (Beatty *et al.*, 2000). The fall in male unemployment has coincided with an increase in male inactivity, particularly among those classified as 'long-term sick'. Wales contains both former coalfields and disadvantaged rural areas, where UK studies have found unemployment has been reduced as a consequence of rising inactivity (Fothergill, 2001; Beatty and Fothergill, 1996, 1997 and 2002). Beatty *et al.* (2002) suggest hidden unemployment is particularly severe in the Welsh Valleys, where the 'real' unemployment rate is estimated to exceed 20 per cent (Merthyr Tydfil has the highest level of 'real' unemployment at 28.2 per cent), compared with figures of around 3 per cent in South East England.[9] Indeed, for Wales as a whole the 'real' unemployment rate was estimated at 13.3 per cent in January 2002, more than double the claimant-count rate for the same period.

Other commentators have highlighted the emergence of a grey area around the traditional labour market, in which workers are not fully integrated into employment and yet are not economically inactive; for example, government training schemes (Peck, 1990), informal work (Gershuny, 1979), home-working, hidden or underground work (Finnegan, 1985) or work which is not recognized or unpaid (Morris, 1988). However, measuring the 'black economy' is notoriously difficult and warrants more detailed research.

SUMMARY AND CONCLUSIONS

The 1990s have witnessed an improvement in labour-market performance in Wales and the rest of the UK, driven by an upswing in the wider economy. A number of indicators suggest that Wales still performs badly compared with the rest of the UK. Regional convergence has been identified in unemployment rates. However, these measures have been criticized on the grounds that increases in inactivity and 'hidden' unemployment in Wales may disguise the real level of unemployment and that substantial regional differentials remain (Beatty *et al.*, 2002).

Several main areas of concern for Wales are highlighted in this article. Inactivity remains a serious problem in Wales, having shown no tendency to fall to UK levels. The concentration of inactivity in previously high unemployment areas suggests hysteresis effects may be important.[10] The concentration of inactivity within certain groups, particularly the over 50s and the unskilled, and its spatial concentration (O'Leary *et al.*, 2002), suggest barriers to activity specific to these groups.

In addition, theory suggests that activity levels depend on earnings. The recent trend in average earnings is a matter of particular concern. Average earnings in Wales have actually fallen relative to the UK, thereby increasing the regional wage-gap. This may result from differences in employment structure, for example Wales has a far lower proportion employed in banking and finance, a high-wage industry (see Blackaby *et al.*, 2001, for further earnings breakdowns). However, earnings for the same job may differ across regions, and more detailed investigation is required.

Equally important is the existence of disparities within Wales. The relative position of different areas in Wales shows remarkable consistency over the range of labour-market indicators. High unemployment and inactivity coexist with low levels of education and earnings, contributing to socio-economic divisions within the Welsh economy. These indicators are clearly interlinked; improvements in education may increase activity, employment and earnings; policy initiatives must take this into account.

The poor performance of some areas in Wales, such as Merthyr Tydfil, which has the highest real unemployment rate in the UK (Beatty *et al.*, 2002), is a cause for concern. Attention has focused on industrial decline, particularly in the south Wales valleys, however further divisions are evident. In particular, an east–west division has emerged, with unitary authorities in east Wales performing relatively better than those in the west. The key issue is the extent to which gaps in labour-market performance, both within Wales and across the UK, are likely to change through policy initiatives and Objective 1 schemes.

NOTES

1. The figures for the Objective 1 area were obtained by aggregating data from the following unitary authorities: Isle of Anglesey, Blaenau Gwent, Bridgend, Caerphilly, Carmarthenshire, Ceredigion, Conwy, Denbighshire, Gwynedd, Merthyr Tydfil, Neath and Port Talbot, Pembrokeshire, Rhondda Cynon Taff, Swansea and Torfaen. The following unitary authorities comprise the Objective 3 area: Flintshire, Wrexham, Powys, Monmouthshire, Newport, Cardiff and the Vale of Glamorgan.
2. Inactivity rates are expressed as a percentage of the total population of interest, and not of the working population, as is unemployment.
3. All figures refer to the quarter ending in May of that year.
4. All data refer to the quarter ending in November of that year.
5. The figures for the Objective 1 area were obtained from NOMIS and are not comparable with the *NES* from ONS.
6. The vacancy data were published by ONS until April 2001, but figures after this date are not available due to the introduction of Employer Direct by Jobcentre Plus, which transferred vacancy notification from local to regional level.
7. Wholly unemployed claimants, workforce base estimates. *Source*: NOMIS.
8. Data from Proviser, *http://www.proviser.com/property_prices/*
9. The real unemployment rate is estimated by including those on government schemes, early retirees and sickness claimants, compared to fully-employed benchmarks in the South East.
10. The hysteresis paradigm suggests that short-run variations in labour market conditions can have permanent effects (see Cross, 1988, for an overview).

REFERENCES

Alchian, A. A. (1969). 'Information costs, pricing and resource utilization', *Western Economic Journal*, 7 (2), 109–28.

Baran, D. and O'Donoghue, J. (2002). 'Price levels in 2000 for London and the regions compared with the national average', *Economic Trends*, 578.

Basic Skills Agency (2001). *The Extent of the Problem: Basic Skills in Wales.*

Beatty, C., and Fothergill, S. (1996). 'Labour-market adjustment in areas of chronic industrial decline: the case of the UK coalfields', *Regional Studies*, 30, 627–40.

Beatty, C., and Fothergill, S. (1997). 'Unemployment and the labour market in rural development areas', *Rural Research Series*, 30, London: Rural Development Commission.

Beatty, C., and Fothergill, S., (2002). 'Hidden unemployment among men: a case study', *Regional Studies*, 36 (8), 811–23.

Beatty, C., Fothergill, S., and Macmillan, R. (2000). 'A theory of employment, unemployment and sickness', *Regional Studies*, 34 (7), 617–30.

Beatty, C., Fothergill, S., Gore, T., and Green, A. (2002). *The Real Level of Unemployment*, Sheffield: Centre for Regional Economic and Social Research, Sheffield Hallam University.

Bivand, P. (2001). *The Cost of Unemployment*, Unemployment Unit Working Brief 120, January.

Blackaby, D., Charles, N., Davies, C., Murphy, P., O'Leary, N., and Ransome, P. (1999). W*omen in Senior Management in Wales*, Research Discussion Series, Manchester Equal Opportunities Commission, 130.

Blackaby, D., Moore, N., Murphy, P., and O'Leary, N. (2001). *The Gender Pay-Gap in Wales*, Manchester: EOC Research Discussion Series.

Blackaby, D., Murphy P. D., and O'Leary, N. C. (1999). 'The payment of public sector workers in the UK: reconciliation with North American findings', *Economics Letters*, 65 (2), 239–43.

Boheim, R., and Taylor, M. P. (2002). 'The search for success: do the unemployed find stable employment?', *Labour Economics*, 9 (6), 699–20.

Brown, S., and Sessions, J. G. (1997). 'A profile of UK unemployment: regional versus demographic influences', *Regional Studies*, 31 (4), 351–66.

Cameron, G., Muellbauer, J., and Snicker, J. (2002). 'A study in structural change: relative earnings in Wales since the 1970s', *Regional Studies*, 36 (1), 1–11.

Cross, R. (1988). *Unemployment, Hysteresis and the Natural Rate Hypothesis*, Oxford: Blackwell.

Dickey, H. (2001). 'Regional earnings inequality in Great Britain: a decomposition analysis', *Regional Studies*, 35 (7), 605–12.

Evans, P., and McCormick, B. (1994). 'The new pattern of regional unemployment: causes and policy significance', *Economic Journal*, 104, 633–47.

Feldstein, M. S. (1978). 'The effect of unemployment insurance on temporary layoff unemployment', *American Economic Review*, 68, 834–46.

Felstead, A., Gallie, D., and Green, F. (2002). *Work Skills in Britain 1986–2001*, London: DFES and SKOPE.

Fothergill, S. (2001). 'The true scale of the regional problem in the UK', *Regional Studies*, 35 (3), 241–6.

Finnegan, R. (1985). 'Working outside formal employment', in Deem, R. and Salaman, G. (eds), *Work, Culture and Society*, Milton Keynes: Open University Press, 130–49.

Forsythe, F. P. (1995). 'Male joblessness and job search: regional perspectives in the UK, 1981–1993', *Regional Studies*, 29 (5), 453–63.

Future Skills Wales (1998). *Future Skills Wales Project Summary Report for Wales.*

Gershuny, J. (1979). 'The informal economy and its role in post-industrial society', *Futures*, 10, 103–14.

Gregg, P. (2001). 'The impact of youth unemployment on adult unemployment in the NCDS', *Economic Journal*, 111, F626–53.

Hansard (2002). *17 July 2002: Column 319W.*

Henley, A. (1998). 'Residential mobility, housing equity and the labour market', *Economic Journal*, 108, 414–27.

Hughes, G. A., and McCormick, B. (1981). 'Do council house policies reduce migration between regions?', *Economic Journal*, 91, 919–37.

Manning, N., and Burdett, K. (1996). 'Do older workers drop out of the labour market? Some recent British evidence', *Bulletin of Economic Research*, 48 (2), 167–71.

Minford, P., and Stoney, P. (2001). 'The UK and with it Cheshire and North Wales are on a good wicket but will Labour's re-regulation ruin it?', North Wales and Cheshire Business Prospect, *Liverpool Research Group in Macroeconomics*, 7 (1).

Morris, J., and Wilkinson, B. (1989). 'Divided Wales: Local Prosperity in the 1980s', report prepared for HTV Wales, Cardiff Business School.

Morris, J., and Wilkinson, B. (1993). 'Poverty and prosperity in Wales', report prepared for HTV Wales, Cardiff Business School.

Morris, L. (1988). 'Employment, the household and social networks', in Gallie, D. (ed), *Employment in Britain*, Oxford: Basil Blackwell, 376–405.

National Assembly for Wales (2000a). *Welsh Local Area Statistics*, Table 7.7, 'Employment in overseas-owned manufacturing plants, 2000'.

National Assembly for Wales (2000b). *Employment in the Hi-Tech Industries Within the EU, 2000*, National Assembly for Wales Statistical Bulletin 2000.

National Assembly for Wales (2001a). *National Curriculum Assessment Results in Wales – Key Stages 2 and 3.*

National Assembly for Wales (2001b). *Welsh Housing Statistics 2001*, Table 1.3.

National Assembly for Wales (2002a). *National Economic Development Strategy.*

National Assembly for Wales (2002b). *Digest of Welsh Statistics*, Table 7.12, 'Industrial stoppages at work'.

National Assembly of Wales (2002c). *Mapping Social Exclusion in Wales.*

O'Leary, N., Murphy, P., Moore, N., Manning, N., Jones, M., Harris, S., and Blackaby, D. (2002). 'Inactivity and unemployment in Wales and the prosperity gap', Report for the WDA.

ONS (1997). *Adult Literacy in Britain: A Survey of Adults aged 16–65 in Britain*, part of the International Adult Literacy Survey (IALS).

ONS (2001). *Labour Market Trends*, August.

Oswald, A. (1996). 'A conjecture on the explanation for high unemployment in the industrialised nations: part 1', Warwick Economic Research Paper, no. 475.

Peck, J. (1990). 'The youth training scheme: regional policy in reverse?', *Policy and Politics*, 18, 135–43.

Robinson, H. (2001). 'Change in the shires? Regional differences in the gender pay-gap in the advent of the national minimum wage', University of Wales, Cardiff.

Roed, K. (1997). 'Hysteresis in unemployment', *Journal of Economic Surveys*, 11 (4), 389–418.

Wales National Assembly and Basic Skills Agency (2001). *The National Basic Skills Strategy for Wales.*

WEFO (2001). *Equal: Final Wales Implementation Plan.*

11. THE WELSH ECONOMY: A STATISTICAL PROFILE

David Brooksbank

INTRODUCTION

This article is the annual statistical profile of the Welsh economy and mirrors the established format common to volumes 9 through 15 of *Contemporary Wales*. The discussion in the main text covers six topics: Output, Income and Expenditure; Employment; Unemployment; Earnings; House Prices; and Regional Competitiveness. This year there have been some changes to the way in which the Office for National Statistics (ONS) have compiled the data for the regions and this has resulted in changes to some of the tables reproduced below. Where changes have occurred, the accompanying commentary describes the effect on the information. The tables are based on information made available prior to 1 June 2003 and, as noted in previous surveys, compilation and production lag with respect to certain official statistics mean that 'latest' figures occasionally lag by two or three years.

This review has been compiled at the time when Wales has just come through the second round of elections for the National Assembly and when the mid-term review of expenditure under the European Structural Fund arrangements is being compiled. As *Contemporary Wales* goes to press this year, the Single Programming Document (SPD) is undergoing serious scrutiny and local and national partnerships are preparing to support projects under Objectives 1, 2 and 3. The information summarized in the tables below illustrates the profound nature of the economic development challenges that still lie ahead, and the problems that have beset some of the Priorities and Strands of the SPD have done little to move the Welsh economy forward over the past few years. Appropriate data are available at a Unitary Authority (UA) level and where comparisons are made with other UK regions, this review uses Government Office Regions.

OUTPUT, INCOME AND EXPENDITURE

Gross Domestic Product (GDP) is an important indicator of the economic activity of a region and is the generally accepted means of comparing both national and regional performance. It also illustrates the historical impact of competitiveness on a region; a subject we return to in a later section. Table 11.1 gives details of the GDP per head at factor cost figures for the Government Office Regions of the UK in 1999. These are still the latest figures available for the review and are the same as those presented last year. As noted then, GDP per head in Wales was estimated to be £10,400, an increase of 5.2 per cent over the 1998 total. In 1999 Wales continued to slip further behind other regions with only 80.5 per cent of the UK average, a fall of 0.9 per centage points from the previous year.

In 1999, the South East had the highest growth at 5.1 per cent. Annual growth was lowest in the North East at 2.3 per cent. GDP per head in London (£16,900) was 30 per cent higher than the UK average of £13,000. In Northern Ireland and the North East it was 23 per cent lower. The estimates for 1999 saw GDP per head rise above £10,000 in every region of the UK.

Individual consumption expenditure measures expenditure by households and non-profit making institutions serving households resident in a region. There are no estimates of individual expenditure below the regional level (that is below Government Office Regions – NUTS level 1[1]) and hence it is now not possible to repeat the split by unitary authority or former council area in Wales.

Table 11.1 shows that in 1999 Wales had household disposable income per head of £9,113, with only the North East and Northern Ireland having a lower level. This represents a gap of 9.6 per centage points from the UK average. Whilst London and the South East skew most series of economic data, it is still evident that Wales falls behind comparable regions elsewhere in the UK.

The index of production and construction for Wales is shown in Table 11.3. Delays in updating this information still remain and the next update, which involves re-basing the data, is due to be produced in Autumn 2003. Therefore Quarter 4, 2002, is still the most up-to-date set of figures, and the analysis provided last year stands. Reasonably buoyant trading in the first quarter of 2002 meant that both production industries and manufacturing output stayed constant in comparison to the previous year. Output in mining and quarrying continued to fall in the UK, but grew slightly in Wales.

TABLE **11.1**
Regional accounts

	GDP per head at basic prices 1999[1]		Household disposable income per head 1999		Individual consumption expenditure per head 1999	
	£	% of UK	£	% of UK	£	% of UK
London	16900	130.0	12036	119.4	12250	124.2
South East	15100	166.4	11249	111.6	11392	115.5
East	15100	116.2	11255	111.7	10077	102.2
South West	11800	90.8	9825	97.5	9600	97.3
West Midlands	11900	91.7	9195	91.2	9262	93.9
East Midlands	12100	93.6	9346	92.7	9057	91.8
Yorkshire & the Humber	11400	87.9	9305	92.3	8907	90.3
North West	11300	86.9	9375	93.0	9321	94.5
North East	10000	77.3	8353	82.9	8003	81.1
England	13300	102.4	10237	101.6	10057	102.0
Scotland	12500	96.5	9558	94.8	9459	95.9
Northern Ireland	10100	77.5	8659	85.9	8281	83.9
WALES	10400	80.5	9113	90.4	8206	83.2
UNITED KINGDOM	13000	100	10088	100	9864	100

Note 1: Figures are consistent with the 2000 UK National Accounts – provisional figures.
Note 2: The differences between the old Standard Statistical Regions (SSRs) and the Government Office Regions (GORs) are that East Anglia SSR is combined with Essex, Hertfordshire and Bedfordshire to create the new East GOR; London is a separate GOR; and Cumbria transfers from the old North SSR to the new North West GOR with the remainder of the North SSR becoming the North East GOR.
Note 3: Based on the European System of Accounts 1995 (ESA95).
Source: Office for National Statistics.

Within the manufacturing sector the largest falls were in the textile-products category, whilst substantial positive growth was seen in the transport-equipment group. The decision by Marks and Spencer to source a larger proportion of its clothing products abroad and the closure of Baird's factories have had a significant impact on the textile sector in Wales over the past three years, especially in Mid and West Wales. The re-based figures are likely to reflect this with a fall. Construction showed positive growth of 12.2 per cent in the 2002 figures and the substantial building programme in Cardiff has continued apace. Major events that are likely to impact upon these figures include the scaling down of steel production by Corus across Wales. Speculation that the steelworks at Llanwern near Newport, operated by Corus, is scheduled for closure has been constant since announcements of

TABLE 11.2
Index of production and construction for Wales, (a) seasonally adjusted, (b) 1995 = 100

1992 STANDARD INDUSTRIAL CLASSIFICATION			1995 weights per thousand	Annual Indices			Quarterly Indices				Percentage change over latest 4 quarters on	
Section	Sub-Section	Description		2001	2002	2001 Qtr 4	2002 Qtr1	2002 Qtr21	2002 Qtr3	2002 Qtr4	WALES	UK
C-F		Production and construction	1000	93.3	93.3	93.0	92.9	94.2	93.9	92.4	0.0	-1.6
C-E		Production industries	860	95.4	93.8	94.5	93.9	94.9	94.4	92.1	-1.7	-3.5
C		Mining and quarrying	26	62.7	64.5	59.7	60.0	60.0	65.4	72.5	2.8	-2.0
D		Manufacturing	752	96.6	93.7	94.4	93.0	95.2	94.0	92.8	-3.0	-4.0
	DA	Food products, beverages and tobacco	77	102	112	102	107	110	114	116	9.6	1.5
	DB-DC	Textiles, textile products, leather and leather products	21	63	55	58	58	55	55	53	-12.4	-7.3
	DE	Pulp, paper and paper products: printing and publishing	59	98	94	98	92.	99	90	95	-4.1	0.9
	DF	Coke and refined petroleum products	14	83	85	89	88	86	82	84	2.2	1.0
	DG	Chemicals, chemical products and synthetic, fibres	82	101	104	102	104	106	108	98	3.2	1.6
	DI	Other non-metallic mineral products	22	89	89	92	90	92	88	85	-0.3	-3.3
	DJ	Basic metals and fabricated metal products	193	84	77	79	77	81	77	73	-0.9	-4.3
	DK	Machinery and equipment not elsewhere classified	38	99	95	97	91	99	97	93	-3.7	-6.1
	DL	Electrical and optical equipment	106	108	91	101	96	93	89	87	-15.5	-16.7
	DM	Transport equipment	67	127	133	124	125	128	135	146	5.2	-2.9
	DD, DH, DN	Other manufacturing (inc. rubber, plastic and wood)	74	87	89	89	90	86	89	89	2.2	n/a
E		Electricity, gas and water supply	82	95.0	103.9	106.8	113.7	103.0	107.2	91.8	9.4	-0.7
F		Construction	140	80.5	90.3	83.4	86.7	89.8	90.8	94.0	12.2	7.3

Notes: a – Revisions to the series are normally made each quarter to take account both of more recent information and improved seasonal factors.
b – All series are seasonally adjusted unless otherwise stated in the note.

Source: Welsh Office.

TABLE 11.3
Identifiable general government expenditure: 2001–2002

	£ per head					Index (United Kingdom identifiable expenditure = 100)			
	England	Scotland	Wales	Northern Ireland	United Kingdom	England	Scotland	Wales	Northern Ireland
Agriculture, fisheries, food and forestry	76	345	185	398	114	67	302	162	348
Trade, industry, energy and employment	125	210	194	287	141	89	149	138	204
Roads and transport	195	224	177	146	195	100	115	91	75
Housing	62	165	86	102	73	85	226	117	140
Other environmental services	176	368	302	177	199	89	185	152	89
Law, order and protective services	379	438	368	701	393	97	112	94	178
Education	816	986	891	1048	841	97	117	106	125
Culture, media and sport	93	35	94	42	86	107	40	109	48
Health and personal social services	1224	1512	1355	1374	1260	97	120	108	109
Social security	1809	2007	2112	2204	1853	107	40	109	48
Miscellaneous[1]	50	35	111	138	54				
TOTAL	5005	6324	5874	6616	5207	96	121	113	127

Note: [1]– expenditure includes the costs of central administration of the offices of the Secretaries of State of the territorial departments.

Source: HM Treasury.

further job cuts across the UK in general, rather than the actual closure of production facilities.

Table 11.3 indicates that identifiable government expenditure per head was 14 per cent higher than in England for the financial year 2000/1. Once again, the figure of £5,874 was the lowest of the three Celtic regions. The activities that grew most over the past year, relative to the average UK expenditure per head, were agriculture, fisheries, food and forestry, and culture, media and sport. Unlike the previous year, the figures for departmental spending fell below those for England in the areas of Roads and Transport, and Law, Order and Protective Services.

EMPLOYMENT

Comparative information about the workforce in Great Britain is given in Tables 11.4 and 11.5. Table 11.4 shows the seasonally adjusted figures for employees in employment, giving data for Government Office Regions, whilst Table 11.5 illustrates the sectoral breakdown by industry for Wales and Great Britain. Table 11.4 is based on the most up-to-date Labour Force Survey (LFS) data available. These figures are felt, by ONS, to reflect better the actual number of employees and are published quarterly after the completion of each new wave of the LFS. These new data also include the rate of employment that can be used to build comparative information over the next few years. A particularly important aspect of the National Economic Development Strategy for Wales is the creation of new and safeguarding of existing jobs, and targets for these will require close monitoring.

Table 11.4 shows that the numbers of employees in Great Britain increased over the past year by 0.2 per cent and, as unemployment has fallen nationally, every government office region has seen a modest increase in employees. The LFS estimate of employment in Wales was 71.4 per cent in the December 2002 to February 2003 period, compared to 70.6 per cent in the same period a year earlier. The employment level was 1.28 million in the December 2002 to February 2003 period, up from 1.26 million in the same period a year earlier. Examining changes in employment by gender over the last year shows that, whilst male employment rose by 1.0 per cent nationally, in Wales it rose by 3.6 per cent, equivalent to some 18,000 employees. Female employment fell by 0.5 per cent nationally, whereas female employment in Wales fell by 3.5 per cent.

Looking in more detail at the causes of these changes, Table 11.5 shows that again Wales bucks the national trend in terms of the proportions of new jobs that are part-time. Whilst Great Britain shows an increase in male part-time jobs of 8.4 per cent and a fall in female part-time jobs of 1.5 per cent, Wales shows a fall of 5.1 per cent for males and a fall of 10 per cent in the number of part-time jobs for females. This reverses the pattern from the previous year, when the review questioned the ability of Wales to secure full-time jobs as the major component of employment growth. Job creation rates for 2002 in Wales are slightly higher than the national average and the growth is accounted for by full-time male employment. In 2002, male employment exceeded female in Wales and the rate of growth in male employment was higher than that for females. This is the same as the picture on a national scale, although for Great Britain male employment growth was positive whereas for females it was negative. Some commentators have expressed the view that many of the new full-time jobs created in Wales have been in areas where job security and pay rates are low (such as assembly line and call-centre type jobs).

This argument is not well supported by the figures for particular sectors presented in Table 11.5. Again, despite the reported strength of parts of the manufacturing sector in Wales, this sector saw a fall of 5.3 per cent in 2002, equivalent to 10,000 jobs. Wholesale, retail, trade and repairs saw a rise of 4 per cent, or some 7,000 jobs. The overall position for employment was the net loss of some 1,000 jobs, accounted for by falls in manufacturing and rises in service sectors.

Other areas where Wales saw positive growth rates were education (0.9 per cent), public administration (4.1 per cent) and transport (13.9 per cent).

The argument between academics and industrialists alike over the impact and role of Foreign Direct Investment (FDI) in Wales has continued apace over the past year. Fewer new arrivals this year have also intensified the debate about the relative value of sterling against the euro and the closures of plants, with moves to Eastern Europe, have inevitably been blamed on the strong pound and the difficulty of competing in the export market. Table 11.6 illustrates the continuing importance of the foreign-owned plants to the Welsh economy. With some 320 plants, employing 68,000 people directly, they make up approximately 5 per cent of the employed workforce in Wales. It should be noted that this is a fall from some 75,000 jobs last year and the loss of over thirty plants since 1999. However, it is still the case that many more jobs rely on their presence as part of the supply chain that now supports them. Employment in Wales is concentrated, therefore, in small firms, with current figures from the National On-line Manpower Information Service (NOMIS) estimating that 59 per cent of employees work in firms with less than 100

TABLE 11.4
Employment: Wales, Great Britain and regions, Labour Force Survey employment, thousands, seasonally adjusted

	December 2001–February 2002						December 2002–February 2003					
	Male	Rate (%)*	Female	Rate (%)*	Total	Rate (%)*	Male	Rate (%)*	Female	Rate (%)*	Total	Rate (%)*
London	1995	76.8	1549	63.8	3544	70.6	1844	76.1	1560	63.7	3405	69.9
South East	2303	85.7	1876	74.4	4179	80.3	2185	84.1	1873	74.3	4058	79.4
East	1537	85.3	1240	73.3	2777	79.6	1446	82.9	1221	72.7	2667	77.9
South West	1326	82.6	1136	75.2	2462	79.1	1297	82.9	1127	75.2	2425	79.2
West Midlands	1393	79.5	1100	68.9	2492	74.5	1327	78.9	1111	69.3	2438	74.2
East Midlands	1132	81.1	912	71.1	2043	76.3	1091	80.5	918	71.2	2009	76.0
Yorkshire & the Humber	1314	78.7	1033	67.8	2347	73.6	1238	78.3	1050	68.7	2288	73.6
North West	1718	76.3	1424	68.3	3141	72.5	1640	77.4	1414	68.5	3054	73.0
North East	593	71.6	505	65.2	1099	68.6	563	71.1	493	64.6	1057	67.9
Scotland	1253	75.4	1118	70.3	2371	73.0	1254	77.6	1133	71.2	2387	74.4
WALES	699	74.1	559	63.2	1258	68.9	678	74.4	604	68.3	1282	71.4
GREAT BRITAIN	15263	79.5	12450	69.6	27713	74.8	14567	79.2	12504	69.9	27070	74.7

Note 1: Government Office Regions as described for Table 11.1.
Note 2: * – denominator is all persons of working age
Note 3: The data in this table for December–February 2003 have been adjusted to reflect the 2001 census population data.

Source: Labour Market Trends various issues.

TABLE **11.5**
**Employee jobs ('000s) in Great Britain and Wales, by industry (SIC92),
December 2001 and December 2002**

	Great Britain			Wales		
	Dec 2001	**Dec 2002**	*% change*	**Dec 2001**	**Dec 2002**	*% change*
Agriculture, hunting, forestry and fishing (A, B)	237	202	–14.8	13	14	7.6
Mining & quarrying (C)	74	69	–6.8	3	3	0
Manufacturing (D)	3646	3462	–5.0	189	179	–5.3
Electricity, gas and water supply (E)	100	130	30.0	4	6	50
Construction (F)	1210	1106	–8.6	57	51	–10.5
Wholesale, retail, trade and repairs (G)	4480	4518	0.8	176	183	4.0
Hotels and restaurants (H)	1613	1741	7.9	66	76	15.2
Transport, storage and communication (I)	1520	1525	0.3	43	49	13.9
Financial intermediation (J)	1067	1032	–0.3	36	27	–25
Real-estate, renting and business activities (K)	3856	3912	1.5	100	94	–6
Public administration and defence: compulsory social security (L)	1367	1410	3.1	74	77	4.1
Education (M)	2108	2145	1.8	107	108	0.9
Health and social work (N)	2695	2742	1.7	153	153	0
Other community, social and personal activities (O–Q)	1259	1313	4.3	56	54	–3.6
Service industries (G–Q)	19932	20321	2.0	811	823	1.5
Total male	12589	12713	1.0	504	522	3.6
Male part-time	1752	1900	8.4	78	74	–5.1
Total female	12641	12576	–0.5	574	554	–3.5
Female part-time	6179	6083	–1.5	308	278	–10
TOTAL	25230	25289	0.2	1077	1076	0

Note: Not seasonally adjusted.
Source: Labour Market Trends.

workers. The geographical distribution remains concentrated along the northern corridor created by the A55 and the southern corridor created by the M4. Bridgend now accounts for 8.8 per cent of foreign-owned manufacturing jobs, with Rhondda Cynon Taff having 7.6 per cent, Caerphilly 7.1 per cent and Wrexham 9.3 per cent. Newport has continued to attract new FDI and has risen to 9.0 per cent from 8.9 per cent last year. The recent announcement of the closure of the LG Philips plant, however, is likely to have a major impact on these figures for Newport next year.

TABLE **11.6**
Employment in overseas-owned manufacturing plants in Wales, by unitary authority, 2001

	Plants	Employees ('000s)	Percentage of total employees
Blaenau Gwent	22	3.0	4.4
Bridgend	15	6.0	8.8
Caerphilly	32	4.8	7.1
Cardiff	17	3.2	4.7
Carmarthenshire	15	3.2	4.7
Ceredigion	–	0.3	0.4
Conwy & Denbighshire	–	1.9	2.8
Flintshire	35	5.9	8.7
Gwynedd	7	1.2	1.8
Isle of Anglesey	6	1.0	1.5
Merthyr Tydfil	8	1.3	1.9
Monmouthshire	–	1.3	1.9
Newport	17	6.1	9.0
Neath and Port Talbot	14	4.6	6.8
Pembrokeshire	–	1.0	1.5
Powys	8	0.8	1.2
Rhondda Cynon Taff	39	5.2	7.6
Swansea	12	2.9	4.3
Torfaen	14	3.4	5.0
The Vale of Glamorgan	12	4.6	6.8
Wrexham	36	6.3	9.3
WALES	320	68	100

Source: Welsh Register of Manufacturing Employment.
Note:–Figures suppressed to avoid disclosure.

As the earlier commentary stressed, economic regeneration over the next few years will prioritize activities that lead to job creation. Indeed, ambitious targets for new jobs were set out not only in the Single Programming Document (SPD) that supports the case for European Structural Funds, but also in new policy documents produced by the National Assembly for Wales (for example *A Winning Wales*). Just as previous reviews have highlighted the rapid nature of global change (which has been blamed for the failure of some high-profile inward investment projects), commentators are now becoming increasing worried about the methods proposed to create the required new jobs to achieve these targets. Essentially, the debate now centres on the correct recipe for economic regeneration. Should policies and financial effort be directed to support the creation of higher-level, well-paid jobs based on higher value-added production/R & D/skills, which will take a long time to achieve, but raise long-term living standards in Wales? Alternatively, with political pressure to deliver new jobs quickly for a wide cross-section of society, should support be given to the new breed of inward investors and projects which create jobs rapidly? Whilst the final decisions inevitably become clouded by political considerations, Wales has had a number of high-profile successes in the new 'call centre' market, with major new operations in Merthyr Tydfil and Swansea creating many hundreds of new jobs. The failure of BT to fill a site at Nantgarw and the closure of ITV Digital in Pembroke have served as a sharp warning to those who have pursued these types of investments. Critics argue that new technology (such as voice-recognition software) will render these plants obsolete in the near future; proponents argue that they will adapt to the new information age and go forward with it.

UNEMPLOYMENT

Unlike many of its European neighbours, high unemployment has become less of a problem for the UK in recent years. Table 11.8 displays regional unemployment rates in the UK over the last decade. Unemployment was generally fairly low at the end of the 1980s, but rose sharply during the recession of the early 1990s. Since 1993, official unemployment rates have fallen steadily, reaching their lowest levels since 1980 in 2002, at 3.1 per cent. This pattern has been replicated by all of the UK government office regions.

The welcome fall in unemployment in 2002 in Wales to 3.6 per cent (3.9 per cent in 2001), although still 0.5 per cent above the UK average, may indicate that the gap between Wales and the rest of the UK is actually closing once again. Looking at the change in unemployment rates for other regions, Northern Ireland, Scotland, Yorkshire and the Humber and the North East continue to have higher rates than Wales, although all regions witnessed a fall during the year (apart from London where the rate increased slightly).

Table 11.8 shows unemployment for the Government Office Regions in the UK in terms of the claimant count. The table shows the number of job-seekers claiming benefits, broken down by government office region. The count of Job seeker Allowance claimants is mostly derived from the Benefits Agency computer records. However, for various reasons (when a claimant's National Insurance number is not known) a few claims have to be dealt with manually by local offices and these claimants are not then analysed by age and duration. Table 11.8 illustrates claimant-count unemployment for the Government Office Regions in the UK in March 2001 and March 2002 (that

Table 11.7

Annual average unemployment rates, Wales, United Kingdom and regions. Males and females combined, seasonally adjusted, 1993–2002

	1993	1994	1995	1996	1997	1998	1999	2000	2001	2002
South East	8.6	7.3	5.9	5.0	3.4	2.7	2.4	1.8	1.6	1.7
East	9.4	8.1	6.5	5.9	4.1	3.3	3.0	2.3	2.1	2.2
London	11.6	10.7	9.4	8.5	6.4	5.3	4.8	3.7	3.3	3.6
South West	9.5	8.1	6.8	6.1	4.3	3.5	3.1	2.3	2.1	2.0
West Midlands	10.8	9.9	8.1	7.2	5.5	4.7	4.6	4.1	3.7	3.5
East Midlands	9.5	8.7	7.4	6.7	4.9	4.0	3.8	3.4	3.2	2.9
Yorkshire & the Humber	10.2	9.6	8.5	7.8	6.3	5.5	5.1	4.3	4.0	3.7
North West	9.5	8.7	8.5	7.7	6.0	5.3	4.9	4.2	3.7	3.6
North East	12.9	12.4	11.2	10.2	8.4	7.5	7.2	6.3	5.5	5.0
Scotland	9.7	9.3	7.9	7.6	6.4	5.7	5.4	4.6	4.2	4.1
Northern Ireland	13.7	12.6	11.2	10.7	8.2	7.4	6.5	5.4	5.0	4.6
WALES	10.3	9.3	8.4	8.0	6.4	5.6	5.2	4.5	3.9	3.6
UNITED KINGDOM	10.3	9.3	8.0	7.2	5.5	4.7	4.3	3.6	3.2	3.1

Note: Government Office Regions as described for Table 11.1.

Source: Labour Market Trends.

TABLE **11.8**
**Unemployment: Wales, United Kingdom and regions, Claimants, thousands,
not seasonally adjusted, March 2002 and March 2003**

	March 2002			March 2003		
	Male	Female	Total	Male	Female	Total
South East	55.8	18.7	74.4	59.4	20.4	79.8
East	43.7	15.7	59.4	45.6	16.9	62.5
London	120.9	45.7	166.6	125.4	48.6	174.0
South West	41.0	14.1	55.1	39.0	14.2	53.2
West Midlands	74.0	22.8	96.8	95.9	23.5	99.4
East Midlands	47.2	15.8	63.0	46.4	16.2	62.6
Yorkshire & the Humber	73.2	27.7	94.9	69.6	21.4	90.9
North West	99.0	27.5	126.5	94.1	27.0	121.1
North East	50.3	12.8	63.1	45.4	12.5	57.9
Scotland	85.9	24.3	110.2	82.5	24.6	107.2
Northern Ireland	29.2	8.3	37.5	26.9	7.7	34.6
WALES	39.3	11.3	50.6	37.6	11.4	49.0
UNITED KINGDOM	759.5	238.7	998.2	747.9	244.4	992.3

Note: Government Office Regions as described for Table 11.1.

Source: Labour Market Trends.

is, the number of job-seekers claiming benefits, broken down by government office region). Four regions, London, the South East, the East and the West Midlands, saw a rise in the number of claimants in the period. The remainder saw a fall. In addition, this fall was true in most cases for both males and females, providing further evidence that the economy is continuing to perform well. In Wales the stock of claimants fell by 3.1 per cent, compared to a fall of less than 1 per cent for the UK as a whole. This may be the tentative first sign that Wales has begun to buck the trend of being amongst the lowest-performing regions in the UK. Statistics such as these have been grasped quickly by the Welsh Assembly Government and are certainly worthy of following up over time as this review develops over the period of structural funding. Wales appears to have set itself extremely ambitious development targets for the next decade and yet the economic evidence from the data has been that those targets are actually accelerating away every year. Some economists have started to argue that this is the legacy or consequence of the lack of investment in the infrastructure required to support higher-level functions in Wales. This year, for the first time in a decade, there is some evidence that the economy may not be moving away from the rest of the UK as badly as had been predicted.

TABLE 11.9
Male unemployment by duration: Wales, United Kingdom and regions, March
2003

	Unemployed for over 52 and up to 104 weeks	Unemployed for over 104 weeks	Percentage claiming over 1 year
South East	5061	1987	11.9
East	3867	1643	12.2
London	17345	7945	20.4
South West	3124	1458	11.8
West Midlands	7592	4995	16.9
East Midlands	4235	2305	14.4
Yorkshire & the Humber	6450	3092	14.0
North West	9408	5334	15.8
North East	4532	2927	16.5
Scotland	7781	3822	14.2
Northern Ireland	4051	2220	23.5
WALES	3319	2151	14.6
UNITED KINGDOM	76765	39875	15.8

Note: Government Office Regions as described for Table 11.1.

Source: Labour Market Trends.

Table 11.9 provides information about the age of claimants combined with the duration spells of unemployment by Government Office Region. The past year has seen a fall in the numbers of unemployed for more than one year in every government office region. In March 2003 in Wales the per centage of total unemployed who had been out of work for more than one year was 14.6, a fall of 0.7 per centage points over the previous year.

It is not only at the national level where unemployment rates have converged over the last decade, as a similar process has been occurring in Wales, as shown in Table 11.10, which reports unemployment rates by Unitary Authority. The rates range from 1.7 per cent in Monmouthshire to 4.1 per cent in the Isle of Anglesey. Most areas experienced a fall in the overall rate of unemployment between March 2002 and 2003, despite some job losses following closures in a number of areas. These falls are general and not restricted to either urban or rural areas. Looking at the larger towns and cities, Cardiff's rate of unemployment rose from 2.9 per cent to 3.0 per cent, Swansea's fell from 4.0 per cent to 3.0 per cent, Newport's fell again from 3.8 per cent to 3.5 per cent and Wrexham's fell from 2.9 per cent to 2.2 per cent. In the rural areas, for example, Ceredigion's fell from 2.8 per cent to 1.9 per cent and Gwynedd's fell from 5.0 per cent to 3.4 per cent. Male

TABLE **11.10**
Unemployment by Unitary Authority and Wales, unadjusted, workforce base, March 2003

	Male		Female		All	
	Number	Rate	Number	Rate	Number	Rate
Blaenau Gwent	1340	10.7	328	3.6	1668	4.0
Bridgend	1575	5.8	506	1.7	2081	2.7
Caerphilly	2324	7.4	722	2.8	3046	3.0
Cardiff	4630	4.6	1117	1.2	5747	3.0
Carmarthenshire	2014	7.0	647	2.2	2661	2.6
Ceredigion	638	3.7	241	1.7	879	1.9
Conwy	1277	6.6	399	1.9	1676	2.8
Denbighshire	1013	4.6	332	1.5	1345	2.5
Flintshire	1284	3.4	442	1.5	1726	1.9
Gwynedd	1794	7.2	513	2.4	2307	3.4
Isle of Anglesey	1166	9.4	434	3.7	1600	4.1
Merthyr Tydfil	943	8.9	248	2.7	1191	3.6
Monmouthshire	634	3.3	235	1.1	869	1.7
Neath & Port Talbot	1927	6.8	578	2.8	2505	3.1
Newport	2260	5.5	603	1.8	2863	3.5
Pembrokeshire	1790	8.1	672	2.6	2462	3.8
Powys	914	2.8	386	1.5	1300	1.8
Rhondda Cynon Taff	2916	6.4	850	2.2	3766	2.7
Swansea	3213	6.8	874	1.5	4087	3.0
Torfaen	1183	5.8	364	1.7	1497	2.8
The Vale of Glamorgan	1559	5.8	433	1.8	1992	2.8
Wrexham	1299	4.2	430	1.4	1729	2.2
WALES	37643	5.7	11354	1.8	48997	2.8

Source: NOMIS.
Note: Rates are calculated as wholly unemployed claimants as a percentage of the working-age population of the area.

unemployment continues to be a major problem. Table 11.10 shows that in Blaenau Gwent this remains above 10 per cent, with a rate of 9.4 per cent on the Isle of Anglesey. Bridgend has witnessed a large fall, from 12.3 per cent male unemployment in April 1999 to 5.8 per cent in March 2003. Female unemployment rates remain much lower, with no UA having a rate above 3.7 per cent (Isle of Anglesey).

UA unemployment is the lowest level for which unemployment rates are given because unemployment rates for travel-to-work areas (TTW*As*) are not reported in this section, due to the recent debate over the legitimacy of these statistics. The TTWA unemployment rate is defined as the claimant unemployment rate in the area divided by the sum of the employees within the area plus the resident unemployed. Therefore, the unemployment rate in areas with a large number of in-commuters will be underestimated, for example in urban centres, whereas the unemployment rate will be over-estimated in those areas where there is out-commuting, for example in rural areas. UA unemployment rates are also open to the same argument of self-containment, but its effect will be reduced because of the increased geographical size of UAs.

EARNINGS

The decline of Welsh earnings relative to the British average over the past twenty years has been extremely well documented. Indeed, it is the low level of earnings which contributes directly to low GDP and hence the need for European Structural Fund help. Once again, according to the 2002 *New Earnings Survey* (*NES02*), Wales still lags behind every other region of Great Britain in terms of earnings, apart from the North East of England. Table 11.11 provides a broad earnings picture of the main sub-groups of full-time employees in the regions of Britain in 2002. The average weekly wage is £399.70 for Welsh employees, who earn 40 pence more than their counterparts in the North East of England. The gap has narrowed here, as has the difference between Wales and the next most well-paid region of Yorkshire and the Humber. In 2001 the gap was £10.30, which has fallen to £10.20 in 2002; hardly a staggering gain. Employees in Wales saw average earnings growth of 4.7 per cent in the twelve months to April 2002, compared to a national increase of 4.6 per cent. Welsh employees continue to earn far less than 90 per cent of the British average of £464.7 a week. Again, here is evidence that some economic development targets are going to prove more difficult than others to achieve.

The earnings performance of Welsh females has been relatively better than that of males in recent years and this was again marginally the case in 2002. As a region, Wales continues to have the lowest male earnings of any government office region, now trailing behind the North East of England for the fifth year running. Welsh female earnings continue to be relatively better placed, with figures showing a ranking of ninth out of the eleven GB regions. The annual earnings increases for 2001–2 were 4.9 per cent and 5.4 per cent respectively for Welsh males and females, compared with 4.8 per cent and 4.5 per cent for Britain as a whole. Figures in Table 11.11 suggest that it is in the manual occupations where the traditional strength of earnings for both Welsh male and welsh female employees has been eroded. These levels now fall significantly below the national average, whereas a few years ago they were only very slightly below. Manual male earnings are now higher in every other region than they were in Wales, whereas in 1998 they were higher in only five other regions. Relative earnings in the non-manual occupations remain very low, especially for Welsh males, who again appear as the lowest section of the regional earnings table. However, for females, non-manual earnings were worse in only two other regions.

Given the lower average earnings in Wales, one would expect Welsh employees to be more heavily concentrated at the bottom of the earnings distribution than the other regions. This is confirmed by Table 11.12, which reports the per centage of employees earning less than specified lower-earnings thresholds. These were set at £250 a week for males and £180 for females in 2002. Wales had by far the highest per centage of male employees in low-paid jobs in 2002, with 24.1 per cent of full-timers earning less than £250 a week. Both manual and non-manual males had the highest con-centrations of low-paid workers of any of the regions. Welsh females fared slightly better, as the East Midlands and the North East had a greater per centage of their workers earning less than £180 per week. The position of Welsh non-manual female workers' earnings has improved slightly again this year, with six regions (North East, North West, West Midlands, East Mid-lands, Yorkshire and the Humber, and South West) having a relatively worse position. For manual females the situation is less encouraging, with only the North East, North West and East Midlands having a higher per centage earning below the threshold.

Table 11.13 examines the average gross weekly earnings in the main industrial and occupational groupings for Wales and Great Britain. 2002 once again saw the relative fortunes of both manual and non-manual male Welsh workers worsen. Manual male production workers in Wales now earn less than the average for Great Britain, a situation that has occurred only in the past two years. Prior to this, successive reviews have highlighted the fact that Welsh manufacturing workers earned a little more than the average elsewhere. This advantage now appears to have gone. Manual males in production earned £10.40 less than the national average for such businesses in 2002; this compares to a situation in 2000 where they earned 30p more. This decline now appears to be a trend and demonstrates definite erosion of the competitive advantage that Wales once had in competing for manufacturing jobs. The NES02 figures suggest that a larger and growing proportion of production jobs in Wales are low paid and therefore low skill.

In non-manual occupations male workers in Wales continued to perform badly in comparison to the rest of GB, and in 2002 earned on average only

TABLE **11.11**

Average gross weekly earnings: Wales, Great Britain and regions, £s, all industries and services, full-time employees on adult rates, April 2002

	Manual males	Non-manual males	All males	Manual females	Non-manual females	All females	All employees
London	409.1	806.7	704.8	292.8	523.5	503.6	624.1
South East	395.1	636.2	555.3	274.7	417.4	398.6	496.7
East	374.6	597.1	506.3	259.7	394.3	375.1	459.6
South West	350.6	543.9	463.3	245.4	368.3	350.0	421.7
West Midlands	361.3	558.5	469.6	247.8	374.9	353.0	427.3
East Midlands	363.8	531.0	454.2	238.5	357.9	374.8	413.0
Yorkshire & the Humber	360.9	522.2	447.1	234.1	367.0	345.0	409.9
North West	357.8	555.7	471.1	241.4	372.7	354.3	426.8
North East	357.8	516.0	439.1	232.2	349.8	332.1	399.3
Scotland	356.1	560.0	473.7	237.5	381.1	360.1	427.0
WALES	345.2	510.6	432.9	233.0	365.9	345.1	399.7
GREAT BRITAIN	368.2	610.4	513.8	251.0	405.2	383.4	464.7

Source: New Earnings Survey, 2002.

83.7 per cent of the Great Britain figure. Females earned 90.3 per cent of the comparable national figure, a fall from 93 per cent in 2000. Table 11.13 also illustrates significant gaps in relative performance in the service industries. Non-manual males earn only 82.5 per cent of the GB average, a significant fall from 86.3 per cent in 2000. The position of females in all sectors fell slightly over the year and they remain around 10 percentage points lower than the national level.

Table 11.14 illustrates the wide variation of earnings within Wales. Data is presented for all unitary authorities where sample sizes were sufficient in the *NES02* to allow for publication. Simple observation of the figures shows the marked difference in average weekly earnings that exists between even neighboring unitary authorities, and the skewed distribution of income within authority areas is further highlighted by the 90/10 earnings differential. Earnings data were available for seventeen out of the twenty-two UAs in 2002, with Blaenau Gwent, Ceredigion, Denbighshire, Isle of Anglesey, Merthyr Tydfil and Pembrokeshire unable to meet the sampling criteria of the *NES*. In 2002, Cardiff had the highest average earnings of the UAs reported, of £442 per week, although this again fell short of the GB average of £464. Table 11.14 also shows that Swansea remains below the Welsh average with earnings of £383.9. Conwy remained the UA with the lowest average earnings of all, at £353.1 a week.

TABLE **11.12**
**Distribution of gross weekly earnings: Wales, Great Britain and regions, £s,
all industries and services, full-time employees on adult rates, April 2002,
percentage with weekly earnings less than £250 for males and less than £180
for females**

	Manual males	Non-manual males	All males	Manual females	Non-manual females	All females
London	13.4	4.6	6.9	12.7	1.4	2.4
South East	12.8	6.6	8.7	12.6	2.9	4.2
East	16.4	8.1	11.5	18.5	3.7	5.8
South West	19.9	9.3	13.7	21.2	4.6	7.0
West Midlands	17.8	9.3	13.1	24.2	4.7	8.1
East Midlands	18.1	9.4	13.4	25.1	5.2	9.0
Yorkshire & the Humber	18.8	10.9	14.6	22.7	4.9	7.8
North West	19.8	10.9	14.7	25.4	4.7	7.6
North East	23.2	13.3	13.2	26.3	6.3	9.3
Scotland	19.4	11.0	14.6	22.3	3.8	6.5
WALES	24.1	12.4	17.9	24.8	4.2	7.4
GREAT BRITAIN	18.0	8.7	12.4	20.9	3.8	6.2

Source: New Earnings Survey, 2002.

The 90/10 earnings differential, which is expressed as the earnings figure exceeded by the top 10 per cent of workers divided by the respective figure for the bottom 10 per cent, increased slightly in 2002, to 3.14, from 3.12 in 2001. This simple measure suggests that earnings inequality increased very slightly in 2002. Looking at the county-based data, earning inequality worsened in Blaenau Gwent, Flintshire, Newport, Rhondda Cynon Taff, Swansea, Torfaen and Wrexham. In the remaining authority areas the inequality was reduced slightly.

A major drawback of the *NES* data published in the tables is that they exclude part-time workers altogether and miss out many of those with low wages, because they cover only full-time workers who earn in excess of the lower earnings limit. The tables (and the survey itself) also ignore the self-employed, on the grounds that earnings data from this group is highly unreliable. Unfortunately, the problem of 'missing data' is important for Wales, where the proportion of part-time employees is higher and wages are lower than the national averages. The true position in Wales is therefore likely to be worse than that shown. Analysis has revealed that the part-time workforce remains overwhelmingly female and is continuing to grow. Some

TABLE 11.13

Average gross weekly earnings by broad industry and occupational groupings: Wales and Great Britain, £s, full-time employees on adult rates, April 2002

	Manual males			Non-manual males			Manual females			Non-manual females			All males			All females		
	Wales	GB	% GB	Wales	GB	% GB	Wales	GB	% GB	Wales	GB	% GB	Wales	GB	% GB	Wales	GB	% GB
All industries and services	345.2	368.2	93.8	510.6	610.4	83.7	233.0	251.0	92.8	365.9	405.2	90.3						
All index of production industries	381.2	391.6	97.3	545.0	621.0	87.8	246.4	260.9	94.4	342.2	408.3	83.8						
All manufacturing industries	379.0	388.0	96.8	539.1	615.5	87.6	246.9	260.5	94.8	342.4	408.1	83.9						
All service industries	312.3	344.3	90.7	501.7	608.2	82.5	223.3	246.0	90.8	382.2	406.0	94.1						
All occupations													432.9	513.8	84.3	345.1	383.4	90.0
All manual occupations													345.2	368.2	93.8	233.0	251.0	92.8
All non-manual occupations													510.6	610.4	83.7	365.9	405.2	90.3

Source: New Earnings Survey, 2002.

TABLE 11.14
Average gross weekly earnings, £s, and the 90/10 differential, Wales and Unitary Authorities, all industries and services, full-time employees on adult rates, April 2002

	All employees	90/10 differential
Blaenau Gwent	–	–
Bridgend	394.4	3.12
Caerphilly	378.4	3.24
Cardiff	442.1	3.22
Carmarthenshire	374.7	2.95
Ceredigion	–	–
Conwy	353.1	3.03
Denbighshire	–	–
Flintshire	435.7	2.86
Gwynedd	393.4	3.46
Isle of Anglesey	–	–
Merthyr Tydfil	–	–
Monmouthshire	377.1	3.13
Neath & Port Talbot	417.3	3.09
Newport	400.1	2.99
Pembrokeshire	–	–
Powys	371.2	3.02
Rhondda Cynon Taff	385.3	3.45
Swansea	383.9	2.98
Torfaen	387.5	2.84
The Vale of Glamorgan	425.4	3.31
Wrexham	378.7	3.05
WALES	399.7	3.14

Note: – denotes not available as sample requirements were not met.

Source: *New Earnings Survey*, 2002.

45 per cent of all women workers in GB work part-time (fewer than thity hours) compared with 10 per cent of male workers. The female part-time workforce has increased by 28 per cent over the last ten years, while the female workforce as a whole grew by 22 per cent. However, a growing number of men now work part-time. In ten years the male part-time work-force has grown by 138 per cent. Also, whilst the majority of people working part-time do so out of choice, the proportion who do so involuntarily because they cannot find full-time work has risen by 50 per cent in the last ten years, from 8 per cent to 12 per cent. This growth is likely to be accounted for by the large number of unemployed men aged 50 to 60, who may prefer to work part-time rather than not to work at all. Part-time work

is concentrated in three occupations – clerical work, personal and protective services and sales – and together these employ six in ten part-timers. Part-time workers earn just 70 per cent of the average hourly earnings of full-timers, and just 5 per cent of part-timers are in managerial jobs compared with 15 per cent of employees as a whole, but twice as many male part-timers make the managerial grade compared with women part-timers.

There is little empirical research evidence conducted to date that has adequately, or indeed accurately, determined the impact of the minimum wage on workers in Wales. The types of industries most affected are likely to fall in the hospitality and business services areas, as well as care services. Anecdotal evidence suggests that the relatively low level of minimum wage has had little impact on employment levels, but that employers are taking advantage of the ability to offer a minimum wage for a wider, larger number of certain types of employee. One consequence, if this is true, is that earnings will rise only by the amount of any statutory increase in the minimum wage, and thus closing the gap with other regions becomes even more difficult if large numbers of workers are effectively taken out of the equation.

HOUSE PRICES

2002 has seen a dramatic increase in house prices across the UK. The property boom has seen prices rise by 23.4 per cent during the year, according to the *HBOS House Price Index*. The steady rise in prices has been fuelled by the low cost of borrowing and has emanated in waves from London and the South East. At the regional level, prices have risen in every area except for Northern Ireland, with record rises in the South East, where the shortage of properties for sale has created a market where buyers queue to view and the phenomenon of gazumping has returned.

The UK picture again hides substantial regional variations, with house prices continuing to rise fastest in the southern regions. That said, local hotspots have also been created in the more desirable areas of major cities such as Edinburgh, Manchester and Leeds, as well as in certain counties such as Cheshire and Somerset. Prices are still weak in some parts of the North of England and the Midlands.

Recent months have seen only a slight fall in base interest rates by the Monetary Policy Committee of the Bank of England and at the time of writing, June 2003, the major mortgage lenders are beginning to report a slow-down in the volume of borrowing and some falling prices, especially in

TABLE 11.15
Average house prices, first quarter 2003, United Kingdom, regions and former Welsh counties

Regions of the UK	£	Annual % change	Welsh counties and cities[a]	£
South East	195700	26.0	South Glamorgan	143937
East Anglia	135993	24.5	Gwent	99932
South West	154134	25.3	Clwyd	112772
West Midlands	120162	26.8	Mid Glamorgan	79613
East Midlands	114141	33.9	West Glamorgan	79802
Yorkshire & Humberside	82771	27.7	Dyfed	99631
North West	85440	18.9	Gwynedd	84230
North	83833	30.9	Cardiff	149819
Scotland	72604	9.2	Newport	99673
Northern Ireland	77250	–0.6	Swansea	89690
WALES	93596	27.4	Wrexham	121935
UNITED KINGDOM	124770	23.4		

Note: a – Counties figures are average semi-detached prices.

Source: HBOS House Price Index.

the major hotspots. As noted in the previous survey, the current house-price rises appear to be taking place within borrowing limits not outside the limits of current earnings.

Table 11.15 gives seasonally adjusted regional house-price data for the UK regions in the first quarter of 2003. The largest rise has been in the East Midlands, where the cost of an average semi-detached house has risen to £114,141, an annual rise of 33.9 per cent. Outside the South East, the South West saw a rise of 25.3 per cent, with an average house now costing £154,134. Far more modest rises have been evident in Scotland (9.2 per cent) and a slight fall in Northern Ireland (–0.6 per cent).

House prices in Wales have continued to rise steadily, rising by 27.4 per cent in the year to the first quarter of 2003. The rate of house-price inflation was above the UK average of 23.4 per cent. According to the HBOS Bank, the average homebuyer in Wales now spends just over 22 per cent of their gross annual income on mortgage payments, compared to a peak of 33 per cent in 1990. Equally, most of the housing activity has been based on the urban areas, especially Cardiff, Newport and parts of Swansea, where there are now reported shortages of property coming on to the market. Property hotspots continue in the Cardiff area, as demand continues to outstrip supply. The housing market has remained flat in some of the Valleys and parts of West Glamorgan, observations that seem to mirror local economic conditions. As yet, the *HBOS Index* does not provide information on a UA basis; instead, data which are available for some former counties allow for comparison at a sub-regional level.

Demand for property in fashionable areas such as Cardiff and Newport has pushed up the costs of housing, especially for first-time buyers, who are now finding it even harder to find properties within their reach. The difficulties faced by first-time buyers in Wales are, of course, widespread. However, the major regional differences in house-price inflation that have accompanied this boom also make it very difficult for workers of all levels who own properties to relocate out of Wales (and make relocation to Wales from outside relatively inexpensive). Whether this is good or bad for the economy is open to debate.

The figures for county variations in Table 11.15 continue to show evidence of a north–south and east–west divide in Wales. The HBOS Bank figures show that along the M4 corridor in south Wales, average prices for a semi-detached property are £149,819 in Cardiff, £99,673 in Newport and £89,690 in Swansea. In Wrexham in the north, the same property would cost £121,935.

REGIONAL COMPETITIVENESS

This section considers the most recent data from the Department of Trade and Industry's (DTI) Regional Competitiveness Indicators (September 2002). In this year's review there are data series from 1997 through to August 2002 which summarize the variables considered by the DTI to be most important in making regional comparisons of this sort. These are gross domestic product (GDP) per head, household disposable income per head, gross value added per head, total income support claimants and manufacturing investment by foreign and UK-owned companies.

GDP and Household Disposable Income measure different aspects of a region's income. The former gives an indication of the size of the local economy – regardless of where the income from that economy accrues–and the latter gives an indication of the income residents within regions have to spend on goods and services.

GDP per head is here repeated in index form from Table 11.1. It is measured as the income of those working in a region including commuters (workplace basis) and these data are used in international comparisons at sub-national level because they are readily available internationally. Wales

TABLE 11.16
Regional Competitiveness Indicators

Region	GDP per head (UK=100) 1999	Household disposable income per head (UK=100) 1999	Gross value added per head (UK=100) 1999	Total income support claimants (proportion of population over 16) % August 2002	Manufacturing investment by foreign and UK-owned companies (£million) 1997	
					Foreign	UK
London	130.0	119.4	146.3	9.6	450	849
South East	116.4	111.6	110.2	5.6	862	1286
East	116.2	111.7	103.6	6.3	566	1035
South West	90.8	97.5	90.8	6.9	451	977
West Midlands	91.7	91.2	91.7	9.2	1000	1482
East Midlands	93.6	92.7	93.6	7.6	500	1162
Yorkshire & the Humber	87.9	92.3	87.9	9.1	245	1487
North West	86.9	93.0	86.9	10.7	701	2050
North East	77.3	82.9	77.3	11.4	369	774
England	102.4	101.6	102.4	8.3	5145	11102
Scotland	96.5	94.8	96.5	10.5	682	1212
Northern Ireland	77.5	85.9	77.5	13.6	112	378
WALES	80.5	90.4	80.5	10.1	539	888
UNITED KINGDOM	100	100	100	8.7	6478	13579

Source: Regional Competitiveness Indicators (DTI, September 2002).

has the third lowest GDP per head figure (some 80.5 per cent of the UK average), after Northern Ireland and the North East, of all regions in the UK in 1999. The 'Winning Wales' targets are for this gap to narrow to only 10 per centage points. Such a change means that Wales must grow on average by approximately 1 per cent per annum more rapidly than the average for the rest of the UK. Such a growth rate, which to date has not been achieved by Wales, is one that this review must track carefully over the coming years.

Household Disposable Income is here again defined according to ESA95. The figures are for 1999 and show that Wales has a level of 90.4 per cent of the UK average, above that for Northern Ireland and the North East. As the section above on earnings discussed, income levels in Wales continue to lag behind other UK regions and the reduction of unemployment over the last year appears to have been achieved without a consequent increase in relative earnings.

Gross Value Added per employee is the official competitiveness measure of labour productivity in manufacturing for each region. The figures are for 1999 and show Wales with a level of 80.5 per cent of the UK average. In a similar way to Household Income, Wales ranks below all other regions except for Northern Ireland and the North East. This clearly indicates that Value Added remains a major problem when targets for economic regeneration are set.

The number of Income Support Claimants is a measure of social deprivation in a region. The indicator used shows the number of Income Support Claimants as a proportion of the population over 16. Since the introduction of the Job Seeker Allowance the figures for the unemployed are no longer included in the Income Support Claimant figures. This has resulted in the figures being between 3 and 6 per centage points lower than those published earlier in the series. In August 2002, Wales had 10.1 per cent of the population claiming income support, compared to the UK average of 8.7 per cent. This figure was the same as that published a year ago.

Manufacturing Investment and Output by Foreign-owned Companies is a measure of the attractiveness of a region to foreign investors and the importance of foreign investment to the manufacturing base of a region. The table shows the same figures as were presented in last year's review. In 1997 nearly £13.6 billion was invested in the UK, almost half of which was from foreign-owned companies. Investment is measured by Net Capital Expenditure. Individual yearly data should be treated with caution, as large one-off investment decisions by companies can make significant differences to total investment figures in a particular region. This indicator only covers manufacturing; a comparison with the service sector is not possible due to lack of data.

OVERVIEW

Wales has gone through a quite remarkable period of change over the past thirty years. It has been transformed from an economy dominated by a narrow base of mining and metal industries, to a diverse and growing country. Much of this change has been forced on it through economic necessity, and the policies that were pursued to reduce unemployment and regenerate industry were kept in place for many years. These policies generally involved large-scale inward investment and the building of related supply chains. The emphasis has now begun to swing towards the promotion of indigenous businesses and in the space of five years a whole raft of business support programmes and funding opportunities have sprung up to support enterprise and entrepreneurship. In 1999 the National Assembly commissioned an Entrepreneurship Action Plan for Wales, which has now been developed into a series of projects that can be implemented and 'actioned'. Over the next few years the overarching aim is to change the culture of the people of Wales to one which accepts entrepreneurship and sees new business creation as a major ingredient of economic regeneration. The National Assembly has now passed its first election and Labour has been returned with the slimmest of working majorities. Increasingly people are starting to look more closely at the development plans that Labour and its agencies have for Wales. The fundamental challenge is still to make the European Structural Funds work and to put in place a system of monitoring and regulation that will allow the approved projects to achieve their aims.

NOTES

1. NUTS (*Nomenclature des Unites Territoriales Statistiques*) was established by the Statistical Office of the European Union (EUROSTAT) to provide a uniform breakdown of territorial units for the production of regional statistics. NUTS is a five-level hierarchical system, with Wales being NUTS1 and the two sub-regional units of West Wales and the Valleys and East Wales being NUTS2.

REFERENCES

Regional Competitiveness Indicators (2001). September, Department of Trade and Industry.

INDEX TO VOLUMES 11–16

INDEX OF AUTHORS

INDEX OF ARTICLES

INDEX OF SUBJECTS

Economic Change

Economic Development

Economic Development, Peripheral Areas

Economic Development, Rural

Economy

Nationalism

North Wales, Economy

North West Wales, Economy

Objective One

Plaid Cymru

Political Parties in Wales

Political Parties in Wales, Conservative

Is Devolution Succouring Nationalism?, **14:** 80–103
Political Institutions, Policy Preferences and Public Opinion in Wales and Brittany, **15:** 89–110
Ron Davies and the Cult of 'Inclusiveness': Devolution and Participation in Wales, **14:** 21–49
Towards a Parliament – Three Faces of the National Assembly for Wales, **15:** 1–19
Y Cynulliad Cenedlaethol – Blwyddyn mewn Grym? (The National Assembly – A Year in Power?), **14:** 50–6

Privatization
Debt and Disconnection in the Privatized Utilities, **11:** 149–66

Public Sector
A Local Authority Perspective on Objective 1, **15:** 51–5
Public Service Sector Employment and Public–Private Wage Differentials: A Research Note, **13:** 230–8

Referendum, Welsh Devolution (1997)
Local Branch Activity and Organization in the Yes for Wales Campaign, 1997, **12:** 54–76

Refugees
Neither Here nor There: Refugees in Wales, **11:** 200–13

Regeneration
Wales and North Wales: The Nature of Regeneration, **11:** 61–74
How Objective 1 arrived in Wales: The Political Origins of a Coup, **15:** 20–9

Regeneration, Community-led
Using Measures of Social Capital to Monitor the Impacts of Community–led Regeneration Policies in Wales, **14:** 144–63

Regional Development
The Digital Value Chain and Economic Transformation: Rethinking Regional Development in the New Economy, **13:** 94–115

Regional Development
The West Wales and Valleys Objective 1 Programme – A Personal Narrative, **15:** 69–77

Regionalism
Celebrating Globalization and Misreading the Welsh Economy: 'The New Regionalism' in Wales, **11:** 12–60
Celebrating Globalization and Misreading the Welsh Economy: 'The New Regionalism' in Wales, **11:** 12–60
Political Institutions, Policy Preferences and Public Opinion in Wales and Brittany, **15:** 89–110

Religion
The Laity of the Church in Wales: Sex Differences in Religious Practice, Attitude and Involvement, **12:** 37–53

CONTRIBUTIONS TO CONTEMPORARY WALES

The editors are always pleased to receive papers on any topic relating to the economy, society and politics of Wales for consideration for publication in *Contemporary Wales.*

Submission of papers:
All articles are subject to a refereeing process. Contributions should be written in a style which makes them readily accessible to non-specialists. The editors are very willing, if desired, to discuss proposals for papers with intending authors. Further details regarding submission and preparation of articles are to be found on the *Contemporary Wales* website: *www.contemporary-wales.com*

Copyright:
Articles are accepted on the assumption that they have not appeared previously and are not currently being offered to another journal. On acceptance by the editors for publication in *Contemporary Wales*, copyright in the article in printed and electronic forms is assigned to the University of Wales. Authors should obtain any necessary permission to use material already protected by copyright.

Contributors will be sent one complimentary copy of the published journal in which their contribution appears, and the right to reproduce their own contributions is granted to the contributors, provided that the copies are not offered for sale.

Subscriptions:
Subscription for one volume per annum is £6.50, and the price is otherwise £7.50. Payment is required with all orders and may be made by sterling cheque (payable to the University of Wales Press), Giro (account 494 9056), credit card (Visa or Mastercard). Apply to Journal Subscriptions at the University of Wales Press, 10 Columbus Walk, Brigantine Place, Cardiff, CF10 4UP, tel: 029 2049 6899, fax: 029 2049 6109, e-mail *journals@press.wales.ac.uk*

Advertisements:
Advertisements are welcome and rates will be quoted on request. Enquiries should be made to the Deputy Director at the University of Wales Press at the address given above.